PRACTICAL COURSE FOR IMPO
EXPORT BUSINESS

进出口业务

实用教程（第2版）

主编 刘治国
参编 黄相会 李远辉
施 勇 徐 坤

重庆大学出版社

图书在版编目（CIP）数据

进出口业务实用教程：英文 / 刘治国主编．-- 2 版
．-- 重庆：重庆大学出版社，2023.3
ISBN 978-7-5689-2132-9

Ⅰ.①进… Ⅱ.①刘… Ⅲ.①进出口业务—教材—英文 Ⅳ.① F740.4

中国国家版本馆 CIP 数据核字（2023）第 036150 号

进出口业务实用教程（第 2 版）
JINCHUKOU YEWU SHIYONG JIAOCHENG（DI-ER BAN）

主　编　刘治国
责任编辑：张春花　　版式设计：张春花
责任校对：刘志刚　　责任印制：赵　晟

*

重庆大学出版社出版发行
出版人：饶帮华
社址：重庆市沙坪坝区大学城西路 21 号
邮编：401331
电话：（023）88617190　88617185（中小学）
传真：（023）88617186　88617166
网址：http://www.cqup.com.cn
邮箱：fxk@cqup.com.cn（营销中心）
全国新华书店经销
POD：重庆新生代彩印技术有限公司

*

开本：787mm×1092mm　1/16　印张：14.25　字数：441 千
2020 年 8 月第 1 版　2023 年 3 月第 2 版　2023 年 3 月第 2 次印刷
ISBN 978-7-5689-2132-9　定价：42.00 元

前　言

据海关统计，2022 年，我国进出口总值首次突破 40 万亿元人民币关口，在 2021 年高基数基础上继续保持了稳定增长，规模再创历史新高，连续 6 年保持世界第一货物贸易国地位。同期，国家出台了稳定经济一揽子政策和接续措施，在外贸领域涉及保通保畅、加大财税金融支持力度、鼓励外贸新业态发展、支持外贸企业保订单拓市场、不断提升贸易安全和便利化水平等。新政策和新举措的落实要求高校必须加快培养既具有扎实的国际贸易知识又精通外语的复合型人才。

为了应对国际贸易所面临的新环境，我们特修订了《进出口业务实用教程》一书。第二版教材旨在使学生置身于英文环境中系统学习国际贸易交易的各环节操作，从而提高学生的国际贸易和跨境电商的实操能力。如若能配合使用国际贸易单证操作系统，则教材使用效果更佳。

本书特点：

（1）内容全面、重点突出

本书从国际贸易买卖双方业务关系的建立到各个单证的申领或制作，均基于企业工作过程，具有典型性和实用性，突出了实践操作。通过对单证实例、常见条款等的分析，帮助学生加深理解和系统掌握。

（2）应用性广、操作性强

本书设置了大量的操作实务练习题，教学内容和全国国际商务单证员的考试要求密切结合，为学生考证和进行实践提供了有效的保障，也可供跨境电商从业者参考学习。

（3）材料新颖、更新及时

本书的大部分材料为外贸企业、银行、海关、保险公司和货运代理的真实素材，并根据学生学习的需要，在本版中做了更新和修订。

（4）语言精练、表达专业

本书采用英文编写，全方位营造英文环境。学生在使用中，能快速学习到外贸领域中专业用语的表达，提升自己的业务能力。

本书符合高校学生认知规律，有助于实现有效教学，提高教学的效率、效益、效果；编写上打破了传统的学科体系结构，将各知识点与操作技能恰当地融入企业工作过程，实用性和适用性较强。

本书的编写参考了国内外众多相关教材，在此向各位学者表示感谢。本书是四川省首批应用型示范课程和四川省首批一流本科课程《进出口业务》的建设成果之一，也是校企合作的成果。在此，非常感谢四川速达通运国际货运代理有限公司、四川晟睿康国际贸易有限公司、东莞市百叶兴进出口有限公司和宜宾综合保税区提供了大量的操作单据和指导意见。

尽管编者倾心编写，疏漏在所难免，敬请专家学者不吝赐教。

编　者

2022 年 12 月

目 录

Chapter 1

Business Letter

In international trade, all the trade terms should be expressed correctly and definitely in any kind of correspondence as they are essential evidence when disputes need to be settled. So business letters are introduced in any kind of business activities.

A business letter has its special features, especially in format and structure. Considered in its most fundamental terms, a business letter may be defined as a message that attempts to influence its receiver to take some action or attitude desired by the sender. Thus, the ability to write an effective business letter will help those who want to represent themselves positively to their customers, competitors and employers.

1.1 Criteria for a business letter

Business negotiation in international trade is the process in which the seller and the buyer negotiate about the trade terms in order to reach an agreement about the sales of goods. Business negotiations usually undergo four stages: inquiry, offer, counter-offer, and acceptance. Among them, offer and acceptance are the two necessary stages. The business letter plays a very important role in these business stages; it is written to serve a specific purpose and often gives rise to the legal obligations of the writer.

When writing a business letter, you'd better follow the below 7Cs.

1.1.1 Courtesy

Courtesy is not mere politeness. A courteous writer should be sincere and tactful, thoughtful and appreciative. In order to make a business letter courteous, try to avoid irritating, offensive, or belittling statements. To answer letters promptly is also a matter of courtesy. Punctuality will please your customer who dislikes waiting for days before he gets a reply to his letter.

Look at the following sentences and think about whether or not they are well written:

1) You are requested to remit the amount by Dec. 22nd, 2019.

   Please remit the amount by Dec. 22nd, 2019.

2) We must tell you that we can't accept your price.

Unfortunately, we cannot accept your price.

1.1.2 Consideration

Prepare every message with the reader in mind and try to put yourself in his place. Plan the best way to present the message for the reader to receive. Emphasize the You-attitude rather than the We-attitude. When writing a letter, keep the reader's request, needs, desires, as well as his feelings in mind. It is also better to focus on the positive rather than the negative approach.

Look at the following sentences and think about whether or not they are well written:

1) We allow a 2% discount for cash payment. We won't be able to send you the brochure this month.

2) You earn a 2% discount when you pay cash. We will send you the brochure next month.

3) It is regretted that the goods cannot be sent today. We are pleased to inform you that the goods will be sent tomorrow.

1.1.3 Clarity

You must try to express yourself clearly. To achieve this, you should keep in mind the purpose of your letter; and use appropriate words in correct sentence structures to convey your meaning. You should also avoid ambiguous sentences.

For example:

As to the steamers sailing from Hong Kong to San Francisco, we have bimonthly direct services.

The word "bimonthly" has two meanings: *twice a month* and *once two months*. So, this sentence can be rewritten as follows:

1) We have two direct sailings every month from Hong Kong to San Francisco.

2) We have semimonthly direct sailing from Hong Kong to San Francisco.

3) We have a direct sailing from Hong Kong to San Francisco every two months.

1.1.4 Conciseness

Conciseness means saying things in the fewest possible words. A concise business letter should say things briefly but completely without losing clarity or courtesy. To achieve conciseness, try to avoid wordiness or redundancy.

Two points need to be considered:

(1) avoid using wordy expressions

For example:

Wordy: We wish to acknowledge receipt of your letter...

Concise: We appreciate your letter...

Wordy: We have begun to export our electronic toys to countries abroad.

Concise: We have begun to export our electronic toys.

(2) avoid the out-of-date words or jargons

You shouldn't use:	You should use:
subsequent	after
prior to	before
in the event of	if
enclosed please find	we enclose
of even day	of today
on the question of	concerning
at this time	now
due to the fact that	because
a draft in the amount of $1,000	a draft for $1,000

1.1.5 Completeness

Business communication should include all necessary information. It is essential to check the message carefully before it is sent out.

For example:

I write to send my congratulations.

Congratulations to you on your promotion.

1.1.6 Correctness

As applied to a business message, correctness means appropriate and grammatically correct languages, factual information and accurate reliable figures.

Compare the following examples:

1) Our competitors were more successful than ours (us).

2) We have drawn on you as usual under your L/C.

(Rewriting): We have drawn on you our sight draft No.755 for the Invoice amount USD560.00 under your L/C No.126 of the HSBC Bank.

1.1.7 Concreteness

Writing concretely means making your message specific, definite and vivid rather than vague, general and abstract. A business letter should avoid emptiness in contents and vagueness in ideas.

Look at the following sentences and think about whether or not they are well written:

1) These brakes can stop a car within a short distance.

2) These Goodson power brakes can stop a 2-ton car within 26 feet.

1.2 The Structure of a business letter and samples

1.2.1 The Structure of a business letter

1.2.1.1 Standard parts

1) Letterhead/Heading

A printed letterhead contains the company's name, address, postcode, telephone number, fax number, etc. For example:

TAIZHOU IMP. & EXP. Co., Ltd

ADD: NO.12 HAIKOU RD. XD DISTRICT, ZHEJIANG PROVINCE

TEL: 86-546-23218732 FAX: 86-546-23218733

2) Date

The date on a business letter is one of the most important pieces of information and it should be typed in full and not abbreviated (e.g. December for Dec.) and there is a growing tendency to omit the -th, -st, -nd and -rd that follow the day (e.g. October 10, 2017).

3) Inside address

The inside address, which consists of the name and address of the company to which you are writing, usually begins on the top left side and below the sender's address.

4) Salutation

On the second line below the inside address type the appropriate salutation. For example:

Dear sirs, — to a company

Gentleman: (commonly used by Americans) — to a company

Dear sir, — to a man if you don't know his name

Dear Madam, — to a woman if you don't know her name

Dear Mr. Smith, — to a man

Dear Mrs. Smith, — to a married woman

Dear Miss Smith, — to a single woman

Dear Ms. Smith, — to a woman you are not sure whether she is married or not

5) The main body

This contains the actual message of the letter. The letter should be carefully planned and paragraphed, with the first paragraph referring to any previous correspondence and the last paragraph to future actions or plans.

6) Complimentary close

It is merely a polite way of ending a letter. It should match the salutation. The most commonly used sets of salutation complimentary close are:

Formal:

Dear Sir(s)— Yours faithfully; Faithfully

Gentlemen— Yours truly; Truly yours

Informal:

Yours sincerely; or Sincerely yours

7) Signature

A letter should be signed by hand and in ink. Because many handwritten signatures are illegible, the name of the signer is usually typed below the signature and followed by his job title or position.

For example:

Johnson Ford

Sales Manager

1.2.1.2 Optional Parts

Some optional parts of a business letter are:

(1) The reference

Our Ref.: 12301 JS/EW

(2) Attention line

Attention: Sales Manager

(between the inside address and the salutation)

(3) The subject line

Subject: Price Reductions

(between the salutation and the main body)

(4) Enclosure

Enclosures: 3 or Encls. 3

(5) Carbon copy

c.c. to Beijing Office, Global Trade Co.

(6) Postscript

P.S.: The invitation will be mailed to you in a day or two.

1.2.2 Samples of business letters

Letters for establishing business relations

The establishment of business relations is one of the important undertakings in the field of foreign trade as a foreign trade firm needs extensive business connections to maintain or expand its business activities. It is the first step in dealing with and developing mutual trade. So it is a very important part of business communication.

Sample Letter 1

Dear Sirs,

We have obtained your name and address from the Communication Bank of China, who informed us that you are an experienced importer of light industrial products. We are writing to enter into business relations with you and push the sales of our products.

We specialize in the exportation of light industrial products for many years; the products have enjoyed great popularity in the European market.

As to our standing, we are permitted to mention the Commercial Bank of London as a reference.

We enclose a copy of our catalogue for your reference and hope you will give us the specific inquiry at an early date.

Yours faithfully,

Samson Lau

Sales Manager

Sample Letter 2

Dear Sirs or Madams,

We have obtained your name and address from the website: www.alibaba.com. We were informed that you are one of the biggest importers of tea in the UK and you are now in the market for tea.

We take this opportunity to approach you in the hope of establishing business relations with you.

To give you a general idea of our products, we enclose herewith a copy of our brochure covering the main items available at present.

If you are interested in any of our products or have other products you would like to import, please contact us with your requirements. We look forward to providing you with high quality products and superior customer service.

Yours faithfully,

Samson Lau

Sales Manager

Inquiry Letter

The letter of inquiry is one of the most important types of business letter. When a buyer wishes to get some information about the quantity, price, availability, etc. of goods to be bought or about the terms of sale, payment ,etc., he writes a letter of inquiry to the seller. It may fall into two categories: general inquiry and specific inquiry.

If the importer wants to have a general idea of the commodity, he may make a request for a price list, a catalogue, samples and other terms. This is a general inquiry. Otherwise, if the importer intends to purchase goods of a certain specification, he may ask the exporter to make an offer or a quotation for the goods. That is a specific inquiry.

Sample Letter 3

Dear Ward,

We learned from the Commercial Counselor's Office of our Embassy in your country that you are a leading exporter of all cotton bedspreads and pillowcases in your country. We take this opportunity to approach you in the hope of establishing business relations with you.

We are a large dealer in textiles, located at the east of Copenhagen, having many years of experience in this line and there is a promising market in our country for your products.

We shall appreciate it if you send us your catalogue and price list at your earliest convenience.

We shall place large orders if your prices are reasonable.

Best regards,

Samson Lau

Sales Manager

Sample Letter 4

Dear Sir,

We are one of the leading importers of sweaters in China. We have seen your products displayed at the Canton Fair.

At present, we are in the market for your sweater, Item No. GE-0756. Will you please quote the lowest price CIF Xingang, inclusive of our 5% commission, stating the earliest date of shipment and terms of payment? We would find it the most helpful if you could provide us with the samples of different colors, and how about the minimum quantity per color and per design?

Should your price be found competitive and the delivery date acceptable, we intend to place a large order with you.

Your prompt attention to this matter will be much appreciated.

Yours faithfully,

Samson Lau

Sales Manager

Sample Letter 5

DHAKA COMMERCIAL LTD.

241 CITY SQUARE, RM 121 DHAKA, BANGLADESH

TO: SHANGHAI NEW CENTURY CO., LTD.

FM: DHAKA COMMERCIAL LTD.

DD: AUG. 8, 2022

Dear sirs,

We are importers of textiles and manufactured cotton goods. We have recently concluded some satisfactory business with CHINA TEXTILE GOODS IMPORT AND EXPORT CORP. LTD. We now have a good demand for ladies' blouses 400 DOZs and therefore write to you in the hope of establishing business relations.

From your recently published catalog, we notice that you are able to supply ladies' blouses, and we should be grateful if you would kindly send us some samples of the goods which you can supply together with a comprehensive price list giving details of packing and specification the time of shipment so as to enable us to go fully into the possibilities of business.

We look forward to your early offer and trust that through our mutual cooperation, we shall be able to conclude some transactions with you in the near future.

Yours Faithfully,

Dhaka Commercial Ltd.

Offer Letter

An offer refers to a promise to supply goods on the terms and conditions in which the seller not only quotes the terms of price but also indicates all necessary terms of sales for the buyer's consideration and acceptance. In addition, an offer may be classified into a firm offer and a non-firm offer.

A firm offer is made when a seller promises to sell goods at a stated price within a stated period of time. Once it has been accepted it cannot be changed or withdrawn and the transaction will be concluded. When the validity is overdue, this offer will cease to be effective and the offeror will no longer take the responsibility of carrying out the commitments stipulated in the offer.

Sample Letter 6

Dear Sampson,

Subject: 90% Cashmere Sweaters

Thank you very much for your enquiry of July 1 for our 90% Cashmere Sweaters.

We are now making you a firm offer subject to your reply reaching us before Aug.15, 2019:

Men's	large	USD 23.50 per piece
ditto	medium	USD 22.00 per piece
ditto	small	USD 20.60 per piece

The above prices are based on the CIF Vancouver basis net.

Payment: By a confirmed irrevocable L/C payable by draft at sight.

Shipment: October 2019 provided the L/C reaches the seller one month before the time of shipment.

We are glad to inform you that our products are selling fast because of their unique design and superior quality. They are just what you want for the fashionable trade like yours. They will appeal to discriminating buyers.

We have received some repeat orders. Our factories are fully committed for months ahead. We suggest you place your order as soon as possible.

We are looking forward to hearing from you soon.

Yours faithfully,

Jerry

The non-firm offer is an informal offer made by the offeror, which has got no validity terms but with clear indications of its confirmation conditions, such as "subject to our final confirmation". It can be considered as an offer which is not upon binding the seller and the details of the offer may change in certain situations.

Sample Letter 7

SHANGHAI NEW CENTURY CO., LTD.
RM 56-120 111 MAOYE MANSION, JIN XIN ROAD, XUHUI DISTRICT, SHANGHAI CHINA

TO: DHAKA COMMERCIAL LTD.
FM: SHANGHAI NEW CENTURY CO., LTD.
DD: AUG. 12, 2022
Dear sirs,
We were delighted to receive your inquiry letter on August 8. Enclosed is our price list with the details you requested. And also, we are sending you some samples by separate post. We are confident that when you have examined you will agree that the goods are both excellent in quality and reasonable in price.
Because of their softness and durability, our all ladies' blouses are rapidly becoming popular and after studying our prices, you will learn that we are finding it difficult to meet the demand.
We look forward to the pleasure of receiving an order from you.
Yours
SHANGHAI NEW CENTURY CO., LTD

Sample Letter 8

Dear Mr. Thomas,
I have received your request for quotation dated Jan. 20, 2019. We are pleased to present you with the following non-firm offer for our products.

Name of Commodity	Price
All Wool Melton	USD 12.50/PC CIF HONGKONG
All wool gabardine	USD 30.20/PC CIF HONGKONG

The minimum quality for an order is 2,000 pcs. Shipment is to be made in three equal monthly installments beginning from May, 2019. Payment is by an irrevocable letter of credit at sight. All the commodities must be packed in cartons.
Prices are valid for one month. We hope you find our offer satisfactory as usual and look forward

to receiving your order promptly.

Sincerely,

Sampson

Sales Manager

Counteroffer Letter

A counteroffer is legally called a partial rejection of the original offer. It also means a counter proposal put forward by the offeree, who could propose some material amendments or alterations for the offer maker to consider. In fact, the counteroffer is a reply that adds to, limits and materially amends the original offer and is regarded as a new offer. Once a counteroffer appears, the original offer has been invalid and replaced by it. Then the counteroffer becomes a new offer and the foundation of business negotiation.

A counteroffer may come from or be made by the buyer when he receives the offer and makes material alterations in reply or the seller when he receives the counteroffer from the buyer and makes some changes of or alterations to the counteroffer, thus being called a re-counteroffer or a counter-counteroffer.

Sample Letter 9

Dear Jerry,

Re: Your offer of 90% Cashmere Sweaters

Thank you for your letter of July 10, in which you offered us 90% Cashmere Sweaters.

Regrettably, we are unable to accept your offer as your prices are too high. We operate on small margins. It means a heavy loss for us to accept your prices. We also have similar offers from American make. They are 25% lower than yours.

We like the quality and design of your products. We accept that the quality of your products is better, but it does not justify such a large difference in price. We might do business with you if you could make us some allowance, say 20%, on your prices. Otherwise we have to decline your offer.

We hope you will consider our counteroffer most favorably and let us have your reply soon.

Yours faithfully,

Sampson

Sales Manager

Sample Letter 10

Dear Mr. Zhang,

Re: Green Tea Extract and Porcelain Tea Set

We acknowledge with thanks receipt of your offer of May 8 for the subject goods.

In reply, we regret to say that we can't accept it. Your prices are rather on the high side and out of line with the world market. Information indicates that some parcels of Japanese make have been sold at a much lower level.

We have seen your samples and admit that they are of high quality, but there should not be such a big gap between your prices and those of other suppliers.

In order to conclude the transaction, we suggest that you reduce the prices of both products by, say 30%.

We hope you can accept the counteroffer and wait for your favorable reply.

Truly yours,

Global Tea Bags (Pvt) Ltd

Sample Letter 11

DHAKA COMMERCIAL LTD.

241 CITY SQUARE, RM 121 DHAKA, BANGLADESH

TO: SHANGHAI NEW CENTURY CO., LTD.

FM: DHAKA COMMERCIAL LTD.

DD: AUG. 20, 2022

Dear sirs,

Thank you for your letter dated August 12, 2022 and the attached quotation.

After careful examination and comparison with similar products of other brands, we found that your price is higher than the average in the market. In order to allow us a better-competing position, we shall be grateful if you could reduce the price to USD 50.00 per DOZ CIF LESS 3 PCT DISCOUNT CHITTAGONG. Moreover, we advise you to make some adjustments to your terms of payment L/C to D/P at sight and that the time of shipment should be on or before Nov. ember 20th, 2022.

We hope we can enter into a lasting business relationship with you and look forward to receiving your reply.

Yours Faithfully,

Dhaka Commercial Ltd.

Acceptance Letter

In business law, an acceptance letter is a final and unconditional expression of assent to the terms and conditions put forward by the offeror or the offeree. It must be tendered only by the person to whom the offer is made, and must confirm any conditions concerning it that are set forth in the offer. In accordance with the usual practice in international trade, an acceptance should confirm the following conditions. An acceptance can only be made in the form of a statement or any other conduct by an offeree, the particular person or a group of persons, who are clearly stipulated in the firm offer. Either a verbal or written statement is good for this purpose. The conduct that the seller delivers the goods or the buyer makes the payment also serves. On the contrary, silence or inactivity is by no means an acceptance.

An acceptance must be unconditional. It should be an unreserved assent to all the terms designated in the offer. In principle, if additions, modifications or limitations to the offer are made, it is a counteroffer, not an acceptance.

It is necessary that an offeree should make an acceptance with the firm offer. An acceptance, as a rule, takes effect when it reaches the offeror. An order can also be an acceptance of an offer or sent voluntarily by a buyer. It should be clearly and accurately written out and state all the terms of transaction. Many buyers now use printed order forms which ensure that no important information will be neglected.

Sample Letter 12

Dear Jerry,

We are pleased to receive your order No.135 Canned Fruit. We accept the order and are enclosing our Sales Confirmation No.354 in duplicate of which please sign and return one copy to us for our file. We trust you will open the relative L/C at an early date.

As to items A and B, we shall arrange delivery as soon as we get your L/C, and for items C and D we shall ship accordingly.

Hoping the goods will turn out to be your entire satisfaction and we may have further orders from you.

Yours faithfully,

Sampson

Sales Manager

Order Letter

When a customer has decided to purchase a product, he will place an order. An order in foreign trade is defined as "a request by a customer for a company to supply goods or service" . It is the result of an offer or a counteroffer with a positive acceptance. An order letter is important and widely used. When writing an order letter, you must be very careful, especially with items, quantities and prices, because a minor mistake may mislead the goods or service providers, which may finally result in the failure of a transaction.

Sample Letter 13

SHANGHAI NEW CENTURY CO., LTD

RM 56-120 111 MAOYE MANSION, JIN XIN ROAD, XUHUI DISTRICT, SHANGHAI CHINA

TO: DHAKA COMMERCIAL LTD.

FM: SHANGHAI NEW CENTURY CO., LTD.

DD: AUG. 26, 2022

Dear sirs,

Thank you for your fax of August 24, 2011.

Enclosed are two copies of your sales confirmation No. 22SCC-22-04. Please sign and return one copy for our file.

We can assure you of the high quality as well as the punctuate delivery so long as the relative L/C reaches our end in time. We suppose the conclusion of this transaction will lead to more business in the future.

We appreciate your co-operation and look forward to receiving your further orders.

Yours

SHANGHAI NEW CENTURY CO., LTD.

Sample Letter 14

DHAKA COMMERCIAL LTD.

241 CITY SQUARE, RM 121 DHAKA, BANGLADESH

TO: SHANGHAI NEW CENTURY CO., LTD.

FM: DHAKA COMMERCIAL LTD.

Dear Sir,

Thank you so much for your letter of August 24, 2022 and the catalogs. Pursuant to our Telex since that date, we have decided to place an initial order as follows:

Item	Item No.	Color	U/P (USD)	Quantity	Subtotal
Blouse	642	Red	52.50	100DOZS	5,250.00
		Blue	52.50	100DOZS	5,250.00
		Yellow	52.50	100DOZS	5,250.00
		White	52.50	100DOZS	5,250.00
Total				400DOZS	21,000.00

CIF CHITTAGONG

If this order is executed successfully, we will be placing large orders in the future.

Please deliver the goods to our warehouse at 6400 Front Drive, Dhaka. We understand you will be shipping from stock and should expect delivery within the stipulated date. The letter of credit will be prepared as soon as we get your confirmation.

We look forward to a long and successful cooperation.

Yours Sincerely,

John Bush

Purchasing Manager

Dhaka Commercial Ltd.

Sample Letter 15

Dear Mr. Zhang,

We are in receipt of your counteroffer of May 19 and have the pleasure of confirming our acceptance of it.

The enclosed is our purchase order in duplicate. Would you please acknowledge immediately by returning a copy of it signed and/or stamped and dated?

We look forward to your cooperation and hope that both our businesses can grow together for our long-range mutual benefits.

Truly yours,

Global Tea Bags (Pvt) Ltd

1.3 Exercises

1. Write a letter making an offer according to the following situation.

The letter will be from China Textile Corporation, 33 Ningxi Rd, Guangzhou, to Clothing Company, 23 Royal Rd, Taiwan. The offer is for the purchase of 980 women's suits and 400 men's suits in blue and black. Women's suits are USD340.00 and men's suits are USD450.00. A discount offered is 5% from the listed price. Prices are CIF Gaoxiong. Terms of payment are by an irrevocable sight letter of credit. Delivery should be arranged eight weeks after the receipt of the letter of credit. Each item is to be packed in plastic with 10 to the carton.

2. Write a letter from Samson Textile Company, 23 Royal Rd, Taiwan to China Imp. & Exp. Corporation Ltd. (Henan Branch), 128 Beijing Rd, Zhengzhou, Henan Province, to place a trial order.

1,000 yards of #77 cotton cloth (blue) at USD12.80/yd

1,500 yards of #88 cotton cloth (green) at USD21.70/yd

1,200 yards of #99 cotton cloth (grey) at USD10.60/yd

Terms of payment: an irrevocable sight letter of credit. All other conditions are followed by the quotation.

3. Please write the inquiry, offer, counter-offer, and acceptance letters according to the following telexes between SHANGHAI NEW CENTURY CO., LTD. and DHAKA COMMERCIAL LTD.

Aug. 8, 2022

Incoming telex

INTERESTED IN LADIES' 55 PCT ACRYLIC 50 PCT COTTON KNITTED BLOUSE 500 DOZS SHIPMENT AS SOON AS POSSIBLE PLEASE QUOTE.

Aug. 12, 2022

Outgoing telex

LADIES' 55 PCT ACRYLIC 50 PCT COTTON KNITTED BLOUSE 400 DOZS PACKED IN CARTONS USD 62.50 PER DOZ CIF LESS 5 PCT DISCOUNT CHITTAGONG SHIPMENT ON OR BEFORE DEC. 20, 2022 SIGHT CREDIT SUBJECT REPLY HERE

SIXTEENTH.

Aug. 18, 2022

Incoming telex

YOUR TLX TWELFTH REGRET UNABLE ACCEPT COMPETITORS QUOTING SIMILAR QUALITY USD 50.00 PLEASE REPLY IMMEDIATELY.

Aug. 20, 2022

Incoming telex

YOURS EIGHTEENTH ACCEPT PROVIDED USD 50.00 CIF LESS 3 PCT DISCOUNT D/P AT SIGHT SHIPMENT IN NOV. PLEASE CONFIRM.

Aug. 23, 2022

Outgoing telex

YOURS TWENTIETH BEST USD 52.50 SIGHT CREDIT SUBJECT REPLY REACHING HERE TWENTY-FIFTH.

Aug. 24, 2022

Incoming telex

YOURS TWENTY-THIRD ACCEPT BOOK ADDITIONAL 100 DOZS SAME TERMS REPLY PROMPTLY.

Aug. 26, 2022

Outgoing telex

YOURS TWENTY-FOURTH CONFIRMED PLEASE OPEN L/C IMMEDIATELY.

Aug. 28, 2022

Incoming telex

YOURS TWENTY-SIXTH CREDIT WILL BE OPENED BY DHAKA COMMERCIAL BANK.

Chapter 2

International Sales Contract

The international sale contract is the most used commercial contract and among the governing trade relations between two different nations, which is generally given in writing. The agreement includes the rights, duties, obligations, and remedies for breach of the parties to the contract. The parties can be either an exporter/seller or an importer/buyer.

The international sale contract should have details like quantity and type of product, delivery time, conditions of payment, price, governing body of law, the forum where the dispute has to be solved (if any arises), and the method of dispute resolution.

2.1 Formation of a sales contract

There are five basic requirements that need to be satisfied in order to make a sales contract:

- An agreement between the parties (which is usually shown by the fact that one has made an offer and the other has accepted it).
- An intention to be legally bound by that agreement (often called intent to create legal relations).
- Certainty as to the terms of the agreement.
- Capacity to contract.
- Consideration provided by each of the parties—put simply, this means that there must be some kind of exchange between the parties. If I say I will give you my car, and you simply agree to have it, I have voluntarily made you a promise (often called a gratuitous promise), which you cannot enforce in law if I change my mind. If, however, I promise to hand over my car and you promise to pay me a sum of money in return, we have each provided consideration.

In addition, in some cases, the parties must comply with certain formalities. Remember that, with a few exceptions, it is not necessary for a contract to be in writing—a contract is an agreement, not a piece of paper.

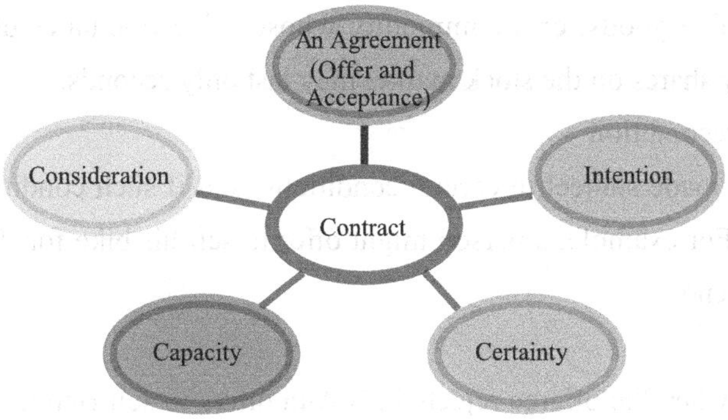

For a contract to exist, usually one party must have made an offer, and the other must have accepted it. Once acceptance takes effect, the contract will usually be binding on both parties, and the rules of offer and acceptance are typically used to pinpoint when a series of negotiations have passed that point, in order to decide whether the parties are obliged to fulfil their promises. There is generally no halfway house—negotiations have either crystallised into a binding contract, or they are not binding at all.

2.1.1 Offer

The person making an offer is called the offeror, and the person to whom the offer is made is called the offeree. A communication will be treated as an offer if it indicates the terms on which the offeror is prepared to make a contract (such as the price of the goods for sale), and gives a clear indication that the offeror intends to be bound by those terms if they are accepted by the offeree.

Offeror = the person making the offer Offeree = the person receiving the offer

An offer may be express, when Annie tells Bennie that she will sell her Kindle for CNY 1,020.00, but it can also be implied from conduct—a common example is taking goods to the cash desk in a supermarket, which is an implied offer to buy the goods.

How long does an offer last?

An offer may cease to exist under any of the following circumstances.

• Specified time

Where an offeror states that an offer will remain open for a specific length of time, it lapses when that time is up.

• Reasonable time

Where the offeror has not specified how long the offer will remain open, it will lapse after a reasonable length of time has passed. Exactly that how long this is will depend upon whether the means of communicating the offer is fast or slow and upon its subject matter—for example, offers to buy perishable goods, or a commodity whose price fluctuates daily, will lapse quite quickly. Offers to buy shares on the stock market may last only seconds.

• Failure of a precondition

Some offers are made subject to certain conditions, and if such conditions are not in place, the offer may lapse. For example, a person might offer to sell his bike for £ 50 if he manages to buy a car at the weekend.

• Rejection

An offer lapses when the offeree rejects it. If Ann offers to sell Ben her car on Tuesday, and Ben says no, Ben cannot come back on Tuesday and insist on accepting the offer.

• Counteroffer

A counteroffer terminates the original offer.

• Death of the offeror

The position is not entirely clear, but it appears that if the offeree knows that the offeror has died, the offer will lapse; if the offeree is unaware of the offeror's death, it probably will not.

• Death of the offeree

There is no English case on this point, but it seems probable that the offer lapses and cannot be accepted after the offeree's death by the offeree's representatives.

• Withdrawal of an offer

The withdrawal of an offer is sometimes described as the revocation of an offer.

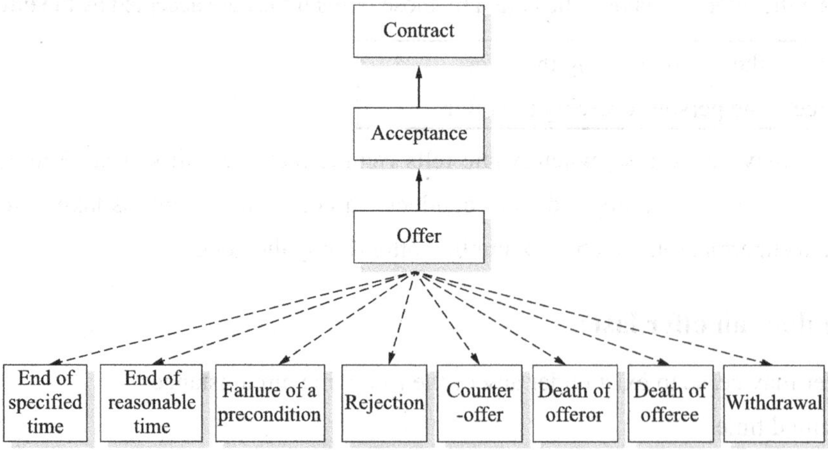

Termination of an offer

2.1.2 Acceptance

In international trade practice, acceptance should abide by the following requirements:

• Acceptance must be absolute and unconditional. It should be an unreserved assent to all the terms put forward in the offer. In principle, in any additions, modifications or limitations to the offer are made, it becomes a counteroffer instead of acceptance.

- Acceptance can be made by an act performed by an offeree, such as one relating to the dispatch of the goods or the payment of the price.
- Acceptance must be clearly expressed by the offeree's verbal or written statement. Silence or inactivity is by no means acceptance.
- Acceptance must be made by the offeree within the valid period of an offer. As a rule, acceptance goes into effect immediately as soon as it reaches the offeror.

2.1.3 Time of the formation of the contract

Normally a contract is formed when effective acceptance has been communicated to the offeror. An exception to this is the postal rule, where the contract is formed at the time acceptance is posted and there is no need for communication.

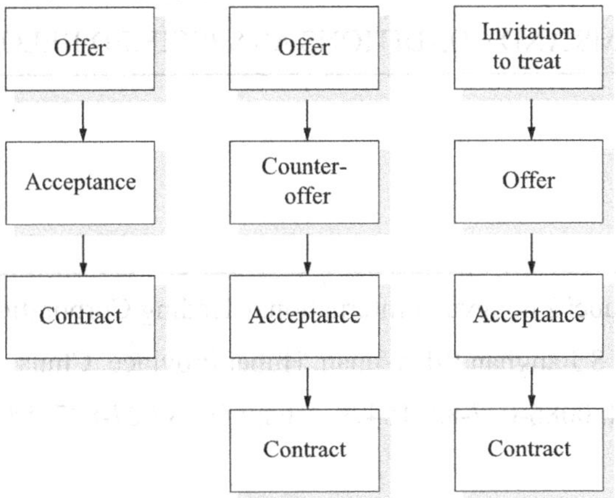

Three examples of how a contract can be made

2.2 The Structure of a sales contract

No matter what name and what type the contract is, a formal business contract usually consists of three parts: the preamble, the body and witness clauses.

2.2.1 The preamble

The preamble is a preliminary statement to introduce the general reasoning of the agreement, the principle of reaching the agreement, or the scope of authority. It usually includes a title, the registered name of the company, the address of operation/residence and the contract information, the date and place for signing of the contract and the preface or recitals of WHEREAS clauses, etc.

Sample 1

售货确认书

SALES CONFIRMATION

卖方 THE SELLER: 合同号 (NO.): 0609030

SHANDONG TRADING IMP. & EXP. CO., LTD. 合同日期 (DATE): APRIL 12, 2019

买方 THE BUYER:

W/W TEXTILES

兹确认售予你方下列货品其成交条款如下：

DEAR SIRS. WE HEREBY CONFIRM HAVING SOLD TO YOU THE FOLLOWING GOODS ON THE TERMS AND CONDITIONS AS SPECIFIED BELOW:

Sample 2

Hubei Zhongyuan International Trading Corporation

8 Jianghan Rd, Wuhan, Hubei Province, China

Tel: 0086-027-82715409 Fax: 0086-027-82715410

Sales Confirmation

To: Iveli Products PJC S/C No.: IP340-2

10 Cambridge Str. London, UK Date: Jan. 24, 2019

We hereby confirm having sold to you the following goods on the terms and conditions as stated below:

2.2.2 The body

The main body is the core of a contract. It mainly includes basic clauses and general terms and conditions of the contract, reflecting duties and obligations of both parties. Generally speaking, the basic clauses are: the name of commodity, the quality, the quantity, the unit price, the packing, the payment, the shipment, the commodity inspection, the insurance, etc. Usually for purchase or sales confirmation or short-form contracts, only these basic clauses are included.

Detailed contracts also include general terms and conditions as inspection, claim, arbitration, force majeure, etc., which may vary on different occasions and be printed overleaf.

2.2.3 Witness clauses

The witness clauses, as final clauses of a contract, usually include contract validity, language validity, copies, signature, seal, and so on.

Usually, the parties concerned in a contract will stipulate that the contract comes into effect when it is signed and sealed. The legal language used for composing the contract should be determined. If two or more languages are adopted, the prevailing language should also be determined in case of discrepancy between or among the different versions. Original copies of the contract should be determined by specifying the number of copies. Usually, each party keeps one original copy of the contract.

Sample

The Seller	The Buyer
Hubei Zhongyuan	Iveli Products PJC
International Trading Corporation	

2.3 Contents of a sales contract

2.3.1 Name of commodity

This is one of the main clauses in a sales contract, as a buyer always prefers a detailed and more precise description of the goods from the seller, and if the goods are not described precisely enough that satisfy the buyer, then those goods are unsatisfactory for the buyer's commercial purposes.

Usually, the name of a commodity, being clearly stipulated and trying to give a specific and widely accepted name, is specified in contracts under the subject "Name of Commodity" and is listed with the quality clause together.

E.g. Changhong Brand Color Television Set

Model SC023

Points for attention when drawing up the clause:

- *Be clear and specific.*
- *Be practical and realistic.*
- *Try to adopt the name of a commodity which is internationally accepted.*
- *Select an appropriate name for the commoditiy to facilitate importing and reduce customs duties and freight charges.*

2.3.2 Quality of goods

The quality of a commodity is the combination of the intrinsic quality and the outside form or the shape of the commodity, such as the structure, the taste, the chemical composition, etc. In international trade, the methods of expressing the quality of a commodity may generally be classified into two kinds: by description and by actual quality.

	Mode of Transaction		Method of Expressing Quality
Sale by actual quality	Sale by inspection		Inspect the seen goods
	Sale by sample	Sale by seller's sample	Seller's sample
		Sale by buyer's sample	Buyer's sample
Sale by description	Sale by specification, grade or standard		Specification, grade or standard
	Sale by brand name/ trade mark		Brand name / trade mark
	Sale by description		Instructions, drawings, etc.
	Sale by name of origin		Name / place of origin

2.3.3 Quality tolerance

In trading agricultural products, industrial raw materials or some products of light industry, a tolerance clause is usually stipulated in the sales contract. Tolerance means the permissible range within which the quality supplied by the seller may be either superior or inferior to the quality stipulated in the contract. The tolerance may be that agreed upon between the seller and the buyer beforehand, or that generally recognized by trade associations. Such tolerance can be compensated by the increase or decrease of the price in proportion to the degree of the tolerance. Sometimes, a price adjustment is not needed if the tolerance is within a certain limit.

Example 1:

Chinese Groundnut 2009 Crop, F.A.Q.

Moisture (max.) 12%

Admixture (max.) 4%

Oil content (min.) 45%

Example 2:

Fresh Hen Eggs: Shell light brown and clean, even in size

Grade A A: 60-65g per egg

Grade A: 55-60g per egg

Grade B: 50-55g per egg

Grade C: 45-50g per egg

2.3.4 Quantity of goods

It is evident that a business deal cannot be completed without caring for the quantity of the goods sold or bought. The quantity of goods refers to the weight, the number, the length, the volume, the area, the capacity, etc., which are indicated by different measuring units.

Units of Measurement	
Weight	gram(g), kilogram(kg), ounce(oz), pound(Ib), metric ton(M/T), long ton, short ton, etc.
Number	piece(pc), package(pkg), pair, set, dozen(doz), gross(gr), ream(rm), etc.
Length	meter(m), centimeter(cm), foot(ft), yard(yd), etc.
Area	square meter(sqm), square foot(sqft), square yard(sqyd), etc.
Volume	cubic meter(cbm), cubic foot(cuft), cubic yard(cuyd), etc.
Capacity	liter(l), gallon(gal), pint(pt), bushel(bu), etc.

2.3.5 More or less clauses

At the time of the conclusion of a contract, the quantity clause should be clearly and definitely stipulated so as to avoid possible disputes thereafter. However, it is very difficult to accurately measure some agricultural and mineral products like corn, soybean, wheat, coal, etc. What's more, influenced by natural conditions, packing patterns, and loading and unloading methods, the quantity of goods delivered by the seller usually does not conform to the quantity definitely stipulated in the contract. In order to facilitate the processing of the contract, the seller and the buyer, generally, agree to use the "more or less clause", which means over-load and under-load are permitted without surpassing a certain percentage of the stipulated quantity. A more or less clause usually contains three parts: the quantity of the deal, the measurement unit and a more or less clause. For example, "dehydrated garlic flackes, 450 M/T with 5% more or less at seller's option" "Chinese peanut 1,000 metric tons, gross for net, 5% more or less at buyer's option at contract price".

2.3.6 Unit price

In international trade, the price term lies at the core of the terms and conditions of a contract and often results in some of the key problems which the exporter and the importer have to solve.

The price of a commodity usually refers to the unit price. A unit price consists of four parts: the type of currency, the price per unit, the measurement unit and trade terms. The details are as follows:

- **Type of currency:** Conventionally, the currency is indicated in abbreviations in the contract with 3 capital letters. For example, CNY, USD, GBP, EUR, JPY, etc.
- **Price per unit:** Generally, it consists of the purchasing cost of the goods, inland freight, packing expenses, inspection fees, tariffs, warehousing, etc. In some cases, ocean freight and insurance premiums should be covered in the quotation. The price margin, of course, should also be considered when a price is quoted.
- **Measurement unit:** The specific measurement unit has been mentioned in the "Quantity".
- **Trade terms:** Two new 2010 Incoterms rules—DAT and DAP—have replaced the Incoterms 2,000 rules DAF, DES, DEQ AND DDU, that is, the number of Incoterms rules has been reduced from 13 to 11.

The 11 Incoterms 2010 rules are presented in two distinct classes: rules for any mode or modes of transport—EXW, FCA, CPT, CIP, DAT, DAP, DDP and rules for sea and inland waterway transport—FAS, FOB, CFR, CIF.

Examples:

1) EUR 231.00 PER DOZEN CIF ANTWERP

2) HKD 11.40 PER SET FOB SHANGHAI

3) USD 20.04/PC CIP LONDON

4) USD 500.00 PER METRIC TON CIFC3 NEW YORK

2.3.7 Packing

Packing is very important in international trade because it must help the goods travel all along across oceans or continents to finally reach the buyer safe and sound. The packing terms in a contract usually include packing materials, packing methods, packing specifications, packing marks, packing fees, etc.

Examples:

1) Packed in cartons of 50 kilos net each.

2) In international standard tea cartons, 10 cartons on a pallet, 10 pallets in an FCL container.

3) To be packed in poly bags, 25 pounds in a bag, 4 bags in a sealed wooden case, which is

lined with metal. The cost of packing is for seller's account.

2.3.8 Shipment

Shipment refers to the carriage of the goods from the seller to the buyer, which includes the time of shipment, the port of loading, the port of destination, the partial shipment, the transshipment, the demurrage, the dispatch, etc.

Examples:

1) Shipment is effected on or before/not latter than/latest on August 12, 2019.

2) Shipment to be made within 30 days after the receipt of the L/C. The relevant L/C must reach the sellers not later than July 30, 2019.

3) Shipment from Shanghai, China to Genoa, Italy during July, 2019 with partial shipment allowed, transshipment not permitted.

2.3.9 Payment

In international trade, payment is a complicated and risky procedure that both the exporter and the importer concern most. The main modes of payment in international trade can be generally divided into three categories: Letter of Credit, Remittance and Collection. The letter of credit is a bank credit while remittance and collection are commercial credits.

Examples:

1) Our term of payment is by a confirmed, irrevocable letter of credit, available by draft at sight for the full amount of the invoice value to be established in our favor through the bank approved by us.

2) Payment is by an irrevocable L/C at 75 days from the B/L date in the seller's favor issued by a prime bank acceptable to the seller, for 100% of the invoice value.

2.3.10 Insurance

In international trade, insurance is essential. It should be indicated in the contract whether the seller or the buyer covers insurance on the goods. Under contracts, on the basis of FOB or CFR, insurance is to be covered by the buyers.

Examples:

1) Insurance is to be covered All Risks and War Risk for the CIF invoice value plus 10%.

2) Insurance to cover WPA plus TPND and War Risk for 110% of the CIF value and to provide for claims, if any, payable in Boston in the US currency.

2.4 Contract drafting

Given materials:

SELLER:	SHANDONG TRADING IMP. & EXP. CO., LTD.
BUYER:	W/W TEXTILES
CONTRACT DATE:	APRIL 12, 2019
S/C NO.:	0609030
DESCRIPTION OF GOODS:	COTTON TEA TOWELS
QUANTITY:	10,000 DOZS
UNIT PRICE:	GBP0.318/DOZ CFR SOUTHAMPTON
AMOUNT:	GBP3,180.00
PACKING:	ONE DOZEN IN A PLASTIC BAG, TEN BAGS TO A CARTON
N.W.:	1,940KGS
G.W.:	2,000.5KGS
MEASUREMENT:	54.120CBM
SHIPPING MARK:	W/W SOUTHAMPTON C/NO.1-UP
SHIPMENT:	FROM QINGDAO, CHINA TO SOUTHAMPTON, BRITAIN VIA HONGKONG NOT LATER THAN JUNE 10, 2019
INSURANCE:	TO BE COVERED BY BUYER
PAYMENT:	BY IRREVOCABLE LETTER OF CREDIT AT SIGHT

售货确认书
SALES CONFIRMATION

卖方 THE SELLER: 合同号 (NO.): 0609030

SHANDONG TRADING IMP. & EXP. CO., LTD. 合同日期 (DATE): APR 12, 2019

买方 THE BUYER:

W/W TEXTILES

兹确认售予你方下列货品，其成交条款如下：

DEAR SIRS. WE HEREBY CONFIRM HAVING SOLD TO YOU THE FOLLOWING GOODS ON THE TERMS AND CONDITIONS AS SPECIFIED BELOW:

(1)品名 NAME OF COMMODITY	(2)数量 QUANTITY	(3)单价 UNIT PRICE	(4)毛重 G.W.	(5)净重 N.W.	(6)体积 MEAS	(7)金额 AMOUNT
COTTON TEA TOWELS	10,000 DOZS	GBP0.318 PER DOZ	2,000.5 KGS	1,940 KGS	54. 120 CBM	GBP3,180.00
TOTAL AMOUNT 总金额	SAY GREAT BRITAIN POUND THREE THOUSAND ONE HUNDRED AND EIGHTY ONLY					GBP3,180.00

CFR SOUTHAMPTON

(8)装运期限：从中国青岛运至英国南安普顿，经香港转运，不迟于2019年6月10日装出。

TIME OF SHIPMENT: FROM QINGDAO, CHINA TO SOUTHAMPTON, BRITAIN VIA HONGKONG NOT LATER THAN JUNE 10, 2019

(9)包装条款：每打装一塑料袋，十袋装一箱

PACKING: ONE DOZEN IN A PLASTIC BAG, TEN BAGS TO A CARTON

(10)付款条件：

TERMS OF PAYMENT:

不可撤销的即期信用证

BY IRREVOCABLE LETTER OF CREDIT AT SIGHT

(11)保险：

INSURANCE:

买方自理

TO BE COVERED BY BUYER

(12)装运标志：

SHIPPING MARK:

W/W
SOUTHAMPTON
C/NO.1-1000

卖方签署
THE SELLER
SHANDONG TRADING IMP. & EXP. CO., LTD.
SAMPSON JOHN

买方签署
THE BUYER
W/W TEXTILES
ALICE JUDY

Sample of sales confirmation:

售货确认书

SALES CONFIRMATION

卖方 THE SELLER:
JINZHE TRADING CO., LTD

合同号 (C/NO.): JZ-DRGSC01
合同日期 (DATE): APRIL 1st, 2019

买方 THE BUYER :

DRAGON TOY CO., LTD
兹确认售予你方下列货品，其成交条款如下：
DEAR SIRS. WE HEREBY CONFIRM HAVING SOLD TO YOU THE FOLLOWING GOODS ON THE TERMS AND CONDITIONS AS SPECIFIED BELOW:

ITEM NO.	COMMODITY& SPECIFICATIONS	QTY (PC)	U/P (USD)	AMT (USD)
TELECONTROL RACING CAR		CIFC3 NEW YORK		
1.	ART.18812	2,400	19.88	47,712.00
2.	ART.18814	2,000	20.66	41,320.00
3.	ART.18817	2,000	21.94	43,880.00
4.	ART.18819	2,400	23.06	55,344.00
TOTAL		8,800		188,256.00
TOTAL CONTRACT VALUE: SAY US DOLLARS ONE HUNDRED EIGHTY-EIGHT THOUSAND TWO HUNDRED AND FIFTY-SIX ONLY				

PACKING:

ART. NO.18812 &18819 TO BE PACKED IN CARTONS OF 12 PIECES EACH
ART NO.18814 & 18817 TO BE PACKED IN CARTONS OF 20 PIECES EACH
ALL PRODUCTS IN FOUR 20' CONTAINERS.

TIME OF SHIPMENT:

SHIPMENT IN MAY 2019 AFTER RECEIVING THE RELEVANT LETTER OF CREDIT WITH PARTIAL SHIPMENT AND TRANSSHIPMENT ALLOWED.

PORT OF LOADING & DESTINATION:

FROM DALIAN CHINA TO NEW YORK USA

PAYMENT:

THE BUYER SHALL OPEN AN IRREVOCABLE L/C IN FAVOR OF THE SELLER BEFORE APR.15, 2019. THE SAID L/C SHALL BE AVAIL BY DRAFT AT SIGHT FOR FULL INVOICE VALUE AND REMAIN VALID FOR NEGOTIATION IN CHINA FOR 15 DAYS AFTER SHIPMENT.

INSURANCE:

TO BE COVERED BY THE SELLER FOR 110% OF TOTAL INVOICE VALUE AGAINST ALL RISKS AND WAR RISK AS PER THE OCEAN MARINE CARGO CLAUSES OF THE PEOPLE'S INSURANCE COMPANY OF CHINA, DATED JAN. 1ST, 1981.

SHIPPING MARK:

D.R.G.
JZ-DRGSC01
NEW YORK
C/NO.: 1-600

THE SELLER	THE BUYER
JINZHE TRADING CO., LTD	DRAGON TOY CO., LTD
GRACE ZHANG	THEOBALD. TIAN

Remarks:

1. The buyer shall have the covering letter of credit, which should reach the seller 30 days before shipment, failing which the seller reserves the right to rescind without further notice, or to regard as still valid the whole or any part of this contract not fulfilled by the buyer, or to lodge a claim for losses thus sustained, if any.

2. In case of any discrepancy in quality/quantity, a claim should be filed by the buyer within 30 days after the arrival of the goods at the port of destination; while for quantity discrepancy, the claim should be filed by the buyer within 15 days after the arrival of the goods at the port of destination.

3. For transactions concluded on the CIF basis (Incoterms 2010), it is understood that the insurance amount will be for 110% of the invoice value against the risks specified in the *Sales Confirmation*. If an additional insurance amount or coverage is required, the buyer must have the consent of the seller before shipment, and the additional premium is to be borne by the buyer.

4. The seller shall not hold liable for non-delivery or delay in delivery of the entire lot or a portion of the goods hereunder by reason of natural disasters, wars or other causes of Force Majeure. However, the seller shall notify the buyer as soon as possible and furnish the buyer within 15 days by a registered airmail with a certificate issued by the China Council for the Promotion of International Trade attesting such event(s).

5. All deputies arising out of the performance of , or relating to this contract, shall be settled through negotiation. In case no settlement can be reached through negotiation, the case shall then be submitted to the China International Economic and Trade Arbitration Commission for arbitration in accordance with its arbitral rules. The arbitration shall take place in Dalian. The arbitral award is final and binding upon both parties.

6. The buyer is requested to sign and return one copy of this contract immediately after the receipt of the same. Objection, if any, should be raised by the buyer within it, or it is understood that the buyer has accepted the terms and conditions of this contract.

7. Special conditions (These shall prevail over all printed items in case of any conflict.).

2.5 Exercises

1. Please translate the following sentences into Chinese.

1) To be covered by the seller for 110% of the total invoice value against all risks and the war risk as per and subject to the relevant Ocean Marine Cargo Cleases of the PICC dated 1981/1/1.

2) This contract is made out in two originals in both Chinese and English, each language being legally of equal effect. Each party keeps one original of the two after the signing of the contract.

3) The buyer shall duly accept the documentary draft drawn by the seller at 30 days sight upon first presentation and make the payment on its maturity. The shipping documents are to be delivered against payment only.

2. Please draw a contract according to the emails between Xinya Imp. & Exp. Co. Ltd, Shanghai, China and Global Trading Corp, Sydney, Australia.

JAN. 9, 2019 INCOMING

XINYA MP3 PLAYER ART NO. NY 101 PLEASE CABLE PRESENT PRICE AND AVAILABLE QUANTITY FOR FEB.

JAN. 10, 2019 OUTGOING

YOUR NINTH XINYA MP3 PLAYER ART NO. NY 101 IN CARTONS OF TEN PIECES EACH REFERENCE PRICE USD 22.00 PER PIECE CIFC5 SYDNEY SHIPMENT FEB.

JAN. 11, 2019 INCOMING

YOUR TENTH INTERESTED 800 CARTONS PLEASE OFFER FIRM.

JAN. 12, 2019 OUTGOING

YOUR ELEVENTH OFFER SUBJECT REPLY HERE THIRTEENTH 800 CARTONS USD 22.00 PER PIECE CIFC5 SYDNEY PAYMENT BY IRREVOCABLE SIGHT LETTER OF CREDIT SHIPMENT WITHIN 30 DAYS AFTER RECEIPT L/C.

JAN. 13, 2019 INCOMING

YOUR TWELFTH USD 19.80 PER PIECE CIFC5 SYDNEY INSURANCE 110 PERCENT INVOICE VALUE AGAINST ALL RISKS AND WAR RISK PAYMENT BY L/C AT 30 DAYS SIGHT PLEASE CABLE REPLY IMMEDIATELY.

JAN. 14, 2019 OUTGOING

YOUR THIRTEENTH USD 20.60 PAYMENT AS USUAL SIGHT CREDIT REPLY HERE FIFTEENTH.

JAN. 15, 2019 INCOMING

YOUR FOURTEENTH L/C OPENING PLEASE CABLE CONTRACT NUMBER.

JAN. 16, 2019 OUTGOING

YOUR FIFTEENTH S/C NUMBER 01 XDTTD-1498.

3. Please draw a contract according to the following materials.

THE SELLER: HANGZHOU INTERNATIONAL TRADING CORPORATION, 8 JIANGHAN ROAD, ZHEJIANG PROVINCE, CHINA

THE BUYER: TIVOLI PRODUCTS PLC 100 CAMBRIDGE STREET, LONDON, UK

USUAL TERMS:

GOODS TO BE PACKED IN CLOTH BALES OF 10 PIECES OF 120.5 YARDS EACH. WHEN BUSINESS IS DONE ON CIF BASIS, THE SELLER SHALL COVER INSURANCE FOR 110 PCT OF CIF INVOICE VALUE AGAINST ALL RISKS AND WAR RISK. THE PAYMENT IS MADE BY IRREVOCABLE SIGHT LETTER OF CREDIT.

MAIN ITEMS OF BUSINESS CONTRACT:

1. COMMODITY NAME AND SPECIFICATION: COTTON BLUE SHIRTING, ART NO.102 23 × 45 72 × 70 38 in. × 120.5 yds

2. QUANTITY: 8,000,000 YDS (8,000BALES)

3. UNIT PRICE: USD 1.80 PER YARD CIF LONDON

4. PACKING: GOODS TO BE PACKED IN CLOTH BALES OF 10 PCS OF 120.5YDS EACH

5. SHIPMENT: TO BE EFFECTED DURING SEPTEMBER/OCTOBER 2019 FROM HANGZHOU TO LONDON IN EQUAL MONTHLY

6. PAYMENT: BY IRREVOCABLE SIGHT LETTER OF CREDIT

Chapter 3

Checking and Amending Letter of Credit

3.1 Introduction to a L/C

A letter of credit is a letter from a bank guaranteeing that a buyer's payment to a seller will be received on time and for the correct amount. In the event that the buyer is unable to make a payment on the purchase, the bank is required to cover the full or remaining amount of the purchase. A letter of credit, often abbreviated as LOC or L/C, is also referred to as a documentary credit.

International transactions often use letters of credit to ensure that payment will be received. They have become an important aspect of international trade, due to differing laws in each country and the difficulty of knowing each party personally. The bank also acts on behalf of the buyer, or the holder of the letter, by ensuring that the supplier will not be paid until the bank receives confirmation that the goods have been shipped.

3.1.1 How a L/C works

A letter of credit is a document from a bank that guarantees payment. It provides security when buying and selling.

Seller protection: If the buyer fails to pay the seller, the bank that issued the letter of credit will pay the seller if the seller meets all of the requirements in the letter. This provides security when the buyer and the seller are in different countries.

Buyer protection: Letters of credit can also protect buyers. If you pay somebody to provide a product or service and he fails to deliver, you might be able to get paid using a standby letter of credit. That payment can be a penalty to the company that was unable to perform, and it's similar to a refund, allowing you to pay somebody else to provide the product or service needed.

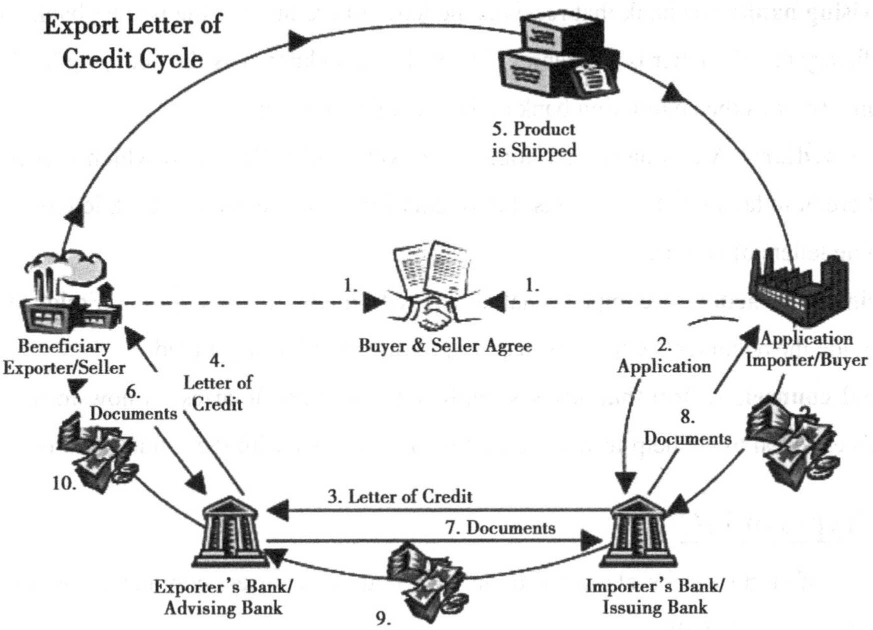

3.1.2 Parties involved in a L/C

To better understand the letter of credit, the below terminology helps.

Applicant: The party who requests the letter of credit. This is the person or company that will pay the beneficiary. The applicant is typically (but not always) an importer or a buyer who uses the letter of credit to make a purchase.

Beneficiary: The party who receives payment. This is usually a seller or exporter who has requested that the applicant use a letter of credit (because the beneficiary wants more security).

Issuing bank: The bank that creates or issues the letter of credit at the applicant's request. It is typically a bank where the applicant already does business (in the applicant's home country, where the applicant has an account or a line of credit).

Negotiating bank: The bank that works with the beneficiary, and which is generally located in the beneficiary's home country, or a bank where the beneficiary already conducts business. The beneficiary will submit documents to the negotiating bank, and the negotiating bank acts as a liaison between the beneficiary and other banks involved.

Confirming bank: The bank that "guarantees" payment to the beneficiary as long as the requirements in the letter of credit are met. The issuing bank already guarantees payment, but the beneficiary may prefer a guarantee from a bank in her home country (with which she is more familiar). This may be the same bank as the negotiating bank.

Advising bank: The bank that receives the letter of credit from the issuing bank and notifies the beneficiary that the letter is available. This bank is also known as the notifying bank, and may be the same bank as the negotiating bank and the confirming bank.

Intermediary: A company that connects buyers and sellers, and which sometimes uses letters of credit to facilitate transactions. Intermediaries often use back-to-back letters of credit (or transferable letters of credit).

Freight forwarder: A company that assists with international shipping. Freight forwarders often provide the documents exporters need to provide in order to get paid.

Legal counsel: A firm that advises applicants and beneficiaries on how to use letters of credit. It's essential to get help from an expert who is familiar with these transactions.

3.1.3 Types of L/C

Letters of credit can be classified under two main categories: commercial letters of credit and standby letters of credit.

Commercial letters of credit are mainly used as a primary payment tool in international trade. It is the correct type of credit that should be used when an importer pays the transaction amount directly to an exporter via a letter of credit. The majority of commercial letters of credit are issued subject to the latest version of UCP. Commercial letters of credit are primary payment tools that need to be utilized when the beneficiary performs its duties and makes a complying presentation.

One point that needs to be stressed is that standby letters of credit have their own rules, which are called *The International Standby Practices 1998 (ISP 98)* published by ICC. However, a standby letter of credit can be issued subject to either the UCP or the ISP.

Other types of L/C are listed below:

Revocable Letters of Credit

Under a revocable letter of credit, the issuer can either amend or cancel the letter of credit any time without prior notice to the beneficiary. Since revocable letters of credit do not provide any protection to the beneficiary, they are not used frequently. In addition, UCP 600 has no reference to revocable letters of credit. All credits issued subject to UCP 600 are irrevocable unless otherwise agreed between the parties.

Irrevocable Letters of Credit

Irrevocable letters of credit cannot be amended or cancelled without the agreement of the credit parties.

Unconfirmed irrevocable letters of credit cannot be modified without the written consent of both the issuing bank and the beneficiary.

Confirmed irrevocable letters of credit also need the confirming bank's written consent so that any modification or cancellation is to be effective.

Unconfirmed Letters of Credit

An unconfirmed letter of credit can be described as a letter of credit, which has not been guaranteed or confirmed by any bank other than the bank that opened it. In these types of credits, the only bank that undertakes to honor a complying presentation is the issuing bank.

Confirmed Letters of Credit

It would be easier to understand the confirmed letter of credit, if we start from the definition of confirmation.

Confirmation means a definite undertaking of the confirming bank, in addition to that of the issuing bank, to honor or negotiate a complying presentation.

If the payment undertaking in a letter of credit is guaranteed by a second bank, in addition to the bank originally issuing the credit, this kind of credit is called the confirmed letter of credit.

The confirming bank agrees to pay or accept drafts against the credit even if the issuer refuses to do so. Only irrevocable credits can be confirmed.

Clean Letters of Credit

Clean letters of credit are payable upon presentation of the draft, without any supporting document being required. A L/C does not require any document other than a written demand for payment by its beneficiary. In effect, a draft. Clean letters of credit are issued only by the request of the highest credit standing companies.

There are also some other forms of letters of credit, which deserve special attention.

Transferable Letters of Credit

A transferable letter of credit is a documentary credit that is issued with the option to allow a trader to transfer its rights and obligations to a new supplier.

Back-to-Back Letters of Credit

Arrangement in which one irrevocable letter of credit serves as the collateral for another; the advising bank of the first letter of credit becomes the issuing bank of the second L/C.

Unlike transferrable letters of credit, there are two separate letters of credit existing in back-to-back letters of credit transactions.

Advance Payment (Red Clause) Letters of Credit

It's a letter of credit that carries a provision (traditionally written or typed in red ink) which allows a seller to draw up to a fixed sum from the advising or paying bank, in advance of the shipment or before presenting the prescribed documents.

3.1.4 Major contents of L/C

1. The number of the credit and the place and time of its establishment

2. The type of credit

3. The contract on which it is based

4. The major parties relevant to the credit, such as the applicant, the opening bank, the beneficiary, the advising bank, etc.

5. The amount or value of the credit

6. The place and date on which the credit expires

7. The description of the goods including the name of commodity, the quantity, specifications, packing, the unit price, price terms, etc.

8. Transportation clauses including the port of shipment, the port of destination, the time of shipment, whether allowing partial shipment or transshipment

9. Stipulations related to the draft

10. Stipulations concerning the shiping documents required

11. Certain special clauses if any, e.g. restrictions on the carrying vessel and the route

12. Instructions to the negotiating bank

13. The seal or signature of the opening bank

14. Whether the credit follows the uniform customs and practice for documentary credits

3.2 Analysis of a L/C

27: Sequence of Total: 1/1

40A: Form of a Documentary Credit: IRREVOCABLE WITHOUT OUR CONFIRMATION

20: Sender's Reference

21: The Documentary Credit Number

IMLC0191000177

31C: Date of Issue

190326

40E: Applicable Rules

UCP LATEST VERSION

31D: Date and Place of Expiry

190611SHENZHEN

52A: Issuing Bank

DCBLINBB061

51D: Applicant Bank

DCB BANK LTD.

M.R.A MARG

OPP. CRAWFORD MARKET

50: Applicant

SWINGTEL COMMUNICATIONS PVT. LTD.

15—16, MISTRY BLDG, 3RD FLR, 635—637 J.S.S. ROAD, NR.METRO ADLAB MARINE LINES MUMBAI 400002, INDIA

59: Beneficiary

DONGGUAN BESTRADING IMP. AND EXP. CO. LTD

1503, HUAKAI TOWER, SHENGHE RD, NANCHE DONGGUAN, GUANGDONG, CHINA

32B: Currency Code, Amount

USD45,900.00

41D: Available... By...

ANY BANK IN CHINA BY NEGOTIATION

42C: Drafts at…

45 DAYS FROM THE DATE OF BILL OF LADING

42A: Drawee

DCBLINBB061

43P: Partial Shipment

ALLOWED

43T: Transshipment

ALLOWED

44E: Port of Loading

SHENZHEN

44F: Port of Discharge

NHAVA SHEVA, INDIA

44C: Latest Date of Shipment

190521

45A: Description of Goods and/or Services

1,350,000 PCS OF ELECTRONICS COMPONENTS TO BE USED IN INVERTER, AUTOMOTIVE, INSTRUMENTS, CFL AND LED MANUFACTURING COMPANIES AS END USED COMPONENTS OF CHINA, ORIGIN AS PER PROFORMA INVOICE NUMBER CS01903070102 DTD 07.03.2019 OF DONGGUAN BESTRADING IMP. AND EXP. CO.. LTD., FOB SHENZHEN

46A: Documents and Required

THE FOLLOWING DOCUMENTS IN ENGLISH MUST BE ACCOMPANIED ALONG WITH THE DRAFTS QUOTING OUR L/C NO.(IN DUPLICATE UNLESS OTHERWISE SPECIFIED).

1. SIGNED COMMERCIAL INVOICE IN QUADRUPLICATE CERTIFYING THAT THE GOODS AND ADDRESS MENTIONED IN THE INVOICE ARE AS PER PROFORMA INVOICE NO. CS01903070102 DTD 07.03.2019.

2. FULL SET CLEAN ON BOARD OCEAN BILLS OF LADING DATED NOT LATER THAN 21.05.2019 MADE TO THE ORDER OF DCB BANK LIMITED, MOHAMEDALI ROAD BRANCH TFU, M.R.A. MARG, OPP. CRAWFORD MARKET, MUMBAI 400,001, INDIA, AT DESTINATION AND NOTIFY DCB BANK LIMITED, MOHAMEDALI ROAD BRANCH TFU, AND THE APPLICANT.

3. LLOYDS CERTIFICATE STATING THAT THE CARRYING VESSEL IS SEAWORTHY AND NOT MORE THAN 20 YEARS OLD.

4. INSURANCE COVERED BY THE APPLICANT POLICY NO.0830019040-18-04-363 DATED 18.03.2019 ISSUED BY TATA AIG GENERAL INSURANCE COMPANY LTD.

5. CERTIFICATE ISSUED BY THE BENEFICIARY TO THE EFFECT THAT ONE SET OF PHOTOCOPIED SHIPPING DOCUMENTS HAS BEEN AFTER SHIPMENT OR DISPATCH.

6. PACKING LIST IN QUADRUPLICATE.

47A: Additional Conditions

1. A TRANSPORT DOCUMENT BEARING A DATE OF ISSUANCE PRIOR TO THAT OF THE CREDIT IS NOT ACCEPTABLE.

2. DISCREPANCY FEE OF USD 50.00 WILL BE DEDUCTED FROM THE PROCEEDS OF BILL FOR EACH DISCREPANT PRESENTATION.

3. SEPARATE DRAFT AND INVOICE FOR INTEREST AMOUNT REQUIRED.

4. INVOICE SHOULD QUOTE IMPORT LICENCE/OGL REFERENCE AND CERTIFY

THAT THE GOODS SUPPLIED ARE AS PER PURCHASE ORDER OF THE APPLICANT. GROSS FOB CIF CFR VALUE OF THE GOODS BEFORE DEDUCTION OF AGENTS COMMISSION, IF ANY, MUST NOT EXCEED THE MAXIMUM CREDIT AMOUNT.

5. ALL DOCUMENTS MUST BE IN ENGLISH.

6. ALL DOCUMENTS MUST MENTION OUR L/C NUMBER AND DATE AND THAT THE GOODS ARE FREELY IMPORTABLE UNDER EXIM POLICY 2009—2014 AND ARE IMPORTED UNDER LICENSE NUMBER.

7. ALL BANKING CHARGES OUTSIDE INDIA, INCLUDING CONFIRMATION CHARGES, ARE FOR BENEFICIARY'S ACCOUNT.

71D: Charges

REFER POINT NO 7 OF 47A

48: Period for Presentation in Days

21

49: Confirmation Instructions

WITHOUT

78: Instructions to the Paying

NEGOTIATIONS UNDER RESERVE NOT PERMITTED. NEGOTIATING BANK SHOULD FORWARD ALL SHIPPING DOCUMENTS TO US IN ONE SET BY COURIER AT THE FOLLOWING ADDRESS, DCB BANK LTD., MOHAMEDALI ROAD BRANCH TFU, M.R.A. MARG, OPP. CRAWFORD MARKET, MUMBAI 400,001, INDIA. WE ENGAGE WITH THE DRAWERS, ENDORSERS AND BONAFIDE HOLDERS OF DRAFTS DRAWN UNDER AND IN COMPLIANCE WITH THE TERMS OF THIS CREDIT THAT SUCH DRAFTS SHALL BE DULY HONOURED ON DUE DATE AND DELIVERY OF DOCUMENTS AS SPECIFIED ABOVE. EXCEPT AS OTHERWISE EXPRESSLY STATED THIS DOCUMENTARY CREDIT IS SUBJECT TO THE UNIFORM CUSTOMS AND PRACTICE FOR DOCUMENTARY CREDITS 2007 REVISION, INTERNATIONAL CHAMBER OF COMMERCE PUBLICATION NO.600. REIMBURSEMENT SUBJECT TO URR 725.

57A: Advise Through Bank

CIBKCN

72Z: Sender to Receiver Information

ON RECEIPT OF THE DOCUMENTS STRICTLY AS PER L/C TERMS WE SHALL REMIT THE PROCEEDS AS PER YOUR INSTRUCTIONS.

Analysis Sheet for L/C

	项目	项目性质（英文）	项目性质（中文）	具体内容（英文）	具体内容（中文）
信用证本身说明	27	SEQUENCE OF TOTAL	电文页次，如果该信用证条款能够全部容纳在该MT700报文中，那么该项目内显示“1/1”，如果该证由一份MT700报文和一份MT701报文组成，那么在MT700的报文项目“27”中显示“2/2”，以此类推	1/1	一页
	40A	FORM OF DOCUMENTARY CREDIT	跟单信用证形式	IRREVOCABLE	不可撤销信用证
	40E	APPLICABLE RULES	适用规则	UCP LATEST VERSION	UCP 最新版本
	20	DOCUMENTARY CREDIT NUMBER	信用证号码	IMLC01919000177	IMLC01919000177
	31C	DATE OF ISSUE	开证日期	190326	190326
	31D	DATE AND PLACE OF EXPIRY	信用证的有效期和有效地点	190611SHENZHEN	有效日期：2019 年 6 月 11 日 有效地点：深圳

当事人	51A	APPLICANT BANK	信用证开证的银行	DCB BANK LTD. M.R.A MARG OPP. CRAWFORD MARKET	DCB BANK LTD. M.R.A MARG OPP. CRAWFORD MARKET
	57A	ADVISE THROUGH BANK	通知行	CIBKCN	CIBKCN
	50	APPLICANT	开证申请人	SWINGTEL COMMUNICATIONS PVT. LTD.	SWINGTEL COMMUNICATIONS PVT. LTD.
	59	BENEFICIARY	受益人	DONGGUAN BESTRADING IMP. AND EXP. CO. LTD	DONGGUAN BESTRADING IMP. AND EXP. CO. LTD
金额	32B	CURRENCY CODE, AMOUNT	结算的货币和金额	USD45,900.00	45 900.00 美元
兑用	41A	AVAILABLE WITH … BY…	指定的有关银行及信用证的兑付方式	ANY BANK IN CHINA BY NEGOTIATION	中国内的任何银行议付
汇票	42C	DRAFTS AT…	汇票付款日期	45 DAYS FROM THE DATE OF BILL OF LADING	提单日期后的 45 天
	42A	DRAWEE	汇票付款人	DCBLINBB061	DCBLINBB061
装运条款	43P	PARTIAL SHIPMENT	分装条款	ALLOWED	允许
	43T	TRANSSHIPMENT	转运条款	ALLOWED	允许
	44A	PORT OF LOADING	装运港	SHENZHEN	深圳
	44B	FOR TRANSPORTATION TO	货物发运的最终地	NHAVA SHEVA, INDIA	印度孟买新港
	44C	LATEST DATE OF SHIPMENT	最迟装船期	190521	2019 年 5 月 21 日

Continued

	项目	项目性质（英文）	项目性质（中文）	具体内容（英文）	具体内容（中文）
货物描述	45A	DESCRIPTION OF GOODS AND/OR SERVICES	货物 / 服务描述	1,350,000 PCS OF ELECTRONICS COMPONENTS TO BE USED INVERTER, AUTOMOTIVE, INSTRUMENTS, CFL AND LED MANUFACTURING COMPANIES AS END USED COMPONENTS OF CHINA, ORIGIN AS PER PROFORMA INVOICE NUMBER CS01903070102 DTD 07.03.2019 OF DONGGUAN BESTRADING IMP. AND EXP. CO. LTD., FOB SHENZHEN.	国内用于逆变器、汽车、仪表、节能灯、LED 制造企业的电子元器件 1,350,000 件，原产地为 BESTRADING IMP. AND EXP. CO. 于 2019 年 7 月 3 日开的形式发票（编号 CS01903070102）所示。深圳港码头交货。
单据条款	46A	DOCUMENTS REQUIRED	单据要求	THE FOLLOWING DOCUMENTS IN ENGLISH MUST BE ACCOMPANIED ALONG WITH THE DRAFTS QUOTING OUR L/C NO.(IN DUPLICATE UNLESS OTHERWISE SPECIFIED). 1. SIGNED COMMERCIAL INVOICE IN QUADRUPLICATE CERTIFYING THAT THE GOODS AND ADDRESS MENTIONED IN THE INVOICE ARE AS PER PROFORMA INVOICE NO. CS01903070102 DTD 07.03.2019 2. FULL SET CLEAN ON BOARD OCEAN BILLS OF LADING DATED NOT LATER THAN 21.05.2019 MADE TO THE ORDER OF DCB BANK LIMITED, MOHAMEDALI ROAD BRANCH TFU, M.R.A. MARG, OPP. CRAWFORD MARKET, MUMBAI 400 001, INDIA, AT DESTINATION AND NOTIFY DCB BANK LIMITED, MOHAMEDALI ROAD BRANCH TFU, AND THE APPLICANT. 3. LLOYDS CERTIFICATE STATING THAT THE CARRYING VESSEL IS SEAWORTHY AND NOT MORE THAN 20 YEARS OLD. 4. INSURANCE COVERED BY THE APPLICANT POLICY NO.0830019040-18-04-363 DATED 18.03.2019 ISSUED BY TATA AIG GENERAL INSURANCE COMPANY LTD. 5. CERTIFICATE ISSUED BY THE BENEFICIARY TO THE EFFECT THAT ONE SET OF PHOTOCOPIED SHIPPING DOCUMENTS HAS BEEN AFTER SHIPMENT OR DISPATCH. 6. PACKING LIST IN QUADRUPLICATE.	下列单据必须用英文拟写，所有单据连同汇票必须注明信用证号码（除非有其他具体的要求，所有单据均一式两份）。 1. 签名商业发票一式四份以证明所有的货物和地址均按照形式发票号码为 CS01903070102 日期为 07.03.2019 上所列。 2. 全套清洁已装船海运提单不能迟于 2019 年 5 月 21 日。做成凭 DCB BANK LIMITED, MOHAMEDALI ROAD BRANCH TFU, M.R.A. MARG, OPP. CRAWFORD MARKET, MUMBAI 400 001, INDIA 指示。在目的港通知 DCB BANK LIMITED, MOHAMEDALI ROAD BRANCH TFU 和开证申请人。 3. 劳合社证明文件证明运输船只适宜航海，且船龄不超过 20 年。 4. 保险由开证申请人购买，保险单号为 NO.830019040-18-04-363，日期为 18.03.2019。保险公司为 TATA AIG GENERAL INSURANCE COMPANY LTD 5. 受益人证书要证明一套运输单据的复印件已经在装运后寄出。 6. 装箱单一式四份。

特殊条款	47A	ADDITIONAL CONDITIONS	附加条款	1. A TRANSPORT DOCUMENT BEARING A DATE OF ISSUANCE PRIOR TO THAT OF THE CREDIT IS NOT ACCEPTABLE. 2. DISCREPANCY FEE OF USD 50.00 WILL BE DEDUCTED FROM THE PROCEEDS OF BILL FOR EACH DISCREPANT PRESENTATION. 3. SEPERATE DRAFT AND INVOICE FOR INTEREST AMOUNT REQUIRED. 4. INVOICE SHOULD QUOTE IMPORT LICENCE/ OGL REFERENCE AND CERTIFY THAT THE GOODS SUPPLIED ARE AS PER PURCHASE ORDER OF THE APPLICANT. GROSS FOB/ CIF/CFR VALUE OF THE GOODS BEFORE DEDUCTION OF AGENTS COMMISSION, IF ANY, MUST NOT EXCEED THE MAXIMUM CREDIT AMOUNT. 5. ALL DOCUMENTS MUST BE IN ENGLISH. 6. ALL DOCUMENTS MUST MENTION OUR L/C NUMBER AND DATE AND THAT THE GOODS ARE FREELY IMPORTABLE UNDER EXIM POLICY 2009-2014 ARE IMPORTED UNDER LICENSE NUMBER. 7. ALL BANKING CHARGES OUTSIDE INDIA INCLUDING CONFIRMATION CHARGES ARE FOR BENEFICIARY'S ACCOUNT.	1. 一份早于信用证开证日期的运输单据是不可接受的。 2. 提示的不符单据，每个不符点则会从汇票中扣除 50 美元。 3. 需要利息金额的单独汇票和发票。 4. 发票应被注明进口许可证或者 OGL 参考号以证明所买货物是按照开证申请人的购买合同来执行的。在扣除代理商佣金前的 FOB/CIF/CFR 总金额不能超过信用证金额。 5. 所有的单据必须用英文。 6. 所有单据必须注明信用证号码和日期，以便货物能顺利通关。在 2009—2014 的 EXIM 政策下，所有的单据要注明许可证号码。 7. 印度之外的费用包括保兑费由受益人承担。
交单	48	PERIOD FOR PRESENTATION	交单期限	21	21 天
费用	71B	CHARGES	费用情况	REFER POINT NO.7 OF 47 A	按照 47A 中的第 7 条来执行。

Continued

	项目	项目性质（英文）	项目性质（中文）	具体内容（英文）	具体内容（中文）
指示	78	INSTRUCTIONS TO THE PAYING	付款行的指示	1.NEGOTIATIONS UNDER RESERVE NOT PERMITTED. 2.NEGOTIATING BANK SHOULD FORWARD ALL SHIPPING DOCUMENTS TO US IN ONE SET BY COURIER AT THE FOLLOWING ADDRESS, DCB BANK LTD., MOHAMEDALI ROAD BRANCH TFU, M.R.A. MARG, OPP. CRAWFORD MARKET, MUMBAI 400 001, INDIA. 3.WE ENGAGE WITH THE DRAWERS, ENDORSERS AND BONAFIDE HOLDERS OF DRAFTS DRAWN UNDER AND IN COMPLIANCE WITH THE TERMS OF THIS CREDIT THAT SUCH DRAFTS SHALL BE DULY HONOURED ON DUE DATE AND DELIVERY OF DOCUMENTS AS SPECIFIED ABOVE. 4.EXCEPT AS OTHERWISE EXPRESSLY STATED THIS DOCUMENTARY CREDIT IS SUBJECT TO THE UNIFORM CUSTOMS AND PRACTICE FOR DOCUMENTARY CREDITS 2007 REVISION, INTERNATIONAL CHAMBER OF COMMERCE PUBLICATION NO.600. 5.REIMBURSEMENT SUBJECT TO URR 725.	1. 凭保议付不允许。 2. 议付行应当通过快递的方式一批次把所有的运输单据寄给 DCB 银行。 3. 兹对出票人、背书人和善意持票人保证，凡按本信用证开具并符合该信用证条款的汇票到期即付款。单据提交的日期如上述详细说明。 4. 除非另有规定，本信用证根据国际商会 2007 年修订本第 600 号出版物“跟单信用证统一惯例”办理。 5. 本信用证项下的偿付遵循 URR725。
	49	CONFIRMATION INSTRUCTIONS	保兑指示	WITHOUT	没有保兑

3.3 Amendment to a L/C

3.3.1 Necessity of amendment

The letter of credit is a balance payment method in international trade. Both exporters and importers are protected by the letter of credit in a certain amount, if they act properly.

Of course, varieties of risks exist in a international trade leading to the damages to and/or losses of the parties involved. Therefore, it is of crucial importance to avoid any problems and/or risks arising from the operation of the L/C to protect traders against various risks when working with a L/C.

3.3.2 Procedures of amendment

Article 10 of UCP 600 has established the rules how the amendment to a L/C can be made.

Parties entitled to amend the L/C

It is stated that except as otherwise provided by article 38, a credit can neither be amended nor canceled without the agreement of the issuing bank, the confirming bank, if any, and the beneficiary.

Therefore, only the buyer/applicant/issuer of the L/C or the exporter/beneficiary can decide whether to amend or accept the amendment to the L/C or not.

Responsibilities

An issuing bank is irrevocably bound by an amendment as of the time it issues the amendment. A confirming bank may extend its confirmation to an amendment and will be irrevocably bound as of the time it advises the amendment. A confirming bank may, however, choose to advise an amendment without extending its confirmation and, if so, it must inform the issuing bank without delay and inform the beneficiary in its advice.

The terms and conditions of the original credit (or the credit incorporating previously accepted amendments) will remain in force for the beneficiary until the beneficiary communicates its acceptance of the amendment to the bank that advised such amendment. The beneficiary should give notification of acceptance or rejection of the amendment. If the beneficiary fails to give such notification, a presentation that complies with the credit and to any not yet accepted the amendment will be deemed to be notification of acceptance by the beneficiary of such amendment. As of that moment the credit will be amended.

A bank that advises an amendment should inform the bank from which it received the amendment of any notification of acceptance or rejection.

Acceptance

Partial acceptance of an amendment is not allowed and will be deemed to be notification of rejection of the amendment.

Exception

A provision in an amendment to the effect that the amendment shall enter into force unless rejected by the beneficiary within a certain time shall be disregarded.

Procedures of L/C amendment

First, the beneficiary decides to have the L/C amended after checking the contents of the L/C because of non-compliances. Second, the importer makes an amendment application to the issuing bank when he agrees to amend. Third, the issuing bank amends the L/C accordingly and sends the amendment notice to the advising bank. Fourth, the advising bank transfers the amendment notice to the exporter/beneficiary. Fifth, the exporter/beneficiary will have the amendment notice and the original L/C combined to be a full document of binding force.

Procedures of L/C amendment have been illustrated in the following two ways as often taking place in practice.

The seller sends the amendment notice to the buyer first; then the buyer applies to amend the L/C; the issuing bank amends the L/C and sends it to the advising bank, the notifying bank transfers the amendment to the seller. Initiated by the seller, the L/C is amended as illustrated below.

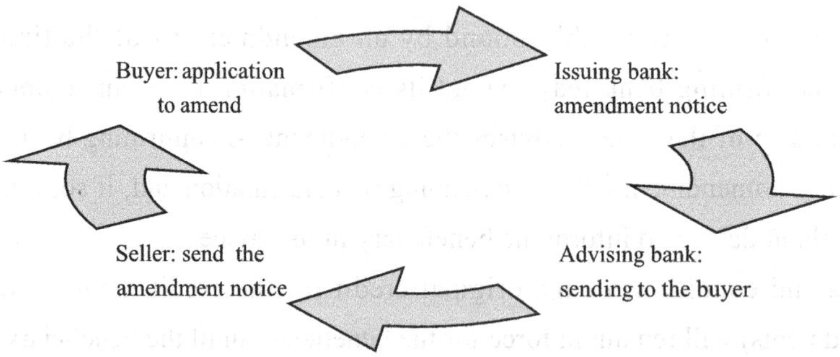

The seller sends the amendment notice to the notifying bank, and the latter sends or telegrams the notice to the issuing bank. Then, the issuing bank informs the buyer to apply to amend the L/C. The issuing bank amends the L/C according to the request of the buyer and sends it to the advising bank. Finally, the notifying bank transfers the amendment to the seller. Initiated by the seller, the L/C is amended as illustrated below.

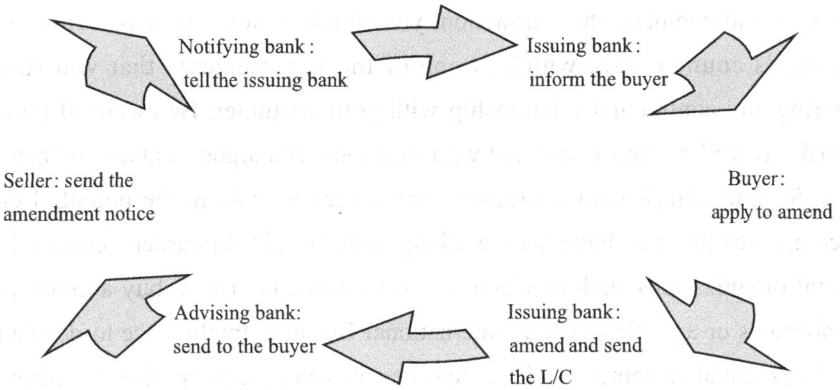

Points concerning the amendment to a L/C

1) Accept all or none: Partial acceptance of the amendment is ineffective.

2) Make an appropriate notice: The notice of amendment must be made by the beneficiary/ exporter via the original advising bank to the traders, and any other forms of amendments are ineffective because the advising bank is responsible for the checking of the L/C.

3) Immediate check: The amendment must be checked upon the arrival of the L/C in order to decide whether to accept or further amend.

4) Clarify fees: Make it clear by whom the amendment fees are borne.

5) Make all amendments at one time: Efforts should be made to ensure that all the amendment requests are made together on time.

6) Effectiveness of amendment to the L/C: once the amendment(s) is (are) accepted, it is binding upon all the parties concerned.

3.4 Points to checking a L/C as an exporter

As an exporter, he must pay close attention to the credit-control process via three stages: check his partners' or customers' background and credibility at the preliminary investigation stage, draft and sign a sales contract at the sales contract stage and control the letter of credit draft at the letter of credit control stage.

3.4.1 Preliminary investigation stage

This stage is centered around the learning of who your customer really is: Nothing can protect you against an ill-will customer.

As a result, you need to make sure that your customer is a valid company with a proven track of business and has the financial credibility to complete the transaction.

In order to understand that you are dealing with a genuine customer, who has the financial strength to start and complete the transaction, you should follow the steps below: First, check your customer's country risk, which is one of the key elements that you should check before entering any contractual relationship with your customer. Be aware of political risks, economic risks as well as risks associated with sanctions, embargoes and anti-money laundering regulations. Second, check your customer's references by asking the potential customer to the other companies that you have been working with, freight forwarders, custom brokers and governmental organizations such as Commercial Counselors. Third, buy a credit report from some organizations or agencies such as International Business Intelligence to decide how much credibility the potential customer has. This does benefit you especially when the payment will be made via an open account, documentary collections or a letter of credit.

3.4.2 Sales contract stage

After you investigate your customer, you can proceed to the sales contract drafting stage.

The letter of credit is not a sales contract. As a result you must have a sales contract regardless of the payment method you will be choosing.

3.4.3 L/C control stage

When it comes to the letter of credit control stage, it is necessary that a "draft letter of credit" from the importers is demanded in order to make a revision without paying extra costs for the amendment. A draft letter of credit prepared by the issuing bank in the swift format contains all the aspects of the actual letter of credit with a couple of exceptions.

It must be clarified that the draft letter of credit does not secure the issuance of an actual letter of credit and it is not an operative instrument because the issuing bank intentionally indicates so.

Step 1 Check the irrevocable structure of the letter of credit

Irrevocable means that the issuing bank cannot amend or cancel the letter of credit without the written consent of the beneficiary. As per UCP 600 all letters of credit are irrevocable unless otherwise explicitly stated in the credit.

Make it clear and precise that the letter of credit issued is subject to the latest version of the uniform rules of documentary credits, UCP 600 and that there is no indication in the credit that the letter of credit is "revocable".

Step 2 Verify the date of issue, the latest date of shipment and the date of expiry

Each letter of credit should contain the date of issue, the latest date of shipment and the date of expiry.

All the regulations must be fully complied with, i.e., shipment must be made before the latest date of shipment. Documents must be presented before the expiry date of the letter of credit.

Close attention must be paid to the expiry location of the letter of credit so as to have or require extra time for forwarding the documents to the issuing bank. Furthermore, some letters of credit will state that documents must not be dated before the letter of credit issuance date.

Step 3 Verify the issuing bank

According to the letter of credit rules, both banks and non-bank organizations are in the position to issue letters of credit, and the latter situation leaves exporters vulnerable to fraud risk originating from the non-bank letter of credit issuers.

The following items must be checked and verified in order to protect the beneficiaries against risks. First of all, the bank that has the L/C established must be a valid and trustworthy bank which is comfortable to work with. Second, a bank appointed as the advising bank is a reputable one located domestically. Third, the letter of credit is in the swift format through an advising bank in your country.

Step 4 Check the name and address of the beneficiary and the applicant

To avoid the errors committed by the issuing bank in indicating the beneficiary's name and address, it must be ensured that both the full name and address of your company and the full name of the importer's company and its address are correctly stated in the letter of credit.

Step 5 Check the currency and amount

The amount and currency stated in the letter of credit must match the amount and currency stated in the sales contract and shown correctly by the right symbols or codes used in international trade finance. For example, the symbol $ stands for US dollar, Canadian dollar, and Singaporean dollar. Therefore, it must be stated clearly in the way known and applied to practices.

Step 6 Check the description of goods/services

The description of goods and services is a fundamental item in the sales contract and a very important article especially when completing the commercial invoice.

According to the letter of credit rules, the commercial invoice must contain an exact description of goods and services that the letter of credit states. Be it right that the description of goods and services is corresponding to the sales contract and that all goods have been covered under the commercial invoice.

Also it is not possible to write additional goods on the invoice even if you mention them free of charge.

Step 7 Check the documents requested by the letter of credit

In international trade, most of the time, it is a kind of transaction of documents, i.e., documentary transaction. Documentation is the core of a letter of credit. Banks decide to pay or reject the presentation by checking the documents only.

Payment shall be made against a complying set of documents. Any discrepancy will lead to dishonor except for the applicant's approval.

Enough attention must be given to the documents which have been covered specifically under the letter of credit rules and international standard banking practices such as transport documents, insurance documents, bills of exchange, commercial invoices, the certificate of origin, packing lists and certificates.

All documents required under the letter of credit shall be provided on time and the signature, issuance and authentication requirements of the documents must be complied with.

Attention should be paid to the fact that there is no document which should be issued or countersigned by the applicant.

Step 8　Check the payment terms

Payment terms in a letter of credit transaction define how sooner the beneficiary can reach the payment. It is of significance that payment terms quoted in the letter of credit agree with those stated in the sales contract.

According to the latest letter of credit rules, all letters of credit must state whether they are available by sight payment, deferred payment, acceptance or negotiation.

The payment term "At Sight" indicates that the exporter will be paid within a reasonable time after the documents are found complying by the issuing bank or the confirming bank. The payment term "Deferred Payment" indicates that the exporter will be paid after a certain amount of time indicated in the letter of credit. The payment term "Acceptance" indicates that the letter of credit consists of a draft either "sight" or "usance" or "time". The payment term "Negotiation" indicates that the beneficiary could get his payment from the nominated bank before the maturity date.

Step 9　Check the incoterms

Trade terms have been grouped into two main categories under the Incoterms 2010 rules: Incoterms that can be used only by sea transportation (FAS, FOB, CFR and CIF) and Incoterms that can be used with all modes of transport (EXW, FCA, CPT, CIP, DAT, DAP and DDP).

First, Incoterms and the shipment mode must match each other in a letter of credit transaction.

Furthermore, "Freight Collect" and "Freight Prepaid" expressions must be used in conjunction with the applied Incoterms.

Finally, if Incoterms are stated in the "description of goods and services" part of the letter of credit, the commercial invoice must exactly reflect the stated Incoterms.

For example, if the letter of credit states "FOB New York Port, USA, Incoterms 2010" in the "description of goods and services" part of the L/C, the commercial invoice must show this exact definition as indicated.

The Incoterms stated in the letter of credit decide the traders' respective responsibilities.

Step 10 Check the port of loading / the port of discharge

The port of loading and the port of discharge are the two main elements of a marine bill of lading, being the fundamental contents of a sales contract.

According to the letter of the credit rules, the port of loading and the port of discharge must be in compliance with the ones stated in the letter of credit and the port of loading and the port of discharge are consistent with what stated in the sales contract.

The use of a very generalized port of loading definition in the letter of credit definitely benefits the exporter, such as "Any U.S. West Coast Port" or "Any China port" or even "Any North American Port". And the actual port of loading to the bill of lading must be stated where the goods are dispatched.

Step 11 Check the letter of credit fees

Fees will be charged while the letter of credit is taken as a payment option.

Enough attention should be paid to the letter of credit charges as an exporter because it is significantly related to your profit margin.

The approximate cost of working with a letter of credit at the beginning of the transaction should be reflected in the goods while offering a price. In practice, importers pay only letter of credit issuance costs and force exporters to pay the remaining L/C charges though theoretically all L/C fees must be paid by the importer.

Fees regarding the L/C are as follows: the courier fee/postage fee, the advising fee, the discrepancy fee, the handling fee/negotiation fee, the amendment commission, the confirmation fee, the reimbursing bank charges and so on.

Step 12 Check the presentation period

According to the current letter of credit rules, 21 days are given to the exporters to make their presentations to the nominated banks, which starts with the date of shipment except that a letter of credit contains a special presentation period clause.

Then, the presentation must be completed within this specially allowed time frame. For example, in some cases issuing banks arrange special presentation periods for each letter of credit by inserting clauses such as "Documents must be presented for negotiation within 15 days after the onboard validation date of the ocean bill of lading and within the validity of the letter of credit", hereby, the exporter must obey this specific presentation period for the letter of credit, not the standard 21 day presentation period.

Step 13 Check the partial shipments

The letter of credit rules usually allows partial shipment.

Making partial shipment is a huge advantage for the exporter. It is in the exporter's favor if the letter of credit is kept in a way that it is allowing partial shipment. It should be understood that partial shipment is allowed if the letter of credit is silent concerning partial shipment. Otherwise, it should be explicitly expressed.

That either partial shipment is allowed or not under the letter of credit must be in strict agreement with the sales contract.

Step 14　Check the transshipment

Usually transshipments are allowed by the letter of credit rules since transshipments are arranged by the carrier and the shipper has no influence. Actually, transhipments are not controlled by the exporters and almost all the container carriers do practice several transshipments between the ports of loading and ports of discharge. Only in very rare situations the letter of credit transaction leads to the prohibition of transshipment.

What is more practical is to make sure that transshipment is allowed under the letter of credit.

Step 15　Check the reimbursement instructions

Reimbursement instructions are very important to the exporter, as they determine how and when the payment will be received. Bear in mind that reimbursement instructions do not block you from receiving payment via unreasonable restrictions.

These four types of reimbursement instructions are usually used in international documentary credits:

The issuing bank authorizes the nominated bank to debit its account;

The issuing bank instructs the nominated bank to claim reimbursement from a reimbursing bank;

The issuing bank requires the nominated bank to send a swift message notifying the issuing bank that the documents have been received and found to be in compliance with the L/C terms, only then the issuing bank remits funds to the nominated bank;

The issuing bank requires the nominated bank to send documents to the issuing bank for payment (the very rare and slowest reimbursement method of payment).

Step 16　Non-documentary conditions

A non-documentary condition can be defined as any instruction or condition that is not clearly attributable to a document to be stipulated in a documentary credit. Make sure that you have identified all non-documentary conditions in the letter of credit because non-documentary conditions are a great source of confusion and disputes between the issuing banks and exporters.

Some documentary condition examples are as often the cases as "Certificate of origin issued in 1 original and 1 copy legalized by the local chamber of commerce attesting that goods are of China origin" "Certificate of origin must show that goods are of China origin"; and some non-documentary condition examples are "Exported goods must be Australian Origin", and "Any of the presented documents must not show that goods are originated from a country other than Australia".

Step 17 Jocker Clause

A credit should not require presentation of documents that are to be issued, signed or countersigned by the applicant. If any document that requires such action should be treated as a "Jocker Clause".

One of the main reasons checking the letters of credit as an exporter is to locate the "Jocker Clauses". All detected "Jocker Clauses" should be removed.

Step 18 Check the confirmation

Confirmation means a definite undertaking of the confirming bank, in addition to that of the issuing bank, to honour or negotiate a complying presentation. A confirming bank is requested by the issuing bank to add its guarantee of payment or acceptance to the letter of credit instrument.

Various risks under the letter of credit transaction can be avoided by having the letter of credit confirmed by one of the prime banks in your country.

Step 19 Check the reimbursement bank

Make sure that the reimbursement bank identified in the letter of credit is one of the most reputable banks around the world such as Bank of China, Commerzbank, HSBC Bank, the Bank of America, etc.

3.4.4 Conclusion

Do not assume anything when working with a letter of credit. Any doubt or uncertainty must be addressed in the operation of the L/C.

3.5 Effectiveness of amendment to a L/C

When amendments are made accordingly, all the parties concerned are bound upon by it and must fulfill their duties and obligations respectively.

Sample of amendments to a L/C

SALES CONTRACT

SELLER: GREAT WALL TRADING CO., LTD. CONTRACT NO.: GW2005X06
ADDRESS: RM201, HUASHENG BUILDING, DATE: 2004.4.22
NINGBO, P.R.CHINA SIGNED AT: NINGBO
BUYER: F.T.C. CORP.
ADDRESS: AKEDSANTERINK AUTO P.O. BOX 9, FINLAND

THIS SALES CONTRACT IS MADE BY AND BETWEEN THE SELLER AND THE BUYER, WHEREBY THE SELLER AGREES TO SELL AND THE BUYER AGREES TO BUY

THE UNDER MENTIONED GOODS ACCORDING TO THE TERMS AND CONDITIONS STIPULATED BELOW:

(1) NAME OF COMMODITY AND SPECIFICATIONS: HALOCEN FITTING W500

(2) QUANTITY: 9,600 PCS

(3) UNIT PRICE: CIF HELSINKI USD 3.80/PC

(4) AMOUNT: USD 36,480.00

(5) PACKING: CARTON

(6) DELIVERY FROM NINGBO TO HELSINKI

(7) SHIPPING MARKS: N/M

(8) TIME OF SHIPMENT: WITHIN 30 DAYS AFTER RECEIPT OF L/C ALLOWING TRANSSHIPMENT AND PARTIAL SHIPMENT.

(9) TERMS OF PAYMENT: BY 100% CONFIRMED IRREVOCABLE LETTER OF CREDIT IN FAVOR OF THE SELLER TO BE AVAILABLE BY SIGHT DRAFT TO BE OPENED AND TO REACH CHINA BEFORE MAY 1, 2004 AND TO REMAIN VALID FOR NEGOTIATION IN CHINA UNTIL THE 15TH DAYS AFTER THE FORESAID TIME OF SHIPMENT. L/C MUST MENTION THIS CONTRACT NUMBER OF L/C ADVISED BY BANK OF CHINA NINGBO BRANCH. ALL BANKING CHARGES OUTSIDE CHINA AREA FOR ACCOUNT OF THE DRAWEE.

(10) INSURANCE: TO BE EFFECTED BY THE SELLER FOR 110% OF FULL INVOICE VALUE COVERING F.P.A. UP TO HELSINKI.

(11) ARBITRATION: ALL DISPUTES ARISING FROM THE EXECUTION OF OR IN CONNECTION WITH THIS CONTRACT SHALL BE SETTLED AMICABLE BY NEGOTIATION. IN CASE SETTLEMENT CAN BE REACHED THROUGH NEGOTIATION THE CASE SHALL THEN BE SUBMITTED TO CHINA INTERNATIONAL ECONOMIC & TRADE ARBITRATION COMMISSION. IN SHENZHEN FOR ARBITRATION IN ACT WITH ITS SURE OF PROCEDURES. THE ARBITRAL AWARD IS FINAL AND BINDING UPON BOTH PARTIES FOR SETTLING THE DISPUTE. THE FEE FOR ARBITRATION SHALL BE BORNE BY THE LOSING PARTY UNLESS OTHERWISE AWARDED.

ISSUE OF DOCUMENTARY CREDIT

ISSUING BANK: METTA BANK LTD., FINLAND.

FORM OF DOC. CREDIT: REVOCABLE

CREDIT NUMBER: LRT9802457

DATE OF ISSUE: 040428

EXPIRY: DATE 040416 PLACE FINLAND

APPLICANT: F.T.C. CO.

AKEDSANTERINK AUTO P.O. BOX 9, FINLAND

BENEFICIARY: GREAT WALL TRADING CO., LTD.

RM201, HUASHENG BUILDING, NINGBO, P.R.CHINA

AMOUNT: USD 3,648.00 (SAY U.S. DOLLARS THIRTY-SIX THOUSAND FOUR HUNDRED AND EIGHT ONLY.)

AVAILABLE WITH/BY: ANY BANK IN ADVISING COUNTRY BY NEGOTIATION

DRAFT AT… : DRAFTS AT 20 DAYS' SIGHT FOR FULL INVOICE VALUE

PARTIAL SHIPMENT: NOT ALLOWED

TRANSSHIPMENT: ALLOWED

LOADING IN CHARGE: NINGBO

FOR TRANSPORT TO: HELSINKI

SHIPMENT PERIOD: AT THE LATEST MAY 30, 2004

DESCRIP. OF GOODS: 960 PCS OF HALOCEN FITTING W500. USD 6.80 PER PC AS PER SALES CONTRACT GW2005M06 DD 22 APRIL, 2004 CIF HELSINKI

DOCUMENTS REQUIRED:

* COMMERCIAL INVOICE 1 SIGNED ORIGINAL AND 5 COPIES.
* PACKING LIST IN 2 COPIES.
* FULL SET OF CLEAN ON BOARD MARINE BILLS OF LADING, MADE OUT TO ORDER, MARKED "FREIGHT PREPAID" AND NOTIFY APPLICANT.
* GSP CERTIFICATE OF ORIGIN FORM A, CERTIFYING GOODS OF ORIGIN IN CHINA, ISSUED BY COMPETENT AUTHORITIES.
* INSURANCE POLICY/CERTIFICATE COVERING ALL RISKS AND WAR RISK OF PICC INCLUDING WAREHOUSE TO WAREHOUSE CLAUSE UP TO FINAL DESTINATION AT HELSINKI, FOR AT LEAST 120 PCT OF CIF VALUE.
* SHIPPING ADVICE MUST BE SENT TO APPLICANT WITHIN 2 DAYS AFTER SHIPMENT ADVISING NUMBER OF PACKAGES, GROSS & NET WEIGHT, VESSEL NAME, BILL OF LADING NO. AND DATE, CONTRACT NO., VALUE.

PRESENTATION PERIOD: 6 DAYS AFTER ISSUANCE DATE OF SHIPPING DOCUMENT.

CONFIRMATION: WITHOUT

INSTRUCTIONS: THE NEGOTIATING BANK MUST FORWARD THE DRAFTS AND ALL DOCUMENTS BY REGISTERED AIRMAIL DIRECT TO US IN TWO CONSECUTIVE LOTS, UPON RECEIPT OF THE DRAFTS AND DOCUMENTS IN ORDER. WE WILL REMIT THE PROCEEDS AS INSTRUCTED BY THE NEGOTIATING BANK.

信用证审核记录表

信用证号码	LRT9802457		合同号	GW2005X06	
开证行	METTA BANK LTD., FINLAND			开证日期	040428
开证申请人	F.T.C. CORP.				
受益人	GREAT WALL TRADING CO., LTD				
货物名称	HALOCEN FITTING W500	数量	9,600 PCS	金额	USD 36,480.00
装运期	WITHIN 30 DAYS AFTER RECEIPT OF L/C	有效期	DATE 040416 PLACE FINLAND	交单期	装船后的 6 天内
装运港	宁波	目的港	赫尔辛基	可否分批	不允许
贸易术语	CIF	汇票期限	即期汇票	可否转运	允许
特殊条款	议付行要用两批次把单据寄给开证行				

单据种类及份数	汇票	发票	装箱单	重量单	尺码单	保险单	提单正本	提单副本	原产地证	GSP产地证	品质证	重量证	质检证	船行证明	寄单证明	寄样证明	受益人证明	邮包收据
	1	6	2	0	0	1	3	3	0	1	0	0	0	0	1	0	0	0

需要修改的内容	来证条款内容	应修改后条款内容	解析
	1. REVOCABLE L/C	IRREVOCABLE L/C	信用证类型有误
	2. 有效日期：040416 有效地点：芬兰	有效日期：040615； 有效地点：中国	收到信用证的一个月后装船，并在装船后的 15 日内议付
	3. 开证申请人：F.T.C. CO	F.T.C. CORP.	开证申请人名称有误
	4. 金额：USD3,648.00	USD36,480.00	信用证金额有误
	5. AT 20 DAYS DRAFT	BY SIGHT DRAFT	汇票性质有误
	6. 分批装运不允许	分批装运允许	分批装运有误
	7. 960PCS	9,600PCS	数量有误
	8. USD6.80PER PC	USD3.80 PER PC	单价有误
	9. GW2005M06	GW2005X06	合同号码有误
	10. ALL RISKS & WAR RISK	F.P.A	保险险别有误
	11. 120 PCT OF CIF VALUE	110 PCT OF INVOICE VALUE	保险加成有误

Continued

	12. PRESENTATION PERIOD: 6 DAYS AFTER DATE OF SHIPMENT	15 DAYS AFTER THE TIME OF SHIPMENT	交单日期有误
	13. CONFIRMATION: WITHOUT	100% CONFIRMED IRRE. LETTER OF CREDIT	保兑条款有误
审证员签字		部门经理签字	

3.6 Exercises

Please fill in the analysis sheet for a letter of credit.

ISSUE OF DOCUMENTARY CREDIT

27: SEQUENCE OF TOTAL: 1/1

40A: FORM OF DOC. CREDIT: IRREVOCABLE

20: DOC. CREDIT NUMBER: KR370/09

31C: DATE OF ISSUE: 110617

40E: APPLICABLE RULES: UCP600

31D: DATE AND PLACE OF EXPIRY: 110815CHINA

51D: APPLICANT BANK: VALUE TRAINING ENTERPRISE CORP.
ROOM 210 GREEN BUILDING KUWAIT

50: APPLICANT: VALUE TRADE ENTERPRISE CORP.
YARIMCA, KOCAELI325, IZMIT, TURKEY

59: BENEFICIARY: TIANJIN YIMEI INTERNATIONAL LTD.
100 DONGLI RD TIANJIN, CHINA

32B: CURRENCY CODE, AMT: USD 67,500.00

41A: AVAILABLE WITH... BY...: BANK OF CHINA TIANJIN BRANCH

41C: DRAFTS AT... : 90 DAYS AFTER SIGHT

42A: DRAWEE: VALUE TRAINING ENTERPRISE CORP.

43P: PARTIAL SHIPMENT: NOT ALLOWED

43T: TRANSSHIPMENT: NOT ALLOWED

44A: PORT OF LOADING/AIRPORT OF DEPARTURE: ANY CHINESE PORT

44B: PORT OF DESTINATION: KUWAIT

44C: LATEST DATE OF SHIPMENT: 110710

45A: DESCRIPTION OF GOODS AND/OR SERVICES:

5,000PCS WINDBREAKER

STYLE NO. YM088
AS PER ORDER NO. A01 AND S/C NO. YM009
AT USD15.10/PC CIF KUWAIT
PACKED IN CARTONS OF 20 PCS EACH

46A: DOCUMENTS REQUIRED +SIGNED COMMERCIAL INVOICE IN TRIPLICATE INDICATING L/C NO. AND CONTRACT NO. +FULL SET (3/3) OF CLEAN ON BOARD OCEAN BILL OF LADING MADE OUT TO ORDER OF APPLICANT AND BLANK ENDORSEMENT MARKED "FREIGHT TO COLLECT" NOTIFY THE APPLICANT +SIGNED PACKING LIST IN TRIPLICATE SHOWING THE FOLLOWING DETAILS: TOTAL NUMBER OF PACKAGES SHIPPED; CONTENTS OF PACKAGE(S), GROSS WEIGHT, NET WEIGHT AND MEASUREMENT +CERTIFICATE OF ORIGIN ISSUED AND SIGNED OR AUTHENTICATED BY A LOCAL CHAMBER OF COMMERCE LOCATED IN THE EXPORTING COUNTRY. +INSURANCE POLICY/CERTIFICATE IN DUPLICATE ENDORSED IN BLANK FOR 120% INVOICE VALUE, COVERING ALL RISKS AND WAR RISK OF CIC OF PICC (1/1/1981) 71B: ALL CHARGES AND COMMISSIONS ARE FOR ACCOUNT OF BENEFICIARY INCLUDING REIMBURSEMENT CHARGES.

ANALYSIS SHEET

	项目	项目性质（英文）	项目性质（中文）	具体内容（英文）	具体内容（中文）
信用证本身说明	27	SEQUENCE OF TOTAL	电文页次		
	40A	FORM OF DOCUMENTARY CREDIT	跟单信用证形式		
	40E	APPLICABLE RULES	适用规则		
	20	DOCUMENTARY CREDIT NUMBER	信用证号码		
	31C	DATE OF ISSUE	开证日期		
	31D	DATE AND PLACE OF EXPIRY	信用证的有效期和有效地点		
当事人	51A	APPLICANT BANK	信用证开证的银行		
	57A	ADVISE THROUGH BANK	通知行		
	50	APPLICANT	开证申请人		
	59	BENEFICIARY	受益人		
金额	32B	CURRENCY CODE, AMOUNT	结算的货币和金额		
兑用	41A	AVAILABLE WITH… BY…	指定的有关银行及信用证的兑付方式		

Continued

	项目	项目性质（英文）	项目性质（中文）	具体内容（英文）	具体内容（中文）
汇票	42C	DRAFTS AT…	汇票付款日期		
	42A	DRAWEE	汇票付款人		
装运条款	43P	PARTIAL SHIPMENT	分装条款		
	43T	TRANSSHIPMENT	转运条款		
	44A	PORT OF LOADING	装运港		
	44B	FOR TRANSPORTATION TO	货物发运的最终地		
	44C	LATEST DATE OF SHIPMENT	最迟装船期		
货物描述	45A	DESCRIPTION OF GOODS AND/OR SERVICES	货物 / 服务描述		
单据条款	46A	DOCUMENTS REQUIRED	单据要求		
特殊条款	47A	ADDITIONAL CONDITIONS	附加条款		
交单	48	PERIOD FOR PRESENTATION	交单期限		
费用	71B	CHARGES	费用情况		
指示	78	INSTRUCTION TO THE PAYING	付款行的指示		
	49	CONFIRMATION INSTRUCTIONS	保兑指示		

Chapter 4

Commodity Inspection Certificate

4.1 Inspection and quarantine of import and export commodities

In international trade, the quality, quantity, packing, safety, hygiene and shipping conditions of the goods are inspected by the commodity inspection and quarantine institutions, which is usually called inspection in international trade. Generally speaking, when the seller fulfills the obligation of delivery, the seller has the right to inspect the goods. If the goods are found to be at odds with the contract and it is indeed the responsibility of the seller, the buyer has the right to file a claim against the seller. If the goods are accepted without inspection, the right to refuse to accept the goods can no longer be exercised even if the goods are found to be in question. Commodity inspection is the basis for the settlement of payment of the goods, the filing of claims and the settlement of claims in order to maintain the legitimate rights and interests of the parties concerned in foreign trade relations.

4.2 Time and place of commodity inspection

The time and place of inspection are directly related to the rights and obligations of the buyer and the seller. Determining the time and place of inspection is in fact a matter of determining either the buyer or the seller exercises the right of inspection of the goods, and at the same time, it is also a question of determining which party will provide the certificate of inspection. Therefore, the determination of inspection time and place is one of the core contents of the inspection clauses of both parties, and the regulation of the time and place of commodity inspection is directly related to the vital interests of the buyer and the seller. In real-world operations, there are four ways to verify the time and place.

4.2.1 Inspection in the exporting country

It includes two methods of testing in the place of production (factory) and in the loading port (place).

Survey in the place of production (Factory)

Inspection or acceptance is conducted by the product manufacturing plant or the buyer's acceptance personnel before the product leaves the factory. In this case, the seller shall bear only the responsibility of the product before the product leaves the plant. As for the quality of the goods in transit, the risk of quantity change shall be borne by the buyer. In adopting this practice, some of the buyer's representatives are allowed to supervise the manufacture or shipment in the place of origin or consignment, which is a common practice in international trade and has been affirmed and adopted by the Commodity Inspection Law of our country.

Inspection prior to or at the time of shipment

Prior to shipment at the port of shipment, the quality, weight, quantity and packaging of the exported goods shall be verified by the inspection authority agreed upon by both parties as the final basis for determining the quality and weight of the goods. This is called the way of determination of the offshore quality and weight (Shipping Quality, Weight or Quantity as Final). The buyer can reinspect the goods after the arrival of the goods at the port of destination but no longer has the right to challenge the quality and weight of the goods. This provision is clearly in the seller's favour.

Note:

In the above two methods, the buyer's right to re-inspection has been canceled and so it is unfavorable to the buyer.

4.2.2 Inspection in the importing country

It includes two methods: inspection at the port of destination (the place of destination) and inspection at the buyer's place of business (the location of end-user).

Survey of the port of destination

It's also known as "CIF quality, CIF quantity" (Landed Quality and Weight), which means that the goods shall be inspected by the inspection and quarantine organizations agreed upon by the two parties within the time stipulated in the contract after the goods have arrived at the port of destination or the place of destination. And the inspection and quarantine certificate will be issued as the seller's final basis for the quality and quantity of the delivery of the goods.

Inspection of the buyer's place of business (end-user location)

Usually, after the goods arrive at the buyer's place of business (end-user location), the inspection and quarantine organizations stipulated in the contract shall inspect the goods and issue the inspection and quarantine certificate as the final basis of the quality and quantity of the goods delivered by the seller.

Note: In adopting the above two methods, the seller shall bear the responsibility for the quality or quantity of the arriving goods and it is unfavorable to the seller.

4.2.3 Inspection by the exporting country; re-examination by the importing country

The exporting country inspection serves as the basis of the exporter's documentary negotiation, and the importing country's re-inspection serves as the basis of the importing country's claim. It is the most common method of determining the time and place of inspection in an international contract of sales of goods. It is fair to both buyers and sellers, so it is widely used as the most common method in the import and export business of our country.

4.2.4 Loading port (place) inspection of weight and port (place) of destination inspection of quality

In the inspection of vast quantity commodity transactions, the inspection of the weight of the goods at the port of shipment and the issuance of the weight inspection certificate will be the final basis for the weight of the goods delivered by the seller. The quality inspection certificate issued by the port of destination (place) inspection organization is the final basis of the quality of the commodity. This approach is often applied to trade contracts for commodities of raw materials.

4.3 Commodity inspection clauses in the contract

Under the most common practice of inspection by exporting countries and re-inspection by importing countries, the terms of commodity inspection in the contract are as follows:

The certificates of quality and weight issued by XX (name of the inspection organization) at the port (place) of shipment shall be a part of the documents to be presented for negotiation under the relevant letter of credit. Any claim by the buyers regarding the goods shipped shall be filed within XX days after the arrival of the goods at the port (place) of destination, and supported by a survey issuer by a surveyor approved by the sellers.

4.4 Commodity inspection agencies

There are many kinds of commodity inspection institutions in the world, which can be classified into official inspection institutions, semi-official inspection bodies and non-official inspection institutions.

An official inspection body means an inspection body established by the State to carry out compulsory inspection and supervision and management of basic commodities laid down by the State. For example, the United States Food and Drug Administration (FDA), the German technical inspection agency network—Technischen Uberwachungs Vereine (TUV), and British Standards Association (BSA) all belong to the official inspection agency.

The semi-official inspection body refers to a number of non-governmental organizations which have certain authority and are authorized by the national government to exercise commodity inspection or inspection administration on behalf of the government, such as the Japan maritime verification association —Nippon Kaiji Kentei Kyokai (NKKK), and so on.

The non-official inspection body mainly refers to a notary bank or an inspection company which is founded by a private person and has the ability of professional inspection and technical identification, such as China Certification & Inspection (Group) Co., Ltd. (CCIC), the Swiss notary bank —SGS, the American insurance institute —UL, etc.

China's inspection agencies and their tasks:

The General Administration of Quality Supervision, Inspection and Quarantine of the people's Republic of China is the administrative law enforcement agency in charge of the nation's commodity quality and measurement, entry and exit commodity inspection, entry and exit health inspection, entry and exit animal and plant quarantine, and certification approval and the standardization work. The branches of the provinces, autonomous regions and municipalities directly under the Central Government supervise and administer the inspection of import and export commodities in their regions.

4.5 Commodity inspection certificates

4.5.1 The role of inspection certificates

The inspection certificate is issued after the inspection of import and export commodities by the commodity inspection authority. An inspection certificate has legal consequences, and its functions are as follows:

1. To certify that the quality, quantity and packaging of the goods delivered by the seller are in accordance with the terms of the contract.

2. In the event of trade disputes, it is the proof of the buyer's disagreement, non-acceptance and claim.

3. It is one of the documents by which the seller can get payment through negotiation.

4. For all the goods that belong to the category of legal inspection of the state, the inspection certificate is one of the certificates indicating that the Customs has inspected and released the goods.

5. It is the basis of tariff differential treatments in import and export countries.

4.5.2 Types of inspection certificates

Common certificates of inspection are:

1. The inspection certificate of quality
2. The inspection certificate of weight and quantity
3. The inspection certificate of package
4. The veterinary inspection certificate
5. The sanitary inspection certificate
6. The certificate of disinfection and inspection
7. The certificate of fumigation
8. The inspection certificate on damaged cargo

4.6 The concept of reporting for inspection

4.6.1 The meaning of inspection reporting

Inspection reporting of import and export goods is the whole of process in which consignors or consignees of import and export commodities or their agents, in accordance with relevant laws and regulations of the Commodity Inspection Law, within the time and place prescribed by the inspection and quarantine organizations, for the import and export commodities which need legal inspection, deal with applying for inspection, cooperating with inspection, paying fees, obtaining commodity inspection documents, etc., to the inspection and quarantine organizations.

4.6.2 Reporting units

There are two types of entry-exit inspection and quarantine reporting units: self inspection reporting units and agency inspection units.

Self inspection reporting units

The self reporting and inspection units refer to the units within China including the foreign trade-related units registered by the local entry-exit inspection and quarantine organization and those obtained the code of the inspection reporting, including domestic enterprises with import and export business rights, production enterprises of exporting goods, consignors and consignees of import and export goods, scientific research institutions and transportation units with related business of entry and exit and enterprises registered with the administrative department for industry and commerce and carry out, on their own, according to the law, the entry and exit inspection and quarantine reporting.

Agent inspection reporting units

An agent reporting unit means a lawful person within China registered with the State Administration of Quality Supervision and Inspection, entrusted by an export production enterprise, or entrusted by a consignee or consignor of import and export goods, or by a foreign trade related person, for the purposes of handling entry and exit inspection and quarantine reporting matters in accordance with the law and also registered in the administrative department for industry and commerce.

In the document (2013) 19 *The Decision of the State Council on the Cancellation and Decentralization of a Batch of Administrative Examination and Approval Items*, after canceling the registration of entry-exit express operation enterprises engaged in the registration of business reporting for inspection, registration of entry-exit inspection and quarantine reporter employment and registration of entry-exit inspection and quarantine agent reporting enterprise, the relevant provisions of the regulations on the implementation of the *Import and Export Commodity Inspection Law* have been amended.

Enterprises engaged in import and export trade will not be required to have a registered inspection reporting personnel, and enterprises can take self inspection reporting according to the needs of the inspection. The relevant rules need to be further clarified by the relevant departments.

4.6.3 Basis for inspection reporting

1. *The Law of the people's Republic of China on the Inspection of Import and Export Commodities* and *The Implementing Regulations of the Law of the people's Republic of China on the Commodity Inspection.*

2. *The Health and Quarantine Law of the People's Republic of China* and *The Implementation Rules of the Health and Quarantine Law of the People's Republic of China.*

3. *The Law of the people's Republic of China on the Quarantine of Inbound and Outbound Animals and Plants* and *The Detailed Implementing Rules of the People's Republic of China on Import and Exit Animal and Plant Quarantine Law.*

4. *Food Hygiene Law of the people's Republic of China.*

5. *Regulations of the People's Republic of China on Certification and Recognition.*

6. *Regulations of the People's Republic of China on the Origin of Import and Export Goods.*

4.7 Time limit and places of inspection of entry and exit goods

Outbound goods shall be reported for inspection no later than 7 days before export declaration or shipment, and individual goods with a long inspection and quarantine cycle shall have a corresponding inspection and quarantine time. Quarantine of outbound animals should be reported 60 days before departure and inspected 7 days before quarantine. Goods which need legal inspection and quarantine, in addition to live animals which are inspected and quarantined by the port, in principle, should have inspection and quarantine in the place of production. If the inspection and quarantine site is specified in the relevant government approval papers such as examining and approving documents and licenses, the inspection shall be reported at the specified place.

Imports of plants, seeds, seedlings and other reproductive materials shall be reported for inspection 7 days before entry. Imported microorganisms, human tissues, biological products, blood and blood products, breeding animals, poultry and semen, embryos, and fertilized eggs should be reported for inspection 30 days before entering the country.

If other animals are imported, the report for inspection should be 15 days before entering the country. Bulk commodities, perishable and spoiled commodities, waste goods and goods found to be damaged and have shortages when unloaded at the importing port of discharge, are reported to be inspected for inspection and quarantine at the port of discharge. Other incoming goods shall apply to the inspection and quarantine authorities of the customs declaration place for inspection before or when entering the territory.

4.8 The main contents and rules for filling in the inspection form of outbound goods

The entry and exit inspection and quarantine bureaus at various ports shall print the entry and exit cargo inspection report form. Except for the number which will be specified by the inspection and quarantine authority, the remaining items shall be filled out and sealed by the inspection report unit (refer to sample sheet 1 of "exit goods inspection form"). The contents of the list must be complete, accurate, clear, and must not be altered.

4.8.1 Number

The number in the inspection form should be filled in by the inspection and quarantine authorities' examining and accepting personnel. The first 6 numbers are the inspection and quarantine organization code, the seventh is the report class code, the eighth and ninth numbers are the chronological codes, and the 10th to 15th numbers are the serial numbers. After the implementation of electronic reporting, the number can be automatically generated in the receipt of electronic inspection reporting.

4.8.2 Inspection reporting unit

It is an enterprise that has been audited, licensed and registered by the State Administration of Quality Supervision, Inspection and Quarantine and has obtained Certificate of Registration for the record of the Self-reporting Unit or Certificate of Registration for the record of the Agent Reporting Unit issued by National Bureau of Quality Inspection. This column fills in the Chinese name of the inspection reporting unit, and affixes the official seal consistent with the name of the unit.

4.8.3 The registration number of the inspection reporting unit

Fill in the code of record or registration of the inspection reporting unit in the inspection and quarantine agency. This column fills in the 10-digit registration certificate number, the name of the inspection reporting persons and their contact telephone numbers.

4.8.4 Date of inspection reporting

The date on which the inspection and quarantine organization actually accepts the application for inspection will be filled in by the receiving and checking personnel of the inspection and quarantine authorities with Arabic numerals.

4.8.5 Consignor

Fill in the "Consignor" item according to different conditions. Consignors who need pre-inspection and report for inspection fill in production units. If the export is reported for inspection, the seller or beneficiary of the letter of credit in the foreign trade contract shall be filled in. This column fills in the name of the consignor in separate lines in both Chinese and English.

4.8.6 Consignee

In accordance with the foreign trade contract, the name of the buyer listed in the letter of credit shall be filled in. This column fills in the name of the consignee in separate lines in both Chinese and English.

4.8.7 Description of goods

Fill in the name of the goods in both Chinese and English and the specifications of the goods listed in the letter of credit in accordance with the foreign trade contract.

Note: Waste materials should be indicated in this column.

4.8.8 H.S. code

Fill in the commodity code for this shipment (a 10-digit code). The commodity tax codes published in that year by the Customs House shall prevail.

4.8.9 Place of origin

It refers to the production (processing) place of the goods. Fill in the Chinese names of provinces, cities and counties.

4.8.10 Quantity/Weight

Fill in the inspection and quarantine number/weight according to the actual application. Weight should also be filled in gross/net/tare weight. This column may fill in more than one unit of measurement. Such as the first unit of measurement: "one"; the second unit of measurement: "kilogram", etc.

4.8.11 Total value of goods

The total value and currency of the goods shall be filled in in accordance with the total value of the goods listed in the foreign trade contract and invoice, and no price terms, such as CIF, etc., shall be required.

4.8.12 Type and quantity of packaging

Fill in the type and quantity of the actual outer transportation packing of the goods, indicating the material of the packing. For example, 135 cases. If pallets are used in packing, in addition to the types and quantities of pallets, the quantity and types of the small packaging on the pallet should also be filled in.

4.8.13 Name and number of the transport vehicle

Fill in the name and number of the transport vehicles, such as the name of the ship, the voyage, etc. If the name and number of the transport vehicles are not determined at the time of the application for inspection, the general name of the mode of transport may be filled in, such as "ship" or "aircraft", etc.

4.8.14 Contract number

Fill in the number of the foreign trade contract, the order or the proforma invoice.

4.8.15 Letter of Credit No.

Fill in the L/C number corresponding to this shipment.

4.8.16 Mode of trade

Fill in the mode of import of the goods. The mode of trade refers to the trade nature of the goods, that is, the way through which the buyer and the seller transfer the ownership of the goods. Choose to fill in: general trade, incoming processing, feed processing, barter trade, compensation trade, exhibits, samples, other non-trade goods, other trade goods and so on according to the actual situation.

4.8.17 Place of storage of goods

Fill in the specific location and warehouse of this shipment.

4.8.18 Shipping date

Fill in the actual export shipment date. Omitted if it needs the pre-inspection and inspection reporting.

4.8.19 Export to countries and regions

The country and region where the buyer (importer) is located in the foreign trade contract, or the final delivery country or area specified in the contract. In this column, enter the Chinese name of the destination country/ area.

4.8.20 License / approval number

For goods that have been managed by the license / approval system, fill in the quality license number or the approval form number at the time of inspection reporting. There is no need to fill in this column for outbound goods without a license or an approval document.

4.8.21 Production Unit Registration number

It refers to the registration number of the unit which produces and processes this batch of goods, registered with the inspection and quarantine institutions, such as the health registration number, the quality license number, etc.

4.8.22 Place of departure

Fill in the Chinese name of the port of the departure / city area of the transport vehicles for the shipment of this batch of goods to leave the country, such as "Shanghai Port" and so on.

4.8.23 Port of arrival

It refers to the name of the port at which the goods finally arrive as their destination. When the final destination port can be predicted, this column is filled in according to the Chinese name of the actual port of arrival, and when the final destination port is unpredictable, the final arrival port can be completed as predictably as possible.

4.8.24 Container specification, quantity and number

If the goods are transported by containers, the specifications, the quantity and the number of containers should be filled in. The container number refers to the identification number of the container, which is composed of the master number (the first 3 letters), plus the equipment identification number (U is the sea container), plus the sequence number (6 digits), and plus Check Digit (the last digit). This column indicates the actual container "quantity" × "specification" / "box number", such as "1X20'/ TGHU8491952".

4.8.25 Special terms of contract formation and other requirements

Fill in the relevant clauses such as quality, hygiene, etc. in the foreign trade contract or the special requirements for inspection and quarantine of this batch of goods by the inspection reporting units.

4.8.26 Marking and number

The marking number of the goods shall be consistent with the relevant foreign trade documents such as contracts, invoices and so on. If there is no marked number, fill in "N/M".

4.8.27 Use

Fill in the purpose of this shipment. Choose to fill in: seeds or reproduction, edible, milk, ornamental or performing arts, partner animal, testing, medicinal, feed, and others, according to the actual situation.

4.8.28 Accompanying documents

In accordance with the documents actually provided to the inspection and quarantine institution, type "√" on the corresponding "□" or fill in it.

4.8.29 The name of the certificate required

Type "√" on the corresponding "□" or fill in it according to the certificate issued by the inspection and quarantine institution. And indicate the number of originals and copies of the required certificates.

4.8.30 Signature

The inspection reporting personnel must sign with his or her own hand.

4.8.31 Inspection and quarantine fees

The fee is to be filled in by the billing personnel of the inspection and quarantine institution.

4.8.32 Drawing of the certificate

The inspection reporting personnel fills in the date of drawing of the certificate and signs it at the time of taking it out.

4.9 Samples of inspection certificates

Sample 1

Outbound Cargo Inspection Sheet

中华人民共和国出入境检验检疫出境货物报检单

Declaration of Entry and Exit Inspection and Quarantine Goods of the People's Republic of China

报检单位(加盖公章): × × ×　　　　* 编号________

报检单位登记号: × × ×　联系人: × × ×　电话: × ×　　报检日期:　　年　月　日

发货人	(中文)				
	(外文)				
收货人	(中文)				
	(外文)				
货物名称(中/外文)	H.S. 编码	产地	数/重量	货物总值	包装种类及数量
运输工具名称号码		贸易方式		货物存放地点	

合同号		信用证号		用途	
发货日期		输往国家(地区)		许可证/审批号	× × ×
启运地		到达口岸		生产单位注册号	× × ×
集装箱规格、数量及号码					
合同、信用证订立的检验检疫条款或特殊要求	标记及号码	随附单位(画“√”或补填)			
		√ 合同 √ 信用证 √ 发票 换证凭单 √ 装箱单 厂检单	包装性能结果单 许可/审批文件		
需要证单名称(画“√”或补填)			* 检验检疫费		
品质证书 _正_副 重量证书 _正_副 数量证书 _正_副 兽医卫生证书 _正_副 健康证书 _正_副 卫生证书 _正_副 动物卫生证书 _正_副	植物检疫证书 _正_副 熏蒸/消毒证书 _正_副 出境货物换证凭单 √ 出境货物通关单		总金额(人民币元)		
			计费人		
			收费人		
报检人郑重声明: 1. 本人被授权报检。 2. 上列填写内容正确属实,货物无伪造或冒用他人的厂名、标志、认证标志,并承担货物质量责任。 签名: ________			领取证单		
			日期		
			签名		

注:有“*”号栏由出入境检验检疫机关填写局制 [1-1(2000.1.1)]　　国家出入境检验检疫

Sample 2

Certificate of Quality Inspection

编号: NO.:891213

中华人民共和国出入境检验检疫

ENTRY-EXTT INSPECTION AND QUARANTINE OF

THE PEOPLE'S REPUBLIC OF CHINA

品质检验证书

INSPECTION CERTIFICATE OF QUALITY

发货人:

CONSIGNOR: GUANGZHOU TOP IMPORT & EXPORT TRADING CO., LTD.

ROOM 3019 HUICUIGE, HUABIAO SQUARE, NO.601 TIANHE NORTH ROAD GUANGZHOU, CHINA

收货人:

CONSIGNEE: WENSCO DAILY PRODUCT CO., LTD.
555 HASTINGS SEYMOUR STREET VANCOUVER CENTRE VANCOUVER, BC CANADA

品名:

DESCRIPTION OF GOODS: 3 ITEMS OF DAILY VASE

报检数量 / 重量: **标记及号码**

QUANTITY/WEIGHT DECLARED: **MARK&NO.**

2034PCS/7125.00KGS/23.083M³

WDP

包装种类及数量:

NUMBER AND TYPE OF PACKAGES: 339 CTNS P/O NO.: EX090823A

运输工具: VANCOUVER

MEANS OF CONVEYANCE: WHR MIT/ H.265 CTN NO.: 1-339

检验结果: MADE IN CHINA

RESULTS OF INSPECTION:

经检验，上述货物符合 EX 090823A 号合同规定

WE HEREBY CERTIFY THAT AT TIME AND PLACE OF SHIPMENT THAT GOODS ARE OF CHINESE JIANGXI ORIGIN IN SOUND CONDITION AND ARE FIT FOR HUMAN USE.

印章

OFFICIAL STAMP

签订地方 签订时间

PLACE OF ISSUE: 广州 DATE OF ISSUE: OCT.17, 2017

授权签字人 姓名

AUTHORIZED OFFICE SIGNATURE: WING

我们已尽所知和最大的能力实施上述检验，不能因我们签发本证书而免除卖方或者其他方面根据合同和法律所承担的产品责任和其他责任。

ALL INSPECTIONS ARE CARRIED OUT CONSCIENTIOUSLY TO THE BEST OF OUR KNOWLEDGE AND ABILITY THIS CERTIFICATE DOES NOT IN ANY RESPECT ABSOLVE THE SELLER AND OTHER RELATED PARTIES FROM HIS CONTRACTUAL AND LEGAL OBLIGATIONS ESPECIALLY WHEN PRODUCT QUALITY IS CONCERNED.

Sample 3

Certificate of Quantity Inspection

中华人民共和国出入境检验检疫

ENTRY-EXTT INSPECTION AND QUARANTINE OF THE PEOPLE'S

REPUBLIC OF CHINA

数量检验证书

QUANTITY CERTIFICATE

发货人:

CONSIGNOR: GUANGZHOU TOP IMPORT & EXPORT TRADING CO., LTD.
ROOM 3019 HUICUIGE, HUABIAO SQUARE, NO.601 TIANHE NORTH ROAD GUANGZHOU, CHINA

收货人:

CONSIGNEE: WENSCO DAILY PRODUCT CO., LTD.
555 HASTINGS SEYMOUR STREET VANCOUVER CENTRE VANCOUVER, BC CANADA

品名:

DESCRIPTION OF GOODS: 3 ITEMS OF DAILY VASE

报检数量 / 重量:

QUANTITY/WEIGHTDECLARED:

33350DOZS/199911KGS

包装种类及数量:

NUMBER AND TYPE OF PACKAGES: 367 BALES

运输工具:

MEANS OF CONVEYANCE: PUDONG V.053

标记及号码

MARK&NO.

WDP

P/O NO.: EX090823A

VANCOUVER

CTN NO.: 1-339

MADE IN CHINA

检验结果:

RESULTS OF INSPECTION:

14’ × 14’ PACKED IN 80 BALES OF 200 DOZS EACH

15’ × 25’ PACKED IN 60 BALES OF 100 DOZS EACH

22’ × 32’ PACKED IN 227 BALES OF 50 DOZS EACH

TOTAL: 33350 DOZS

TOTAL: 367 BALES

我们已尽所知和最大的能力实施上述检验，不能因我们签发本证书而免除卖方或者其他方面根据合同和法律所承担的产品责任和其他责任。

ALL INSPECTIONS ARE CARRIED OUT CONSCIENTIOUSLY TO THE BEST OF OUR KNOWLEDGE AND ABILITY THIS CERTIFICATE DOES NOT IN ANY RESPECT ABSOLVE THE SELLER AND OTHER RELATED PARTIES FROM HIS CONTRACTUAL AND LEGAL OBLIGATIONS ESPECIALLY WHEN PRODUCT QUALITY IS CONCERNED.

CHINA INSPECTION AND QUARANTINE BIREAU

中国进入境检验检疫局

丁毅

MAR.10, 2017

4.10 Exercises

1. Judge whether the following statements are true or not.

1)"检验证书"的英文应该翻译成"inspection certificate"。

2)"port of discharge"的意思是"卸货港"。

3)When filling out the exit goods inspection form, fill in the "N/M" in the "mark and number" column to indicate that the goods are unmarked.

4)The unit of measure in the "number/weight" column of the exit cargo inspection form may not be filled out.

5)The buyer listed in the contract or the L/C shall be filled in the "consignee" column of the exit goods inspection form.

6)The "port of departure" column of the exit cargo inspection form should fill in the port of final departure of the goods.

7)Generally, the inspection certificate can only be issued by the state-designated inspection agency, and the export enterprise cannot issue the certificate by itself.

8)Outbound goods shall be reported for inspection no later than 7 days before export declaration or shipment, and individual goods with a long inspection and quarantine cycle shall have a corresponding inspection and quarantine time.

9)Imports of plants, seeds, seedlings and other reproductive materials shall be reported for inspection 15 days before entry.

10)The place of origin in the inspection report form shall be filled out in accordance with the actual place of origin.

2. Translate the following sentences into English.

1)检验证书是具有法律效力的证明凭证，在国际贸易中起到公正性的作用。

2)检验证书的种类很多，分别用以证明货物的品质、数量、重量、卫生条件等方面的情况。

3)检验证书一般由国家指定的检验机构出具，也可根据不同情况，由出口企业或生产企业自行出具。

4)熏蒸证明书。黄曲霉素检验证书。植物检疫证明书。

5)由中国出入境检验检疫局出具的品质和数量检验证明书一式三份。

3. Judge whether the items on the outbound cargo inspection sheet are correct or not based on the documents given.

SHENZHEN TV IMP. & EXP. CO., LTD.

22, ZHONG SHAN RD SHENZHEN, CHINA

TEL: 86-755-82100000 FAX: 86-755-82110000

SALES CONTRACT

S/C NO.: RT05342
DATE: Mar. 20, 2020
P/I NO.: 2020023

TO:

MAMUT ENTERPRISESAV
TARRAGONA76-3AR, BARCELONA, SPAIN

DEAR SIRS,

WE HEREBY CONFIRM HAVING SOLD TO YOU THE FOLLOWING GOODS ON TERMS AND CONDITIONS AS SPECIFIED BELOW:

(1)

MARKS & NO.	DESCRIPTIONS	QTY	U/P	AMT
M.E BARCELONA C/NO.1-1100	TV SET 56CM (CHANGHONG BRAND)	1,100 SETS 1,100 CARTONS	USD 50.00/SET	USD55,000.00 USD55,000.00
TOTAL	SAY UNITED STATES DOLLARS FIFTY FIVE THOUSAND ONLY			USD55,000.00

FOB SHENZHEN

(2) PACKING: ALL THE GOODS ARE PACKED IN CARTONS

(3) PORT OF LOADING: SHENZHEN PORT, CHINA

(4) PORT OF DESTINATION: BARCELONA, SPAIN

(5) DATE OF SHIPMENT: NOT LATER THAN MAY 30, 2020 BY SEA

(6) TERMS OF PAYMENT: LETTER OF CREDIT AND CREDIT NO. ME67340

(7) DOCUMENTS REQUIRED: CERTIFICATE OF QUANTITY ISSUED BY CIQ INDICATING THE NO. OF L/C

THE SELLER: THE BUYER:

SHENZHEN TV IMP. & EXP. CO.,LTD. MAMUT ENTERPRISESAV

CIQ

中华人民共和国出入境检验检疫

出境货物报检单

报检单位（加盖公章）：深圳电视进出口有限公司 *编 号________________

续表

报检单位登记号：3200600018　联系人：李江　电话：888888　报检日期：2020 年 5 月 25 日

发货人	(中文)深圳电视进出口有限公司	
	(外文)SHENZHEN TV IMP. & EXP. CO.,LTD.	
收货人	(中文)猛犸象企业	
	(外文)MAMUT ENTERPRISESAV	

货物名称(中/外文)	H.S. 编码	产地	数/重量	货物总值	包装种类及数量
电视机 TV	8415101000	成都	1000 纸箱	80 美元	1000 台 /1000 箱

运输工具名称号码	船舶	贸易方式	一班贸易	货物存放地点	本公司仓库
合同号	RW05342	信用证号	ME673400	用途	其他
发货日期	2020.5.30	输往国家(地区)	葡萄牙	许可证/审批号	***
启运地	深圳	到达口岸	葡萄牙	生产单位注册号	***
集装箱规格、数量及号码	***				

合同、信用证订立的检验检疫条款或特殊要求	标记及号码	随附单据(画"✓"或补填)	
**********	M.E BARCELONA C/NO.1-1100	☑合同 ☐信用证 ☑发票 ☐换证凭单 ☑装箱单 ☐厂检单	☐包装性能结果单 ☐许可/审批文件 ☐ ☐ ☐ ☐

需要证单名称(画"✓"或补填)				*检验检疫费	
☐品质证书	__正__副	☐植物检疫证书	__正__副	总金额(人民币元)	
☐重量证书	__正__副	☐熏蒸/消毒证书	__正__副		
☐数量证书	__正__副	☐出境货物换证凭单	__正__副	计费人	
☐兽医卫生证书	__正__副	☐			
☐健康证书	__正__副	☐			
☐卫生证书	__正__副	☐		收费人	
☐动物卫生证书	__正__副	☐			

报检人郑重声明：	领取证单	
1. 本人被授权报检。	日期	
2. 上列填写内容正确属实，货物无伪造或冒用他人的厂名、标志、认证标志，并承担货物质量责任。	签名	
签名：李江		

注：有"*"号栏由出入境检验检疫机关填写　◆国家出入境检验检疫局制

[1-2 (2000.1.1)]

Chapter 5

Invoice

Commercial invoice is abbreviated as invoice. In practice the commercial invoice is the price list of the goods dispatched by a exporter to the importer. It is the basis of the account kept by the buyer and the seller, and is also a general statement of the import and export declaration and tax payment. It is the most important document allowing the parties concerned to know the full picture of a transaction. Other documents are based on invoices.

5.1 The role of commercial invoice

The invoice is issued by the seller to the buyer. It is the general description of the goods delivered and it is a list of the prices of the goods dispatched. The importer uses invoices to check the goods and knows the quality, specifications, and the value of the goods. It is the basis of the account keeping for importers and exporters. In the absence of a draft, the exporter may receive the payment by using the invoice. Invoice is the basic basis of customs declaration and tax payment, and it is also the basis of other management.

It is important to note that invoices also serve the following purposes before being used as exchange earnings receipts, that is, when the goods are shipped, there are also the following roles:

- As the basic document among the international business documents, it is the basis of preparing other documents such as customs declaration, the origin certificate, the inspection report form, and the insurance policy.
- As part of customs declaration and inspection reporting documents, in the shipping process, both the inspection report form and customs declaration need to attach invoices so that they can play the corresponding roles.
- After being used as the receiving foreign exchange document, the invoice has the function of writing off foreign exchange. After receiving the foreign exchange, the exporter should provide the invoice when processing the write-off.

5.2 Types of commercial invoice

In addition to commercial invoices, there are other types of invoices, such as customs invoices, proforma invoices, etc.

5.2.1 Customs invoice

Customs invoice is a document issued by the exporter at the request of the customs of the importing country, the basic content of which is similar to that of ordinary commercial invoices, and the format of which is generally formulated and provided by the customs of the importing country in a uniform manner. It is mainly used for the customs statistics, the verification of the place of origin, and the checking of the composition of the price of the imported goods of the importing country.

The main functions of the customs invoice are as follows: it is used by the customs of the importing country to check and ratify the place of origin of the goods in order to adopt different national policies; it is used by the importer to carry out the formalities of customs declaration and tax payment to the customs; it is used by the customs of the importing country to get the information about the prices of imported goods in the market of exporting countries to determine whether they are dumped at low prices in order to levy anti-dumping duties; it is used by the import customs as the basis for statistics.

5.2.2 Proforma invoice

The abbreviated form of proforma invoice is (PI). Exporters sometimes issue, at the request of the importer, an informal reference invoice containing the name, specifications, the unit price, etc. of the goods for sale. This invoice is called a proforma invoice for importers to apply for import licenses or the approval of being given foreign exchange from trade or foreign exchange authorities of their own countries. Its functions are: as a quantitative quotation; as the confirmation of the sales; letting the buyer use this invoice to apply for the import license, the foreign exchange license, and the opening of a letter of credit.

The proforma invoice is not an official invoice and cannot be used for collection or negotiation. The unit price listed in it is also an estimate price made by the importer on the basis of the circumstances at the time, and there is no final binding force on both parties. Therefore, the proforma invoice is only a kind of price valuation list. It is necessary to make another commercial invoice if there is a formal transaction.

However, the proforma invoice is closely related to the commercial invoice. After the description of the goods clause, the letter of credit usually has the clauses "according to the proforma invoice of a certain month and a certain date" or "the goods listed are in accordance with the proforma invoice No. XX" and so on, and requires that it be invoked. When making commercial invoices, the words "as per proforma invoice... dated..." should be typed. In order to distinguish from the formal invoice, the proforma invoice must be clearly marked with the words "proforma invoice". The content of the proforma invoice is generally the same as that of the formal invoice, indicating the terms of trade, the trade name, the quantity, the unit price, the total value, the date of delivery and the validity period of the goods and the words "for the merchant to apply for a permit" or "this transaction is valid with the seller's final confirmation" should be marked.

5.2.3 Consular invoice

Consular invoice is also known as visa invoice. Consular invoice is one of the prerequisites for the import declaration of goods, which is filled out by the exporting party in accordance with the fixed form stipulated by the consulate of the importing country in the exporting country or the consulate in the adjacent region, and it is subject to a consular visa.

The main function of consular invoice is: to serve as the basis for import tariff collection by import customs; to prove the quantity of goods supplied by exporters and the authenticity of prices; to increase consular revenue.

In practice, more often than not, the letter of credit opening from some countries requires their consuls to certify on commercial invoices, the purpose of which is to confirm the exact place of origin of the commodity and to charge a fee for certification. Therefore, in calculating the export price, the cost should be taken into account.

At present, in practice, except for some Latin American, Middle East countries, consular invoices are seldom used. It should be noted that:

If the exporter is unable to provide such invoice, the importer shall be informed as early as possible (if there is such a clause in the L/C but the exporter cannot obtain the document, then the letter of credit shall be amended upon request);

If such documents are processed, they need to be prepared in advance to prevent delays due to non-exporter reasons, thus affecting the exporter's collecting foreign exchange when presenting documents and the importer's customs clearance and picking up the goods.

5.2.4 Manufacturer invoice

Manufacturer invoice is an invoice issued by the manufacturer of export goods in domestic currency to prove the factory price in the domestic market of the exporting country. It is used for customs valuation, checking duties and levying anti-dumping duties in importing countries. If the L/C from foreign countries has this requirement, it should be dealt with in the light of the method of filling in the domestic price of customs invoice. It should be noted that the manufacturer invoice is issued by the manufacturer to the exporter.

5.3 The contents and making-out of a commercial invoice

5.3.1 General contents of a commercial invoice

Commercial invoices are drawn up by the exporting enterprises themselves without a uniform format, but the basic columns are roughly the same. It is divided into three parts: the first part, the body part and the concluding part. The first part includes the invoice name, the number, the date, the place, the payer, the contract number, the transportation route, etc. The body part includes the description of the goods, the unit price, the total amount, the transport sign, etc. The concluding part includes the origin of the goods, the type of packaging, all kinds of clauses for proof, the invoice maker's signature and so on.

In essence, an invoice is the original accounting voucher of importers and exporters in international trade and economic business, so the specific content of invoice is based on the basic content of the original accounting voucher. It includes the following specific elements:

1. The name of the drawer, that is, the name of the person issuing the invoice. It includes the exporter's name and detailed address, telephone, fax, etc. Generally, export enterprises when printing blank invoices, will put the company's name, address, telephone, fax directly on the invoice (as a letterhead). When using the L/C, UCP600 stipulates that the invoice must be issued by the beneficiary.

2. The name of the document, i.e., "commercial invoice" or "invoice" shall be consistent with the letter of credit.

If the letter of credit does not specify the name of the invoice (only "invoice"), then any form of invoice, commercial invoice, customs invoice, consular invoice, etc. may be submitted. However, the name of the invoice must not have the words "provisional invoice" or "proforma invoice". If the letter of credit requires a "certified invoice" or a "detailed invoice", then the invoice name should also be thus displayed.

3. The date of the documents making is the basic information of the documents making, including the making date of the invoice, the invoice number, the contract number, etc.

4. The name of the recipient of the invoice is the addressee of the invoice. The invoice must clearly show the name and address of the addressee, that is, the payer of the invoice. Usually, the invoice addressee becomes an importer, the applicant of the L/C. If the letter of credit requires the addressee to be a third party, this requirement of the letter of credit shall be followed. The invoice title of the transferable letter of credit may replace the name of the issuing applicant of

the original letter of credit with the name of the first beneficiary.

5. A summary of this business activity includes:

1) Descriptions of the goods, indicating the name, the specification, the quantity, the packing type and the number of pieces of the goods. When the letter of credit is used, the description of the goods in the invoice must be consistent with the description in the letter of credit.

2) Transport information, including the place of embarkation, the destination, the transport mark (the identification mark of the goods), etc. If transshipment is allowed, the place of transshipment may be indicated.

6. Quantity and amount. Export invoices must clearly indicate the quantity, the unit price, the gross value and trade terms (price terms), including the quantity and the unit of quantity, the denomination currency name, and the specific price. Sometimes commissions, discounts, freight and premiums are to be listed.

7. The name of the drawer's enterprise and the signer's seal or signature. These are generally typed at the bottom right of the invoice.

8. Other contents, including the business-related specific number, proof, and so on. For example, the buyer's reference number, the import license number, the letter of credit number and the origin of the goods and the exporter's proof of the manufacturing, packing, transportation of the goods, etc. should be indicated in the blank space below the invoice commodity description.

5.3.2 Key points of the making-out of a commercial invoice

The commercial invoice is made by the export enterprise itself, and there is no uniform format, but the basic content and the making method are the same. The main points of making are as follows:

5.3.2.1 Name and address of the drawer

The name and address of the drawer shall be the same as the name and address of the seller of the contract or the beneficiary of the letter of credit. In the making of the invoice, the name and address of the drawer shall be marked prominently in both English and Chinese. Generally, when the blank invoices are printed by the common export enterprises, the name, address, telephone and fax of the company are printed in advance directly in the invoices.

5.3.2.2 Invoice name

The invoice name shall be marked "Commercial Invoice" or "Invoice" in bold. The name of the invoice shall be in accordance with the letter of credit. If the letter of credit requires "Certified Invoice" or "Detailed Invoice", the invoice name should also thus be displayed.

5.3.2.3 Invoice number

The invoice number is compiled by the exporting company according to the actual situation of the company. It is the central number of the full sets of foreign exchange settlement documents.

5.3.2.4 Invoice date

The invoice date shall generally be later than the date of the signing and issuance of the contract and the letter of credit (UCP600 stipulates that the bank may accept invoices dated earlier than the date of the issuance of L/C), but generally not later than the date of the bill of lading, the date of the bill of exchange, the date of presentation and the validity of the letter of credit as stipulated in the letter of credit. Among the settlement documents, it is the earliest issued document.

5.3.2.5 Letter of credit number

Invoices under the letter of credit must be filled in the number of the letter of credit and for the other means of payment, this number may not be filled in.

5.3.2.6 Contract number

The contract number shall be consistent with that specified in the letter of credit. If the letter of credit does not specify the contract number, it may not be filled in. For other forms of payment, this number must be filled in.

5.3.2.7 Consignee

Under the payment of the letter of credit, it should be completed in accordance with the stipulations of the letter of credit. Generally, it is the applicant of the L/C. Under the payment mode of collection, it is usually the buyer. When both are filled in, the name and address should not be placed in the same row, but should be indicated in different rows.

5.3.2.8 Route

Fill in the actual port (place) of departure of the goods and the port (place) of destination. If the goods need to be transshipped, the name of the port(place) of transfer should be indicated. For instance: From Shanghai to London W/T Rotterdam. From Guangzhou to Piraeus W/T Hong Kong by Steamer. If the goods are transported to the port of destination and then re-transferred to the inland city, the words "In transit to" or "In transit" may be typed below the port of destination. If only the country name is indicated in the L/C, a specific place name should be entered at the time the invoice is made (unless the destination has not been determined at the time of shipment of a particular transaction).

5.3.2.9 Shipping mark and piece number

Invoice marks shall be filled in in accordance with the letter of credit or the contract, usually including the consignee's abbreviations, reference numbers, destinations and the total number of goods. If no specific provision is made, fill in N/M.

5.3.2.10 A description of goods

A description of goods generally includes the product name, the quality, the quantity, the packaging, etc. If the letter of credit has been used, then the description of the goods in the invoice must be consistent with that in the letter of credit. Omitting or adding any word or sentence of the name of the goods will result in the non-conformity of the document with the L/C. In the case of other means of payment, the description of goods shall be in accordance with the terms of the contract.

With regard to the description of the goods in the invoice, there are usually the following cases in practice:

1) If only the general title of the goods is specified in the letter of credit, in addition to displaying as usual the general title in the invoice, the invoice may also add the detailed name of the goods but the detailed name shall not contradict the general name. For example: the letter of credit states "blue cotton wears" and the invoice shows "colored cotton wears". This is not allowed.

2) If there are more items listed, when the letter of credit is marked with a general name, the invoice may indicate the general name in the invoice above the specific product name in accordance with the L/C.

3) If the letter of credit does not specify the general name of the goods, but the listed names are very detailed, the invoice should be stated in accordance with the letter of credit.

4) When the name of the goods specified in the letter of credit is not in English, the invoice should also be shown in the original language. (It can also be expressed in English at the same time).

5) If the letter of credit prescribes a variety of names of the goods, one or more of those names should be indicated according to the actual delivery conditions. The names should not be copied blindly.

6) Invoices cannot show other goods (including samples, advertising materials, etc.) other than those specified in the L/C, even if they are noted free of charge.

If one of the letters in the invoice's goods description is incorrectly written, but does not affect the understanding of the word, issuing banks are not allowed to refuse to pay all of them. For example, in the letter of credit it is MACHINE, but the invoice mistakenly typed it into MASHINE. But if the letter of credit writes DIRED GRAPES, and in the invoice it is typed as

RAISIN, then the meaning will be different, and that will form non-conformity. Although the ICC now requires less stringent descriptions of invoice names, exporters should spell correctly when making invoices.

The common words or phrases used in the L/C to describe the contents of the goods are as follows: a. Description of goods; b. Description of merchandise; c. Covering shipment of; d. Covering the following goods by; e. Covering value of; f. Shipment of goods.

5.3.2.11 Unit price and price terminology

The complete unit price shall consist of four parts: the currency, the unit price, the unit of measure and the trade term.

Example: USD100 Per DOZ CIF London (INCOTERMS 2010). A trade term is related to the division of risks and expenses between buyers and sellers, and is also the basis of customs taxation, which must be correctly stated.

5.3.2.12 Total value

The total invoice value shall not exceed the amount of the L/C and the commission and discount shall be dealt with in accordance with the L/C. If the L/C requires to list freight, insurance and FOB price separately, you must follow suit; if the L/C requests to list the net price after separately deducting the commission and discount, you must do so.

Example 1: CIF Tokyo USD 30000.00
Less F USD 250.00, Less I USD 150.00
FOB USD 29600.00

Example 2: CIF Tokyo USD 30000.00
Less C USD 250.00, Less D USD 150.00
NET USD 29600.00

When the amount is lowercase, two decimal places should be retained, such as USD100,000.00. Write the money first in uppercase, then the number. If the USD100000.00 is capitalized, it should read:

SAY U.S.DOLLARS ONE HUNDRED THOUSAND ONLY

If there is a decimal point, then USD100000.30 reads:

SAY U.S. DOLLARS ONE HUNDRED THOUSAND AND CENTS THIRTY/POINT THREE/30/100/30% ONLY

5.3.2.13 Statements and other contents

They should be written in accordance with the provisions of the L/C or in accordance with what particularly needs to be noted in the invoice. For example: some reference numbers, Import

License No., etc. Proof sentences: We hereby declare that the goods are of pure national origin of the exporting country; We hereby certify that the contents of in voice herein are true and correct.

5.3.2.14 Drawer's signature

Usually the drawer signs the name of the export company in the lower-right corner of the invoice and is signed or stamped by the agent. If the L/C requires that the invoice be signed by hand, the letter of credit must be followed. Invoices in exports to Mexico and Argentina must be signed by hand whether or not it has been stipulated in the letter of credit.

5.4 Samples of commercial invoice

Commercial invoices are prepared by exporting enterprises on their own. There is no uniform format. The common forms are as follows:

Sample sheet 1

BEIJING YILIAN CLOTHING MANUFACTURE CO., LTD.
CHANGPING DISTRICT, BEIJING, CHINA

TEL: 0086-10-62387997 INV. NO.:__________

FAX: 0086-10-62387997 DATE:__________

S/C NO.:__________

COMMERCIAL INVOICE

TO:

FROM:__________ TO:__________

L/C NO.:__________ ISSUED BY:__________

MARKS & NO.	DESCRIPTION OF GOODS	QTY	UNIT PRICE	AMOUNT
ABC JA-ABC-231 N.Y. C/NO.:1-25	HYUNDAI (32Gg)	1000PCS	USD2.60/PC CIF HONGKONG	USD2600.00
TOTAL		1000		USD2600.00

TOTAL AMOUNT: SAY UNITED STATES DOLLARS TWENTY SIX HUNDRED ONLY

WE HEREBY CERTIFY THAT THE ABOVE MENTIONED GOODS ARE OF CHINESE ORIGIN.

BEIJING YILIAN CLOTHING MANUFACTURE CO., LTD.

Sample sheet 2

<table>
<tr><td colspan="2">ISSUER
SAMSON CO., LTD.
Room 2901, HuaRong Mansion, GuanJiaQiao 85#, Shanghai
200005, P.R. China
TEL: 021-4711363 FAX: 021-4691619</td><td colspan="3">商业发票
COMMERCIAL INVOICE</td></tr>
<tr><td colspan="2">TO
SAMAN AL-ABDUL KARIM AND PARTNERS CO.
POB 13552, RIYADH 44166, KSA
TEL: 4577301/4577312/4577313 FAX: 4577461</td><td>NO.
DS2001INV205</td><td colspan="2">DATE
May 22, 2001</td></tr>
<tr><td colspan="2" rowspan="2">TRANSPORT DETAILS
SHIPMENT FROM TIANJIN PORT TO DAMMAM PORT
BY SEA</td><td>S/C NO.
DS2001SC205</td><td colspan="2">L/C NO.
LC010986</td></tr>
<tr><td colspan="3">TERMS OF PAYMENT
L/C AT SIGHT</td></tr>
<tr><td rowspan="2">Marks and Numbers</td><td rowspan="2">Number and kind of packages; Description of goods</td><td rowspan="2">Quantity</td><td>Unit price</td><td>Amount</td></tr>
<tr><td colspan="2">USD</td></tr>
<tr><td rowspan="3">N/M</td><td colspan="4">CFR DAMMAM PORT, SAUDI ARABIA</td></tr>
<tr><td>CANNED APPLE JAM
24 TINS × 340 GMS</td><td>2200CTNS</td><td>USD6.80</td><td>USD14960.00</td></tr>
<tr><td>CANNED STRAWBERRY JAM
24 TINS × 340 GMS</td><td>2200CTNS</td><td>USD6.80</td><td>USD14960.00</td></tr>
<tr><td colspan="5">Total: 4400CARTONS USD29920.00
SAY TOTAL: U.S. DOLLAR TWENTY-NINE THOUSAND NINE HUNDRED
AND TWENTY ONLY</td></tr>
</table>

SAMSON CO., LTD.

5.5 Common commercial invoice clauses in a letter of credit

Example 1

Signed commercial invoice 3-fold. (This clause requires the signing of commercial invoices in triplicate.)

Example 2

A 5% discount should be deducted from the total amount of the commercial invoice. (This clause requires that the total amount of the commercial invoice be deducted by 5% as a discount.)

Example 3

Signed commercial invoices in quadruplicate showing a deduction of USD141.00 being ORC charges. (This clause requires the signed commercial invoice to be in quadruplicate and show a deduction of US $141 for ORC expenses on the commercial invoice.)

Example 4

Manually signed commercial invoices in triplicate indicating applicant's ref. No.SCLI-98-0474.(This clause requires a hand-signed commercial invoice to be in triplicate and show the applicant's reference number in the commercial invoice.)

Example 5

Signed commercial invoices in triplicate showing separately the FOB value, the freight charge, the insurance premium, the CIF value and the country of origin.(This clause requires the signed commercial invoices to be in triplicate and show the total value of FOB, the freight, the insurance, the CIF total value and the country of origin, separately.)

Example 6

Signed invoices in triplicate, certifying merchandise to be of CHINESE origin. (This clause requires the signed invoice in three copies certifying the origin of the product in China.)

Example 7

Commercial invoices certifying at the same time origin of goods, contents are true and authentic, prices correct and current, that it is the only invoice issued for the goods described therein and mentioning that it is their exact value without any deduction of payment in advance. One original copy must be certified by CCPIT and legalized by Lebanese Consulate if available at the beneficiary's location. (This clause requires the beneficiary to prove in the invoice at the same time: (1) the origin of the goods, (2) the contents of the invoice are true, (3) the price is correct; (4) it is the only invoice issued for the said goods and (5) the actual price stated does not deduct any advance receipts. The original invoice must be certified by the Council for the Promotion of Trade and, if there is a Lebanese consulate there, it must be certified.)

Example 8

The beneficiary must make the statement in the invoice: "We certify that each piece/each packing unit of the goods has an undetachable label which shows 'Made in China' words." (This clause requires the beneficiary to certify on the invoice that each piece or packing unit of the goods shall be accompanied by an inseparable label with the words "made in China". This statement is required in the invoice, which is the local customs regulation on the import of goods, and must be followed.)

Example 9

Commercial invoices issued for amounts in excess of the amount permitted by the credit are not acceptable, the gross FOB/CIF/C&F/CIP value of the goods before the deduction of the agent's commission if any, must not exceed the credit amount. (This clause indicates that if commercial invoices exceed the L/C in amount, they are not accepted. If the gross value of FOB, CIF, CFR or CIP contains an agent's commission, the amount of the commission shall not exceed that in the L/C until deducted.)

5.6 Exercises

1. Judge whether the following statements are true or not.

1) In the making of invoices, the word "commercial" is not required to be marked, as long as the word "invoice" has been written. But this invoice cannot be the proforma invoice.

2) The description of the goods in the commercial invoice may be inconsistent with the provisions in the letter of credit.

3) The seller of the commercial invoice fills out the seller or the beneficiary of the letter of credit in the contract.

4) The invoice number is drawn up by the exporter itself, and usually the invoice number is inconsistent with the draft number.

5) Generally speaking, the invoice is the document with the earliest date issued in the full set of documents.

6) Unless otherwise provided in the letter of credit, the title of the commercial invoice must be the name of the applicant.

7) The proforma invoice is a formal invoice that can be used for collection and negotiation.

8) If the commercial invoice does not specify the trade terms specified in the letter of credit, it constitutes the non-conformity between the document and the L/C and the bank has the right to refuse to accept the document.

9) When using a L/C as the mode of payment, the invoice shall indicate the corresponding L/C number unless otherwise specified in the L/C.

10) Invoices may be issued later than the date of issuance of the bill of lading.

2. Translate the following sentences into English.

1) 商业发票全面反映了交付货物的状况，因此，是出口商必须提供的主要单据之一。

2) 商业发票是全套出口单据的核心，其他单据均应参照它制作。

3) 商业发票是出口商向进口商的发货凭证，是出口商重要的履约证明文件。

4) 商业发票可以作为索赔和理赔的重要凭证，是出口商凭以结汇的重要工具。

5) 以买方的名义开具，列明商品名称，原产国及其他有关资料，且经签署的受益人的商业发票正本至少一式六份。

3. Please make out an invoice according to the given materials.

— L/C NO.291-11-6222531 DATED APRIL 2ND, 2006

— DATE AND PLACE OF EXPIRY: OCT.15, 2006 IN COUNTRY OF BENEFICIARY

— APPLICANT: WOODLAND LIMITED

450 CASTLE PEAK ROAD, KLN., HONG KONG.

— BENEFICIARY: ZHEJIANG ANIMAL BY-PRODUCTS IMP. & EXP. CORPORATION

76 WULIN RD, HANGZHOU, CHINA

— L/C AMOUNT: USD16663.00

— LOADING IN CHARGE: SHANGHAI PORT,CHINA

— FOR TRANSPORTATION TO: HONGKONG

— LATEST DATE OF SHIP: 060930

— DESCRIPTION OF GOODS: 42500 PIECES OF STUFFED

TOY AS PER SALES CONTRACT 03ZA16IA0019 DATED 06.03.13

STYLE NO. QUANTITY UNIT PRICE

ZEAPEL01 7000PCS USD0.345/PC

ZEAPEL02 500PCS USD0.65/PC

ZEAPEL04 5000PCS USD1.10/PC

ZEAPEL05 30000PCS USD0.31/PC

CIF HONGKONG AS PER INCOTERMS 2006

— DOCUMENTS REQUIRED: + COMMERCIAL INVOICE IN 1 ORIGINAL AND 3 COPIES LESS 5% COMMISSION AND HAND SIGNED BY BENEFICIARY.

+ --------------

— ADDITIONAL COND.: +PACKING IN CARTONS OF 50 PCS EACH.

+ CARTONS TO BE MARKED WITH: Z.J.A.B

HONGKONG

C/NO.1-

+ --------------

ISSUING BANK: HSBC, HONGKONG

Chapter 6

Insurance Documents in Export Business

In export business, if the contracts are concluded on CIP or CIF terms, the exporter should affect insurance and bear the insurance premium. The exporter applies to the insurance company stipulated in the export contract by filling a proposal form and the insurance company will produce the insurance policy or certificate on the basis of the application.

6.1 A general knowledge of the marine cargo insurance

To adapt to the development of the international marine cargo insurance, the People's Insurance Company of China (PICC) has manipulated China Insurance Clauses (CIC) on the basis of international practices and the actual conditions of China. CIC contains The Ocean Marine Cargo Clauses, The Ocean Marine Cargo War Risk Clauses and other special clauses. The Ocean Marine Cargo Clauses are the most widely adopted marine cargo insurance clauses by Chinese trading companies and the most recent revision of the clauses is the 2009 version.

6.1.1 Coverage of the marine cargo insurance under CIC

Marine cargo insurance under CIC falls into two general categories: basic coverage and additional coverage.

6.1.1.1 Basic Coverage

Under CIC, the basic coverage of ocean transportation risks consists of three kinds: Free from Particular Average (FPA), With Particular Average (WPA), and All Risks.

(1) Free from Particular Average (FPA)

FPA is the most limited form of cargo insurance coverage covering the following losses:

1) The actual total loss or the constructive total loss of the consignment caused by natural calamities such as heavy weather, tsunami, earthquake, flood, etc.

2) The total loss or the partial loss caused by fortuitous accidents such as stranding, striking

upon the rocks, icebergs or others, collision, fire and explosion.

3) The partial loss attributable to heavy weather, lightning and/or tsunami, where the ship has been stranded, sunk, or burned, irrespective of whether the event took place after or before such accidents.

4) The partial or total loss consequent on the falling of an entire package or packages into the sea during loading, unloading, and transshipment.

5) Reasonable expenses the insured makes for salvage of the goods insured, and for averting or minimizing the losses, provided the expenses do not exceed the insured amount.

6) Expenses incurred by the discharge of the insured cargoes at a port of distress following a sea peril as well as special charges arising from loading, warehousing at an intermediate port of call or refuge.

7) Sacrifices in and contributions to general average and salvage charges.

8) Losses reimbursed by the insured to the ship-owners as is under the Contract of Affreightment "Both to Blame Collision" clause.

(2) With Particular Average (WPA)

Aside from the risks covered under FPA conditions as above, WPA also covers partial losses of the insured goods directly caused by natural calamities such as heavy weather, lightning, tsunami, earthquake or flood. WPA provides a more extensive coverage against all losses or damages due to marine perils throughout the duration of the policy.

(3) All Risks

Aside from the risks covered under FPA and WPA conditions as above, the coverage of All Risks means that the insurer shall undertake the liabilities to indemnify the insured the total or partial loss on the cargo insured either arising from perils of the sea or general extraneous risks during the course of transit. All Risks is the most comprehensive coverage among the three. However, this coverage shall not cover all risks of loss or damage.

6.1.1.2 Additional coverage

While the basic insurance coverage can be taken out independently, the additional coverage shall be made complementarily with the insurance company according to the actual situation. The additional insurance coverage includes general additional risks and special additional risks.

(1) General additional risks

General additional risks cover the losses caused by general extraneous risks which are covered by All Risks in the basic insurance coverage. There are 11 types of general additional risks: (1) Theft, Pilferage, and Non-delivery (TPND); (2) Fresh Water Rain Damage; (3) Risk of Shortage; (4) Risk of Intermixture and Contamination; (5) Risk of Leakage; (6) Risk of Clash; (7) Risk of Odor; (8) Heating and Sweating Risk; (9) Hook Damage; (10) Risk of Rust;

(11) Breakage of Packing Damage.

(2) Special additional risks

Special additional risks cover losses caused by special extraneous risks. There are eight types of special additional coverage: (1) War Risks; (2) Strike, Riots and Commotions (SRCC); (3) Failure to Delivery Risk; (4) Import Duty Risk; (5) On Deck Risk; (6) Rejection Risk; (7) Aflatoxin Risk; (8) Fire Risk Extension Clause (for Storage of Cargo at Destination Hong Kong, including Kowloon, or Macao).

(3) Special risks

According to the features of certain insured goods in ocean transportation, C.I.C has developed specifically Frozen Products Risks and Bulk Wood-oil Risks. In order to promote foreign trade, C.I.C has also established Seller's Contingent Interest Risks. These special risks can be effected independently by the insured according to the actual demand.

6.1.2 Duration of the marine cargo insurance

The duration of insurance is the period throughout which the insurance company undertakes an insurance liability. In marine cargo insurance, the duration of the basic coverage is generally defined by Warehouse to Warehouse Clause, which means that the insurance takes effect from the time the goods leave the warehouse or the place of storage at the place named in the insurance policy for the commencement of the transit, continues during the ordinary course of transit, and terminates when the goods arrive at the consignee's final warehouse or the place of storage at the destination in the insurance policy. If the goods fail to reach the final warehouse for whatever reason, the insurance terminates 60 days after the goods are discharged from the ship. If within the 60 days the goods are delivered to some other destination than the one specified in the insurance policy, the insurance terminates from the moment the goods start to get transferred.

The Warehouse-to-Warehouse Clause is not suitable for War Risks. The duration for War Risks commences from the time when the goods insured are loaded on board the vessel named in the insurance policy until the insured goods are unloaded from the named vessel at the port of destination in the insurance policy. If the goods remain unloaded, the duration of insurance terminates on the expiry of 15 days after the midnight of the day when the vessel arrives at the port of destination.

6.1.3 Exclusions of the marine cargo insurance

In the marine cargo insurance, the following losses and damages are not covered by the Ocean Marine Cargo Clauses:

Losses or damages caused by the deliberate act or fault of the insured.

1. Losses or damages falling under the liability of the consignor.

2. Losses or damages arising from the inferior quality or the shortage in quantity of the consignment before the insurance takes effect.

3. Losses or damages arising from normal losses, the inherent vice or nature of the insured goods, the loss of market and/or delay in transit and any expenses arising therefrom.

4. Risks and liabilities covered and excluded by the war risks clauses and strike, riot, and civil commotion clauses under C.I.C.

6.1.4 Major types of insurance document

Insurance documents are of many kinds. The commonly used insurance documents are: insurance policy, insurance certificate, open policy and endorsement.

6.1.4.1 Insurance policy

The insurance policy is a document issued by an insurance company to the insured detailing the name of the insured, details of goods, the type and amount of the insurance coverage of an insurance contract. It is the most often used insurance document binding upon the insurer and the insured. On the back of the insurance policy are the set clauses about the obligations and rights of the insurer and the insured while on the front are the main contents. Generally, an insurance policy has a lot of standard clauses.

6.1.4.2 Insurance certificate

The insurance certificate is the simplified version of the insurance policy issued by an insurance company. It has the same legal effect as the insurance policy. It doesn't have the clauses on the back, while on the front it has the same clauses as listed on the insurance policy. The insurance certificate is rarely used in practice.

6.1.4.3 Open policy

Open policy is also called open cover. It is a pre-contract concluded between the insurer and the insured by which the insurer offers insurance to the insured for the consignments he dispatches within a certain period of time. As soon as the carriage for the consignment under the open policy is made, it is under the insurance cover of the open policy in accordance with the terms listed on therein. But every time when the dispatch is made, the insured should present to the insurer a dispatch notice in which there are descriptions of goods, the quantity, the insured amount, the transport vessel or vehicle, the starting place of the voyage, and the dispatch or shipment date.

The open policy saves the insured the trouble of negotiating the terms of a new policy for every shipment, thus it is commonly used in international trade. The exporter has to fill the shipping advice and submit the insurance items under the open policy to the insurer before or at the time of shipment. The importer also has to present the insurance items under the open policy to the insurer after receiving the shipping advice from the exporter. In case that the exporter and importer delay presenting the dispatch notice to the insurer, the open policy is still effective from the time of shipment.

6.1.4.4 Endorsement

Endorsement is a document issued by the insurer to add or change or even eliminate some items of the insurance policy upon the request of the insured. It is an integrated part of the insurance policy.

Insurance documents shall be presented in accordance with the terms of the L/C. If the L/C requires the presentation of an insurance policy, only an insurance policy can be accepted; if a proof of insurance under the open policy is required, an insurance policy may be substituted.

6.2 Documentation of the insurance application form

After selecting an insurance company and deciding on the insurance coverage, the insured should fill out an application form and present it to the insurance company. The insurance company will produce an insurance policy in accordance with the application form.

Every insurance company has its own application form, but the contents are mostly similar. An insurance application form includes the following items.

6.2.1 Insurer

It is to be filled in with the name of the insurance company.

6.2.2 Insured

It is generally filled in with the beneficiary of the L/C (the name of the export company). If the L/C requires otherwise, it is to be filled as per the L/C stipulations:

a. If the L/C specifies ×× company as the insured, it should be filled in with "×× CO., Ltd".

b. If the L/C requires it to be transferred to the issuing bank or a third party, the name of the beneficiary should be written in this column followed by "held to the order of ××× bank/ ×××".

6.2.3 Policy No.

It is usually filled in by the insurance company.

6.2.4 Policy Date

It is to be filled in with the actual date.

6.2.5 Shipping Marks

The shipping marks should be filled in as the same as those in the B/L, especially in strict conformity with the actual marks printed on the outer packing of the goods, so as to avoid the future confusion caused by the inspection, verification and compensation and the determination of liability.

6.2.6 Packing & Quantity

The modes of packing and quantity should be filled in clearly.

6.2.7 Descriptions of goods

Descriptions of goods should be filled in with the specific name of the cargo rather than the general words such as textiles, groceries or general merchandise.

6.2.8 Insured Amount

Generally, the insured amount is 110% of CIF value of the insured cargo. If other percentage is desired, there should be an agreement between the trading parties and the consent of the insurance company. Fractional amount should be rounded up. For example, USD134.01 should be filled in with USD135.

6.2.9 Conveyance

It should be stated clearly with the name of the ship, the transshipment and the modes of combined transport.

6.2.10 Port of Loading & Port of Discharging

It should be filled in with the actual name of the port.

6.2.11 Sailing Date

It should be filled in with the actual date of shipment according to the date of shipment on the shipping company's cargo allocation data.

6.2.12 Conditions

The conditions are to be filled in with the name of the insurance coverage agreed by the trading parties.

6.2.13 Claims Payable at

The claims payable place is generally to be filled in with the place of destination.

6.2.14 Premium

The premium is generally filled in with "as arranged".

6.2.15 Issuing Date

The issuing date should not be later than the date of sailing.

Sample of Insurance Application Form

出口货物运输保险投保单

发票号码	NT001FF004	投保条款和险别
被保险人	客户抬头 NANJING TANG TEXTILE GARMENT CO., LTD. 过户 FASHION FORCE CO., LTD	(√) PICC CLAUSE ( ) ICC CLAUSE (√) ALL RISKS ( ) W.P.A./W.A. ( ) F.P.A. (√) WAR RISKS ( ) S.R.C.C. (√) STRIKE ( ) ICC CLAUSE A ( ) ICC CLAUSE B ( ) ICC CLAUSE C
保险金额	USD (35904.00) HKD ( ) ( ) ( )	( ) AIR TPT ALL RISKS ( ) AIR TPT RISKS ( ) O/L TPT ALL RISKS
启运港	SHANGHAI	( ) O/L TPT RISKS
目的港	MONTREAL	( ) TRANSSHIPMENT RISKS
转内陆		( ) W TO W
开航日期	2017.3.20	( ) T.P.N.D.
船名航次	HUA CHANG V.09981	( ) F.R.E.C.

Continued

赔款地点	CANADA	(　　)	R.F.W.D.
赔付币别	USD	(　　)	RISKS OF BREAKAGE
正本份数	1 份正本，1 份副本	(　　)	I.O.P.
其他特别条款	COVERING INSTITUTE CIVIL COMMOTIONS CLAUSES.		
以下由保险公司填写			
保单号码		费 率	
签单日期		保 费	

投保日期：　2017 年 3 月 16 日　　　　投保人签章：

6.3 Documentation of an insurance policy

An insurance policy is a legal evidence of the insurance contract concluded between the insurer and the insured, serving as the basis of lodging and settling insurance claims. For a CIF/CIP contract, the exporter is obliged to insure the goods and submit the insurance documents to the importer. The exporter must fill out an insurance application form in accordance with the contract terms or the L/C, and the insurance institute or its agent issues formal documents after verification, generally three originals and two copies. Unless otherwise provided by a L/C, the insurance document shall generally be in a transferable form and endorsed by the beneficiary as an applicant.

6.3.1 Contents and documentation of an insurance policy

The contents of insurance documents issued by different insurance companies are much the same, mostly made on the basis of S.G. policy.

6.3.1.1 Parties to an insurance contract

Parties to an insurance contract include the insured, the insurer, the insurance broker, the insurance agent, the inspector, the indemnity agent, etc.

The insured is the title of the policy. Under collection, the insured is to be filled as the exporter; under the L/C, unless otherwise stated in the L/C, the insured can be made out to one of the following:

1) If the L/C stipulates the policy to be "To order of ××× bank" or "In favor of ××× bank", it is to be filled in with "the name of the beneficiary + held to order of ××× bank / in favor of ××× bank".

2) If the L/C requires the title of all documents to be made ××, it is to be filled in according to the stipulation.

3) If the L/C requires the title to be made a third party or in neutral form, it is to be filled in with "To whom it may concern".

4) If the policy is required to be "made out to order and endorsed in blank", it is to be filled "the name of the beneficiary + to order".

The Chinese or foreign insurance company can sign and issue an insurance policy in its name and become an underwriter, and its agent is an insurance broker. An insurance agent represents the owner of the cargo. Generally, an inspector is the one who surveys the loss of goods at the place where the goods are imported. The indemnity agent refers to the designated institution which can accept the claim as stated on the documents, and its address and the contact method shall be specified in detail.

6.3.1.2 Name of an insurance document

This column is to be filled in according to the contract terms and the L/C. For example, if the L/C stipulates "INSURANCE POLICY IN DUPLICATE", it requires an insurance policy rather than an insurance certificate to be issued.

6.3.1.3 Invoice No.

This column is to be filled in with the number of the commercial invoice of the insured goods.

6.3.1.4 Policy No.

Fill in the number of the insurance policy in this column.

6.3.1.5 Descriptions of goods

Descriptions of shipping marks, packing and quantity should be made consistent with those on the B/L.

6.3.1.6 Amount insured

The insured amount is the highest compensation amount undertaken by the insurer to pay for indemnity. Generally, the insured amount is 110% of the CIF/CIP invoice value. If the percentage of addition is over 10%, the additional premium should be borne by the buyer. The insurance policy under the L/C must be consistent with the stipulations of the L/C. If the invoice value includes commission and a discount, the discount must be deducted from the invoice value before calculating the insured amount. The insured amount has to be expressed in both words and figures, and the fractional amount should be rounded up.

6.3.1.7 Amount insured in capital

This column only needs to be filled in with the insured amount in column 6 in capitals and the denomination currency in full. The insured amount shall be in the same monetary unit as in the L/C.

6.3.1.8 Insurance premium and premium rate

The premium and rate are usually printed with "As Arranged" beforehand, both of which may not be specifically displayed on the policy. If the L/C has other stipulation such as "INSURANCE POLICY ENDORSED IN BLANK FULL INVOICE VALUE PLUS 10% MARKED PREMIUM PAID", then fill in this column with "PAID", or delete the words "As Arranged" and type "PAID" after stamping the proofreading stamp.

The premium usually accounts for 1%—3% of the cargo value. Different risks have different rates (The rate of WPA might be 1/2 of that of All Risks), and different countries have different rates. Take "All Risks" for example, they can be 0.5%, 1.5% and 3% for the European and American markets, the Asian market and the African market, respectively.

6.3.1.9 Per Conveyance S.S.

This column is to be filled in with the name of the carrying vessel. All the names of the ships involved in the transportation should be stated. For example, if the first voyage is carried out by "East Wind" while the second voyage by "Red Star", this column is to be filled with "East Wind / Red Star".

6.3.1.10 Date of commencement

It is to be filled in with either the on board date of the B/L or "As Per B/L" or "As Per Transportation Documents". The filling of "the port pf lading" "the port of destination" and "per conveyance" must be consistent with that in the B/L. If the goods are shipped to the destination port and the insurance covers the inland city, the inland city shall be indicated after the destination port. Example: FROM NINGBO TO LIVERPOOL AND THENCE TO BIRMINGHAM.

6.3.1.11 Conditions

Conditions are the essence of an insurance policy, the filling of which must be in strict consistency with those stipulated in the L/C. If there is no statement of conditions in the L/C or the L/C just stipulates " Marine / Fire / Loss Risk" "Usual Risk" or "Transport Risk" etc., the insured may choose one of the basic risks from All Risks, WPA and FAP by taking into consideration the insured goods, trading parties, the shipment route and so on. If the L/C requires the insurance clauses to be used as CIC, ICC or AICC, the insured must insure the goods according to the L/C. The complete form of conditions consists of the type of risks, the insurance clauses and the effective date of that insurance clauses. The insurance policy for some goods may have the stipulation of IOP (no franchise). Most of the sales contracts or L/C require the combination of basic risks, War Risks and Risk of Strike Riots and Civil Commotion (SRCC). The insurance policy for the container or the deck cargo may indicate the risk of JWOB. TPND (Theft, Pilferage, and Non-Delivery) is frequently used to ship goods to areas/ports where theft is serious.

6.3.1.12 Claim payable at

This column is to be filled in according to the contract terms or the L/C. If there is no clear stipulation in the L/C, the claim payable place is always to be the place/port of destination. The currency of indemnity shall be the same currency of the insured amount.

6.3.1.13 Issuing date

The issuing date of the insurance policy signifies the date on which the coverage takes effect. In the marine cargo insurance, the duration of the basic coverage is generally defined by Warehouse-to-Warehouse Clause, so the exporter should effect the insurance before the goods leave the warehouse at the port of loading. The issuing date of the insurance policy should be earlier than the date of cargo's leaving the warehouse at the port of loading or the date of shipment. The issuing date of the insurance policy must be earlier than that of transportation documents, if there is no different stipulations.

6.3.1.14 Issuing place

It is generally to be filled in with the port of loading.

6.3.1.15 Authorized signature

An insurance policy is officially effective when signed and sealed by an insurance company. The insurance policy must be signed by the insurance company, the insurance underwriter or its agent. An insurance document issued on the letterhead of an insurance broker is acceptable provided that the insurance document is signed by the insurance company or its agent, or by the insurer or its agent. UCP provides that a temporary policy issued by an insurance broker will not be accepted by the bank unless specifically authorized by the L/C.

6.3.1.16 Endorsement

Policy endorsement can be divided into blank endorsement (indicating the name of the insured only), full endorsement (less used in business) and To order endorsement (marking "To Order of ×××" and the name of the insured on the reverse side of the policy). A blank endorsement of the insurance policy means that the insured or any insurance policy holder is entitled to claim compensation from the insurer in the event that the subject matter of the insurance suffers from losses arising from the risks covered by the insurance. A To order endorsement indicates that only the endorsee has the right to claim compensation from the insurance company or its agent.

6.3.1.17 Number of copies of policy

Generally, the exporter submits a full set of insurance policies with one original and one duplicate. If the L/C has specific requirements on the original and the copy, the exporter must follow the stipulation. The one bearing the word "ORIGINAL" on its face is the original and the one bearing "COPY" on its face is a copy.

6.3.1.18 Special conditions

If the L/C and sales contract have special stipulations on the insurance policy, they are to be filled in this column. For example, if the L/C states "L/C NO. MUST BE INDICATED IN ALL DOCUMENTS", then this column shall be filled in with "L/C NO. ×××".

6.3.2 Points for attention when filling an insurance policy

1) An insurance policy and an insurance certificate have the same legal effect.The insurance policy has on its back the detailed insurance clauses and is commonly used in practice. If it is required to present an insurance policy, an insurance certificate is not permitted. However, if it is required to submit an insurance certificate, an insurance policy can also work.

2) Open policies are commonly used by companies involved in high volume trade over a long period of time or the imported goods from foreign countries to China. The biggest benefits of an open policy are: preventing missed coverage, facilitating customers and eliminating the need to negotiate insurance terms for every transaction.

3) Under FOB and CFR terms, the seller can affect insurance on behalf of the buyer according to the stipulations of the L/C or contract terms if there is a guarantee of premium.

4) It is significant for the insured to make a sound decision about the insurance coverage. All Risks should not be the only choice. The insured should determine the appropriate insurance coverage by considering the types of goods and different contract terms.

5) The stipulation of the Warehouse-to-Warehouse Clause in the insurance policy doesn't mean that the insurance company will compensate for all the losses in the transit of goods from warehouse to warehouse. Under FOB/CFR terms, the insurance will not cover the goods before the goods have been loaded on board the ship.

6) The insurance application form can be written both in Chinese and English, but the insurance policy must be made in English.

6.3.3 Effecting insurance

1) For goods exported on CIF basis, the exporter should effect insurance before the goods are actually loaded on board the carrying ship after the preparation for goods and determining the date of shipment in accordance with the contract terms or stipulations of the L/C. The exporter is to fill in an insurance application form and submit it to the insurance company together with the relevant documents (the L/C, the contract, etc.). After checking and confirming these documents by the insurance company, a formal insurance contract can be concluded.

2) Upon the receipt of the insurance application form, the insurance company will produce an insurance policy accordingly.

3) If the insured wants to change the items of the policy such as the risks coverage, the insured amount, the transport means and so on after the issuing of the insurance policy, he must apply to the insurance company for the change. The document issued to state the changes of the policy items is known as an endorsement. An endorsement is an integrated part of the insurance policy and should be attached to the policy, and its legal effect is prior to that of the insurance policy.

4) The insured must pay an insurance premium, which is the precondition for the insurance contract to take effect. The insurance company charges a premium for a certain percentage of the insured amount.

5) After issuing a blank insurance policy to the insured by listing the relevant items such as the insurance policy number and so on, the insured has to fill in the insurance policy and submit it to the insurance company for confirmation and signature.

6.3.4 Insurance claims

An insurance claim refers to the act taken by the insured to claim compensation from the insurer in the event that the subject matter of the insurance suffers from losses arising from the risks covered by the insurance. If the insurance is effected by the seller, the insurance policy should be endorsed by the seller and transferred to the buyer or his agent immediately after delivery of the goods. Upon the arrival of goods at the port/place of destination, if the goods are found damaged or lost, the buyer or his agent should lodge a claim against the local insurer. The People's Insurance Company of China has established inspection or claims agencies in more than 100 countries, facilitating the inspection and claims of the goods exported from China at the port/place of destination. The inspection and claims of the imported goods to China are lodged by a professional import company or its agent at the port/place of receipt against the agency of The People's Insurance Company of China. The insured or his agent lodges a claim against the insurer, and he should do the following.

1) In case the goods are found damaged or lost out of the risks covered by the insurance, the insured should immediately notify the insurance company for a joint survey and preserve the spot and the original state of the cargo. The insurer will come to inspect and survey the damage of the goods, the cause of the damage, determine the nature of the damage and insurance liabilities, take necessary rescue measures and issue a joint survey report.

2) Upon the arrival of the goods at the port/place of destination, if the insured goods are found short in entire package or packages or to show apparent traces of damage, the insured or his agent should immediately obtain from the carrier or other relevant authorities the certificate of loss or damage or the short-landed memo. If any third party is involved, the insured or his agent shall firstly claim compensation from a third party liable, and then lodge a claim against the insurance company. After getting compensation, the insured must transfer to the insurance company the right for the damaged goods, so that the insurance company can file a claim to a third party in the name of the insured. Such kind of right granted to the insurer is called the right of subrogation.

3) The insured and the insurer are obliged to take all necessary measures to prevent or mitigate loss or damage of the insured subject matter when an insured event occurs. The expenses incurred from such measures shall be compensated by the insurance company. However, the insurer will not be responsible for any extended loss or even the total loss of the insured subject matter caused by the nonfeasance from the insured.

4) The following documents are usually required for insurance claims: the original of the insurance policy or insurance certificate; the shipping documents; the commercial invoice, the weight memo and the packing list; the survey report; the cargo damage/loss report and the short-landed memo; documents testifying the claim against the third party; the marine accident report; the statement of claim listing the amount claimed for and the specific items of the expenses. According to the international insurance practice, the time of validity of a claim shall not exceed a period of two years counting from the time of completion of discharge of the insure goods from the seagoing vessel at the final port of discharge.

6.3.5 Points for attention when negotiating insurance clauses

1) The exporter should respect the importer's suggestion and requirement. There are more than 40 countries which have the regulation that the insurance for the imported goods from foreign countries must be effected by the importer. These countries are listed as follows: North Korea, Burma, Indonesia, Iraq, Pakistan, Ghana, Yemen, Sudan, Syria, Iran, Mexico, Argentina, Brazil, Peru, Somalia, Libya, Jordan, Algeria, Zaire, Nigeria, Ethiopia, Kenya, Gambia, Congo, Mongolia, Romania, Rwanda, Mauritania, etc. Therefore, the export contracts with these countries should not be concluded on the CIF term.

2) The exporter can accept the importer's requirement for the insurance to be subject to the Institute Cargo Clause (I.C.C) and state it clearly in the contract. The Institute Cargo Clause have exerted great influences on the development of international insurance, and import insurance in many countries is inclined to be subject to I.C.C.

3) The export contracts under collection should be concluded on the CIF term so as to reduce the risks for damage/loss. If the insured goods suffer from damage/loss and the importer refuses to retire the bill, the exporter can get compensation from the insurance company in China and the insurer will lodge a claim against the importer.

6.3.6 Samples of insurance policy

Sample 1

中保财产保险有限公司

The People's Insurance (Property) Company of China, Ltd.

发票号码 保险单号次

Invoice No. NB05111 Policy No. SH043101984

海 洋 货 物 运 输 保 险 单

MARINE CARGO TRANSPORTATION INSURANCE POLICY

被保险人

Insured: NINGBO IMPORT & EXPORT CORPORATION

中保财产保险有限公司（以下简称"本公司"）根据被保险人的要求，及其所缴付约定的保险费，按照本保险单承担的险别和背面所载条款与下列特别条款承保下列货物运输保险，特签发本保险单。

THIS POLICY OF INSURANCE WITNESSES THAT THE PEOPLE'S INSURANCE (

PROPERTY) COMPANY OF CHINA, LTD. (HEREINAFTER CALLED "THE COMPANY"), AT THE REQUEST OF THE INSURED AND IN CONSIDERATION OF THE PREMIUM PAID BY THE INSURES, UNDERTAKES TO INSURE THE UNDER-MENTIONED GOODS IN TRANSPORTATION SUBJECT TO THE CONDITION OF THIS POLICY AS PER THE CLAUSES PRINTED OVERLEAF AND OTHER SPECIAL CLAUSES ATTACHED HEREON.

保险货物项目 Descriptions of Goods	包装　单位　数量 Packing　Unit　Quantity	保险金额 Amount Insured
COTTON TEATOWELS	330CARTONS	USD 96,492.00

ORIGINAL

承保险别　FOR 110% OF THE INVOICE VALUE COVERING　　货物标记 AS PER INVOICE NO. NB05111

Condition ALL RISKS　　Marks of Goods

总保险金额：

Total Amount Insured: SAY U.S. DOLLARS NINETY SIX THOUSAND FOUR HUNDRED AND NINETY TWO ONLY

保费　As arranged　运输工具　开航日期：

Premium ________ Per conveyance S. S DANMIN V.342 Slg.　On or abt OCT. 31, 2009

起运港　目的港

From NINGBO To MONTREAL

所保货物，如发生本保险单项下可能引起索赔的损失或损坏，应立即通知本公司下述代理人查勘。如有索赔，应向本公司提交保险单正本（本保险单共有 2 份正本）及有关文件。如一份正本已用于索赔，其余正本则自动失效。

IN THE EVENT OF LOSS OR DAMAGE WHICH MAY RESULT IN A CLAIM UNDER THIS POLICY, IMMEDIATE NOTICE MUST BE GIVEN TO THE COMPANY'S AGENT AS MENTIONED HEREUNDER. CLAIMS, IF ANY, ONE OF THE ORIGINAL POLICIES WHICH HAS BEEN ISSUED IN TWO ORIGINAL (S) TOGETHER WITH THE RELEVANT DOCUMENTS SHALL BE SURRENDERED TO THE COMPANY. IF ONE OF THE ORIGINAL POLICIES HAS BEEN ACCOMPLISHED, THE OTHERS TO BE VOID.

THE PEOPLE'S INSURANCE (PROPERTY) COMPANY OF CHINA, LTD. MONTREAL BRANCH

98 LSKL MACH MONTREAL CANADA

TEL: 56-543657

中保财产保险有限公司

THE PEOPLE'S INSURANCE (PROPERTY) COMPANY OF CHINA, LTD.

赔款偿付地点

Claim payable at MONTREAL IN USD

日期 在

Date OCT.16, 2009 at NINGBO

General Menager: 凡玲

地址:

Address:

Sample 2

中国人民财产保险股份有限公司货物运输保险单

PICC PROPERTY AND CASUALTY COMPANY LIMITED CARGO TRANSPORTATION INSURANCE POLICY

总公司设于北京 一九四九年创立

Head Office: Beijing Established in 1949

保险单号 (Policy No.)

印刷号 (Printed No.)

合同号 (Contract No.)

发票号 (Invoice No.)

信用证号 (L/C No.)

被保险人 (Insured)

中国人民财产保险股份有限公司（以下简称“本公司”）根据被保险人的要求，以被保险人向本公司缴付约定的保险费为对价，按照本保险单列明条款承保下述货物运输保险，特订立本保险单。

THIS POLICE OF INSURANCE WITNESSES THAT PICC PROPERTY AND CASUALTY COMPANY LIMITED (HEREINAFTER CALLED "THE COMPANY") AT THE REQUEST OF THE INSURED AND IN CONSIDERATION OF THE AGREED PREMIUM PAID TO THE COMPANY BY THE INSURED, UNDERTAKES TO INSURE THE UNDERMENTIONED GOODS IN TRANSPORTATION SUBJECT TO THE CONDITION OF THIS POLICY AS PER THE CLAUSES PRINTED BELOW.

标 记 MARKS & NOS.	包装及数量 QUANTITY	保险货物项目 GOODS	保险金额 AMOUNT INSURED

总保险金额：

Total Amount Insured: ______________________________

保费 (Premium):______________ 启运日期 (Date of Commencement):____________

装载运输工具 (Per Conveyance): ______________________________

自：　　　　经：　　　　到：

From: ______________ Via: ____________ To: ____________

承保险别 (Conditions):

所保货物，如发生保险单项下可能引起索赔的损失，应立即通知本公司或下述代理人查勘。如有索赔，应向本公司提交正本保险单（本保险单共有_____份正本）及有关文件，如一份正本已用于索赔，其余正本自动失效。

IN THE EVENT OF LOSS OR DAMAGE WHICH MAY RESULT IN A CLAIM UNDER THIS POLICY, IMMEDIATE NOTICE MUST BE GIVEN TO THE COMPANY OR AGENT AS MENTIONED. CLAIMS, IF ANY, ONE OF THE ORIGINAL POLICIES WHICH HAS BEEN ISSUED IN __________ ORIGINAL(S) TOGETHER WITH THE RELEVENT DOCUMENTS ALL BE SURRENDERED TO THE COMPANY. IF ONE OF THE ORIGINAL POLICIES HAS BEEN ACCOMPLISHED, THE OTHERS TO BE VOID.

保险人：

Underwriter:

电话 (TEL):

传真 (FAX):

地址 (ADD):

赔款偿付地点

Claim Payable at__________________________　　授权人签字：

签单日期 (Issuing Date)____________________　　Authorized Signature:

核保人：　　制单人：　　经办人：

6.4 Calculation of the insured amount and the insurance premium

Under the CIF/CIP terms, the insurance premium is included in the selling price and calculated according to the insured amount and the premium rate.

6.4.1 Determination of the insured amount

In international practice, the insured amount equals 110% of the invoice value. According to INCOTERMS 2010, the minimum insured amount should equal the CIF/CIP value of the goods plus 10% of the CIF/CIP value. The purpose of this 10% mark-up is to cover the loss of the importer's operation and management expenses or anticipated profits in the event of a cargo accident.

6.4.2 Calculation of the premium

Different premium rates are charged on the basis of the different commodities, different destinations, different modes of transport and different risks. The rate schedule provided by the insurance company can be referred to for the calculation of the premium.

6.4.2.1 Calculation of the general insurance premium

Premium = the Insured Amount × the Premium Rate

Insured Amount = the CIF/CIP value × (1+ the Mark-up Rate)

Here is an example of how a premium is calculated:

Company ABC in China was to export food on the CIF term with a total invoice value of USD 1,000. The L/C stipulated that the insurance was to be effected for 110% of the invoice value against All Risks and War Risk. The premium rates for All Risks and War Risk are 0.6% and 0.4%, respectively. The premium for this transaction is calculated as follows:

Premium = the Insured Amount × the Premium Rate

= USD1000 × 110% × (0.6% + 0.4%)

=USD1100 × 1%

=USD11

6.4.2.2 Calculation of the insurance premium with a discount

Unless there are other stipulations in the contract or the L/C, the insured amount should be calculated on the basis of the net CIF/CIP value minus the discount. The premium can be calculated by the following equation:

Premium = the CIF/CIP value × (1−the Discount Rate) × the Mark-up Rate × the Premium Rate

For example:

Suppose the discount rate in the above example of Company ABC is 3% with other terms remaining the same, then the insured amount and the premium can be calculated as follows:

Insured Amount = the Net CIF value × (1+ the Mark-up Rate)

= USD1000 × (1−3%) × (1+10%)

= USD1067

Premium = the Insured Amount × the Premium Rate

= USD1067 × (0.6% + 0.4%)

= USD10.67

6.4.2.3 Calculation of the additional premium

The insured amount usually equals the CIF/CIP value plus 10% of the CIF/CIP value. Sometimes, the buyer may want a higher percentage of addition, thus increasing the expenses of export to the seller. In practice, the additional premium should be borne by the buyer if there is no other stipulation in the contract. The formula for an additional premium under the CIF/CIP term is:

Additional Premium = the CIF/CIP Value × the Added Percentage × the Premium Rate

For example:

Suppose the L/C from the buyer in the above example of Company ABC requires the insurance to be effected for 130% of the invoice value with other terms remaining the same, then the insured amount and the premium can be calculated as follows:

Additional Premium = the CIF/CIP Value × the Added Percentage × the Premium Rate

= USD1000 × (130%−110%) × (0.6% + 0.4%)

= USD2

6.4.3 Price conversion related with insurance

CIF/CIP Price Converted from CFR/CPT Price

CFR Quoted Price = the CFR Total Cost / (1−the Anticipated Profit Rate)

CIF Quoted Price = the CFR Total Cost / (1−the Premium Rate × the Mark-up Rate−the Anticipated Profit Rate)

CPT Quoted Price = the CPT Total Cost / (1−the Anticipated Profit Rate)

CIP Quoted Price = the CPT Total Cost / (1−the Premium Rate × the Mark-up Rate−the Anticipated Profit Rate)

In the above equations, it is assumed that the anticipated profit is calculated on the basis of the quoted price, according to the profit maximization principle.

For example:

Company ABC in China concluded an import contract on the CFR term with the invoice value of USD 1,000. The foreign exporter notified the delivery of goods and Company ABC had to effect insurance for 110% of the CIF invoice value. The premium rate is 0.6%, the anticipated profit rate is 5%, and the anticipated profit is calculated on the basis of the quoted price. Then the CIF quoted price can be calculated as follows:

CFR Quoted Price = the CFR Total Cost / (1−the Anticipated Profit Rate)

CFR Total Cost = the CFR Quoted Price × (1−the Anticipated Profit Rate)

= USD1,000 × (1−5%)

= USD950

CIF Quoted Price = the CFR Total Cost / (1−the Premium Rate × the Mark-up Rate−the Anticipated Profit Rate)

= USD950 × (1−0.6% × 110%−5%)

= USD1,006.99

The CFR/CPT price is converted from the CIF/CIP price.

For example:

Suppose the above contract for Company ABC was concluded on the CIF term with the quoted price of USD 1,006.99, and other terms remained the same. But now the foreign exporter required Company ABC to effect insurance itself on the CFR term, and the CFR quoted price can be calculated as follows:

CFR Total Cost = the CIF Quoted Price × (1−the Premium Rate × the Mark-up Rate−the Anticipated Profit Rate)

= USD1,006.99 × (1−0.6% × 110%−5%)

= USD 950

CFR Quoted Price = the CFR Total Cost / (1−the Anticipated Profit Rate)

= USD 950 / (1−5%)

= USD 1,000

6.5 Exercises

1. Analyze and translate the following insurance clauses.

1) INSURANCE POLICIES/CERTIFICATE IN TWO FOLD PAYABLE TO THE ORDER OF COMMERCIAL BANK OF LONDON LTD COVERING MARINE INSTITUTE CARGO CLAUSES A, INSTITUTE STRIKE CLAUSES CARGO, INSTITUTE WAR CLAUSES CARGO FOR INVOICE VALUE PLUS 10% INCLUDING WAREHOUSE TO WAREHOUSE UP TO THE FINAL DESTINATION AT SWEDEN, MARKED PREMIUM PAID, SHOWING CLAIMS IF ANY, PAYABLE IN GERMANY, NAMING SETTLING AGENT IN GERMANY.

2) INSURANCE POLICIES/CERTIFICATE IN TRIPLICATE ENDORSED IN BLANK FOR 110% OF INVOICE VALUE COVERING ALL RISKS AND WAR RISKS AS PER CIC WITH CLAIMS PAYABLE AT SINGAPORE IN THE CURRENCY OF DRAFT (IRRESPECTIVE OF PERCENTAGE), INCLUDING 60 DAYS AFTER DISCHARGES OF THE GOODS AT PORT OF DESTINATION (OF AT STATION OF DESTINATION) SUBJECT TO CIC. INSURANCE COVERED BY THE APPLICANT. ALL SHIPMENT UNDER THIS CREDIT MUST BE ADVISED BY THE BENEFICIARY AFTER SHIPMENT DIRECTLY TO PRAGATI INSURANCE LTD JUBILEE ROAD BRANCH, CHITTAGONG, BANGLADESH AND

APPLICANT ALSO TO US QUOTING OUR CREDIT NO. AND MARINE COVER NOTE NO. PIL/JBL/0102005 DATED AUG. 01, 2005 GIVING FULL DETAILS OF SHIPMENT AND COPY OF SUCH ADVICE MUST ACCOMPANY SHIPPING DOCUMENTS.

3) INSURANCE IS TO BE EFFECTED BY THE SELLER FOR 110% OF THE INVOICE VALUE AGAINST WPA AND WAR RISK AS PER OCEAN MARINE CARGO CLAUSES OF THE PEOPLE'S INSURANCE COMPANY OF CHINA.

2. Compose contract clauses in English.

1) 由卖方按发票金额的 120% 投保平安险加保战争险，额外保险费由买方支付。

2) 保险由卖方负责，按中国人民保险公司海洋货物保险条款投保一切险加保战争险，保险费由买方支付。

3. Calculation.

Company ABC in China exported frozen food under the CIF term with a total amount of the invoice value of USD 25,000. The goods were to be insured for 120% of the invoice value against WPA and War Risk at PICC, with the premium rates of 0.6% and 0.3%, respectively.

Please calculate the insured amount and the insurance premium.

Chapter 7

Certificate of Origin

7.1 Ordinary Certificate of Origin

An ordinary certificate of origin (or shortened as certificate of origin) is a document supplied by the exporter and issued by a competent authority, certifying that the goods are originated from a particular country.

Certificate of Origin is legal evidence for the delivery of goods, the payment for goods, the compensation claims, the customs inspection and the collection by the importing country. It also serves as the basis for the exporting country to enjoy quota treatment and for the importing country to apply different trading policies to different exporting countries.

7.1.1 Types of Ordinary Certificate of Origin

There are three kinds of certificate of origin issued by different institutes.

1. Certificate of Origin issued by an inspection bureau. For example, CERTIFICATE OF ORIGIN issued by Inspection and Quarantine Bureau of the People's Republic of China (CERTIFICATE OF ORIGIN).

2. Certificate of Origin issued by a chamber of commerce. For example, CERTIFICATE OF ORIGIN issued by the China Council for the Promotion of International Trade (CCPTT CERTIFICATE OF ORIGIN).

3. Certificate of Origin issued by the manufacturer or the exporter.

Note:

Certificate of Origin issued by an inspection bureau and a chamber of commerce is the most authoritative. In international trade practice, the sales contract or the L/C may specify the institute which will issue a certificate of origin. If the L/C doesn't stipulate an issuing party, banks should accept an ordinary certificate of origin issued by any of the three parties. It is now a common practice for exporters in China to use CCPTT CERTIFICATE OF ORIGIN.

7.1.2 Application for an ordinary certificate of origin

The exporter should apply for a certificate of origin to the certifying authority no later than three days before the date of shipment, and fill in the following documents in a true, complete and correct manner in strict accordance with the requirements.

1. The application form for an ordinary certificate of origin / a detailed list of processing procedures.

2. A certificate of origin, four copies (one original and three duplicates).

3. A commercial invoice (one original).

4. Other required documents.

7.1.3 Documentation of an ordinary certificate of origin

An ordinary certificate of origin contains 12 columns, which are filled in and printed in English by the exporter except for three columns "CERTIFICATE NO." "FOR CERTIFING AUTHORITY USE ONLY" and "CERTIFICATION".

7.1.3.1 Certificate No.

This column must not be left blank, otherwise the certificate is invalid.

7.1.3.2 Exporter

Type the name, the address and the country of the exporter. The name of the exporter refers to the name registered and approved by the China Administration for Industry and Commerce, and it must be the same as the exporter described in the invoice. Under the L/C, the name of the beneficiary is generally typed. Under collection, it is to type the name of the exporter /principal. This box shall not be left blank.

7.1.3.3 Consignee

Type the name, the address and the country of the final consignee. The consignee is generally the buyer or the notify party of the bill of lading stipulated in the L/C. If the L/C requires that the item of consignee on all documents should be kept blank, then it is here to type "TO WHOM IT MAY CONCERN" or "TO ORDER", but this box shall not be left blank. If the name of the re-exporter needs to be filled in this box, the word "VIA" shall be typed after the consignee, and then type the name, the address and the country of the re-exporter.

7.1.3.4 Means of transport and route

Type the port of loading, the port of destination and the means of transport. If transshipment is involved in, it can be indicated as the example: FROM SHANGHAI TO HAMBURG BY VESSEL VIA HONGKONG. The port of loading must be in the Chinese mainland.

7.1.3.5 Country/Region of destination

Type the country/region of destination, which is generally to be in compliance with the country of the final consignee or the final port/place of destination.

7.1.3.6 For certifying authority use only

This box shall be left blank. It is reserved for use by the certifying authority for reissuing a certificate or adding other declaration after issuance.

7.1.3.7 Marks and numbers

Type the shipping marks. It should be identical to the marks and numbers of the packages on the L/C, the contract and the invoice. It should not be typed with "AS PER INVOICE NUMBER" or "AS PER B/L NUMBER". If there is no marks, it is to be typed with "NO MARK". If the marks can't be typed completely in this box, they can be typed in the margin in box 7, 8, 9, or even in an attached sheet which will be manually signed and sealed by the certifying authority. The words such as "MADE IN TAIWAN" other than China should not appear in the shipping marks.

7.1.3.8 Description of goods: number and kind of packages

Type the description of goods and the number of packages. The name of the commodity should be filled in with a specific name rather than a general term such as "GARMENT" "FOOD", etc. The number and kind of packages should be in compliance with those in the L/C and other documents. The packing quantity should be written in capitals after the Arabic numbers like "ONE HUNDRED AND FIFTY CARTONS OF WORKING GLOVES". If the goods are in bulk, the words "IN BULK" should be appended to the name of the commodity. Sometimes, the L/C requires an indication of the contract number, the L/C number, etc. on all documents, and these numbers may be indicated in this box. The last entry of this column must be followed immediately by a line of asterisks (*******), so as to prevent from adding an extra insertion, wording or other remarks.

Notes:

The following contents shall not appear in this box:

The unit price and the total price of the goods;

A customs code different from that in No.8 of this certificate of origin;

The words that a part of the products made in another country;

The goods are under a bilateral or regional preferential trade agreement;
The goods conform to the industry standard of a certain country;
Discriminatory provisions.

7.1.3.9 H.S. CODE

Type in this box the H.S. code, which should be consistent with the customs declaration. If the same certificate contains several commodities, the corresponding tax code should be filled in completely and be in conformity with that shown in the customs declaration. This box shall not be left blank.

7.1.3.10 Quantity

Type the quantity of the export goods and the unit of measurement of the goods. For gross weight only, "G.W" is to be filled in the box like "G.W.400KG". The unit of measurement of the goods should be typed in standard English or abbreviation like: Pieces (PCS), Dozen (DOZ), etc.

7.1.3.11 Number and date of invoice

Type the number and the date of the invoice. This box should not be left blank. The date of the invoice shall be expressed in English like "MARCH 15, 2009". The number and the date of the invoice are typed in separate lines, generally with the invoice number typed in the first line while the date in the second line.

7.1.3.12 Declaration by the exporter

Type the name of the exporter, the place and the date of declaration. This box must be signed by the company's authorized signatory and stamped with Chinese and English seals.

7.1.3.13 Certification

Type the certifying place and date. After examination, the certifying authority will sign and seal in this box (original). Certificate of Origin issued by CCPIT would generally annotate the following.

7.1.4 Samples of application form of C/O and C/O

Sample 1

Application form of Certificate of Origin

一般原产地证明书 / 加工装配证明书

申 请 书

申请单位注册号： 证书号：

申请人郑重声明：

本人被正式授权代表本企业办理和签署本申请书。

本申请书及一般原产地证明书 / 加工装配证明书所列内容正确无误，如发生弄虚作假、冒充证书所列货物、擅改证书，本人愿按《中华人民共和国进出口货物原产地规则》的有关规定接受处罚。现将有关情况申报如下：

<table>
<tr><td colspan="2">企业名称</td><td colspan="3"></td><td colspan="2">发票号</td><td colspan="2"></td></tr>
<tr><td colspan="2">商品名称</td><td colspan="3"></td><td colspan="2">H.S. 编码（六位数）</td><td colspan="2"></td></tr>
<tr><td colspan="3">商品 FOB 总值（以美元计）</td><td colspan="2"></td><td colspan="2">最终目的地国家 / 地区</td><td colspan="2"></td></tr>
<tr><td colspan="2">拟出运日期</td><td colspan="3"></td><td colspan="2">转口国（地区）</td><td colspan="2"></td></tr>
<tr><td colspan="9">贸易方式和企业性质（请在适用处画“√”）</td></tr>
<tr><td colspan="3">一般贸易</td><td colspan="3">三来一补</td><td colspan="3">其他贸易</td></tr>
<tr><td>国有</td><td>三资</td><td>民营</td><td>国有</td><td>三资</td><td>民营</td><td>国有</td><td>三资</td><td>民营</td></tr>
<tr><td></td><td></td><td></td><td></td><td></td><td></td><td></td><td></td><td></td></tr>
<tr><td colspan="3">包装数量或毛重或其他数量</td><td colspan="6"></td></tr>
<tr><td colspan="3">证书种类（画“√”）</td><td colspan="3">一般原产地证明书</td><td colspan="3">加工装配证明书</td></tr>
<tr><td colspan="9">现提交中国出口货物商业发票副本一份，一般原产地证明书 / 加工装配证明书一正三副，以及其他附件　　份，请予审核签证。

申请单位盖章　　　　　　　　申请人（签名）：
电　话：
日　期：　　年　　月　　日</td></tr>
</table>

Sample 2

Certificate of Origin

ORIGNAL

<table>
<tr><td colspan="2">1. Exporter (full name and address)
EAST ASIA (SHANGHAI) TRADING CO., LTD. NO.886 CAOYING RD, QINGPU DISTRICT, SHANGHAI, CHINA.</td><td colspan="3" rowspan="2">Certificate No.
C0943670098
CERTIFICATE OF ORIGIN OF
THE PEOPLE'S REPUBLIC OF CHINA</td></tr>
<tr><td colspan="2">2. Consignee (full name, address, country)
PB TRADING LLC
29, BBC AVENUE DHAKA-1000, BANGLADESH.</td></tr>
<tr><td colspan="2">3. Means of transport and route
FROM SHANGHAI, CHINA
TO CHITTAGONG, BANGLADESH BY SEA</td><td colspan="3" rowspan="2">5. For certifying authority use only</td></tr>
<tr><td colspan="2">4. Country / Region destination
BANGLADESH</td></tr>
<tr><td>6. Marks and Numbers of packages</td><td>7. Description of goods; Number and kind of packages</td><td rowspan="2">8. H.S. Code
9506.91.10</td><td rowspan="2">9. Quantity or weight
14,271.00
G.W.</td><td rowspan="2">10. Number and date of invoices
SHA100186
OCT.15, 2009</td></tr>
<tr><td>PB TRADING LLC</td><td>TWO HUNDRED AND THIRTY
(230)CTNS OF
GYM EQUIPME
NT CREDIT NO.074809010253
DATED AUGUST 12, 2009
ISSUED BY THE CITY BANK LIMITED DHAKA CHAMBER BRANCH, DHAKA, BANGLADESH
IMPORTER'S NAME: PB TRADING LLC
***************************************</td></tr>
</table>

Continued

11. Declaration by the exporter	12. Certification
The undersigned hereby declares that the above details and statements are correct; that all the goods were produced in China and that they comply with the Rules of Origin of the People's Republic of China. EAST ASIA (SHANGHAI) TRADING CO., LTD. 东亚贸易（上海）有限公司 SHANGHAI, OCT. 20, 2009 Place and date. Signature and stamp of the certifying authority	It is hereby certified that the declaration by the exporter is correct. SHANGHAI ENTRY - EXIT INSPECTION AND QUARANTINE BUREAU THE PEOPLE'S REPUBLIC OF CHINA 中华人民共和国上海出入境检验检疫局 SHANGHAI, OCT. 20, 2009 Place and date. Signature and stamp of the certifying authority

7.2 GSP Certificate of Origin

Generalized System of Preference (GSP) was introduced by the fourth special committee on preferences of the United Nations conference on trade and development in 1970. The implementation of this system can help the developing countries expand exports, increase the revenue of export and speed up their economic growth and industrialization.

7.2.1 Definition and principles

Generalized System of Preference (GSP) is a preferential tariff system imposed by the developed countries (preference-giving countries) on the goods from the developing countries (preference-receiving countries/beneficiary countries). GSP is the preferential treatment of further tax reduction or total exemption on the basis of the most-favoured-nation tax rate.

Tariff rates on GSP exports are about a third lower than the most-favoured-nation tax rate. China is a developing country and should enjoy the GSP treatment. The implementation of GSP must follow the three principles: generalized, non-discrimination and non-reciprocity.

7.2.1.1 Generalized

The preference shall be applied to the primary products, semi-finished products and commodities imported by developed countries from developing countries, and preferential treatment shall be given without exception and discrimination.

7.2.1.2 Non-discrimination

The preference is conducted on a non-discriminatory basis. The countries that were formerly called backward and underdeveloped or emerging countries are now collectively referred to as developing countries (also known as beneficiary countries). Those countries that were formerly called advanced or industrialized countries are now collectively referred to as developed countries (also known as preference-giving countries).

7.2.1.3 Non-reciprocity

The preference is granted by the developed countries to the developing countries without any requirements of a counter preference from the developing countries.

7.2.2 Rules of a GSP certificate of origin

The rules of origin are the provisions on the necessary conditions for the export products from preference-receiving countries to enjoy GSP treatment. It is the main component and the core of GSP. To ensure that the benefits of GSP are granted only to products produced, harvested and manufactured in and shipped from developing countries, each preference-giving country has developed detailed rules of origin. Rules of origin include three parts: an origin criterion, direct shipment rules and a written certificate.

Products originating in a third country are generally not eligible for GSP treatment if they are only lightly processed in the preference-receiving country or only transshipped through the preference-receiving country.

7.2.2.1 Origin criterion

Origin criterion is the definition of the original products by each preference-giving country. It classifies original products into two broad categories:

1) Products sufficiently obtained.

It refers to the products that are made and manufactured entirely in the preference-receiving country using all domestic raw materials and components.

2) Products containing imported ingredients.

It refers to the products that are made and manufactured in the preference-receiving country entirely or partially by using the imported raw materials or spare parts (including those with unclear origins), which are fully processed to the degree of being a completely different product through substantial transformation of its nature and characteristics. Such kind of products are regarded as the products sufficiently obtained in the preference-receiving country. Substantial transformation is a necessary condition for products containing imported ingredients to obtain the qualification of original products. But the standards measured by each preference-giving country are different, which are generally processing standards and percentage standards.

7.2.2.2 Direct consignment

Original products from the preference-receiving country must be consigned directly from the preference-receiving country to the preference-giving country. However, for geographical reasons or transport needs, export goods from preference-receiving countries may also be allowed to pass through the territory of a third country, regardless of whether the means of transport are transferred or temporary stocks are made in the transit country. Most preference-giving countries accept passage through intermediate countries subject to certain conditions: The goods have been under the supervision of the customs of the intermediate countries and have not been sold in the local market or delivered for local use and have not undergone any reprocessing there, except for unloading and necessary treatment to keep the goods in good condition. In other words, when the means of transport of goods can't directly reach the preference-giving country and the goods must be transshipped, the goods must be sealed by the customs of the transshipment place to prevent camouflage on the way to the preference-giving country.

Note:

Direct shipment rules are not directly related to the origin of the products. But it is a necessary technical means to ensure that the products shipped to the importing preference-giving country are the same as the original products shipped from the exporting preference-receiving country, thus avoiding any reprocessing or change of package that may occur on the way through the transit country.

7.2.2.3 Written certificate

The claim for GSP treatment must be supported with the documentary evidence which can certify the origin of the export products and serve as the proof of compliance with the direct shipping rules. These documents are as follows:

1) GSP Certificate of Origin Form A is a standard form used worldwide to certify the origin of the export products. While GSP Certificate of Origin Form 59A, Form APR and a simplified certificate of origin can also be used under certain circumstances.

2) Documentary evidence of compliance with the direct shipment rules.

It includes a direct bill of lading and a through bill of lading issued in the export preference-receiving country, and a certificate issued by the customs authority of the transit country. It is used to certify the name of the goods, the date of discharge and loading, the name of vessel, the date of departure and the status of cargo in the transit country.

7.2.3 List of preference-giving countries

There are 40 countries in the world that give GSP treatment to manufactured goods and semi-manufactured goods exported from China. They are EU member states (28), Switzerland, Norway, Japan, New Zealand, Australia, Canada, Russia, Ukraine, Belarus, Kazakhstan, Turkey and Liechtenstein. America is a preference-giving country, but it has never given GSP treatment to China.

Note:

Among the above preference-giving countries, two countries have special requirements for the GSP certificate of origin. New Zealand only uses GSP Certificate of Origin Form 59A. For Australia, the only requirement is adding the specified declaration on the commercial invoice such as: "Declare: A, that the final process of manufacture of the goods for which special parts are claimed has been performed in China and B, that not less than one half of the factory cost of the goods is represented by the value of labour and materials of China."

7.2.4 Application for a GSP certificate of origin

The procedure for applying for a GSP certificate of origin is as follows.

(1) Registration

According to the relevant regulations, all state-owned import and export enterprises and production enterprises, and foreign-funded enterprises that have obtained registration in China's Industrial and Commercial Administrative Departments can apply for registration to the local Entry-Exit Inspection and Quarantine Institution. The following documents are required to submit for registration:

1) A document granted by a competent government department to an enterprise for import and export rights;

2) A copy of the business license;

3) The completed Registration Certificate of the GSP Certificate of Origin and the Registration Form for Enterprises Applying for Issuing GSP Certificate of Origin;

4) The detailed List of Processing Procedures and Costs for Goods (if the goods to be exported containing imported materials or components);

5) Certificate of Origin Manual Signatory Authorization.

(2) Investigation

For an enterprise applying for registration, its products must comply with the rules of origin of the preference-giving country. For the products declared by the enterprise, after receiving the registration application from the relevant enterprise, the Entry-Exit Inspection and Quarantine Institution will send staff to carry out on-site inspection on the production enterprise, check the relevant information provided by the enterprise, examine the raw materials, the production and processing process, calculate the proportion of the value of the imported raw materials in the manufactured products if imported raw materials are used in the products to determine their origin status.

(3) Verification

After verification, if the products' origin qualification meets the relevant regulations, the Entry-Exit Inspection and Quarantine Institution will register the enterprise and grant the registration number. Then, this enterprise can apply for a GSP certificate of origin to the Entry-Exit Inspection and Quarantine Institution.

(4) Issuance

The GSP certificate of origin is a combined form of declaration by the exporter and the certificate by certifying authority. Therefore, the GSP certificate of origin should be made by the applicant, signed and sealed in the required column, and submitted to the Entry-Exit Inspection and Quarantine Institution. The Entry-Exit Inspection and Quarantine Institution shall check and verify the certificate of origin according to the invoice and other relevant documents, sign and seal the relevant column of the certificate.

Enterprises should apply for a GSP certificate of origin at least five days before shipment, and submit the following documents:

1) Application Form for GSP Certificate of Origin;

2) Three copies of GSP Certificate of Origin Form A filled and signed by the exporter;

3) The commercial invoice;

4) Other required documents.

7.2.5 Documentation of a GSP certificate of origin

7.2.5.1 Goods consigned from

Type the exporter's business name, address and country in this box.

For example:

NINGBO SKYLAND GROUP CO., LTD

ROOM 1209, ZHONGSHAN MANSION, 93 EAST ZHONGSHAN ROAD, NINGBO CHINA

Note:

This item is compulsive, requiring the complete information of the exporter's business name and address to be supplied. The exporter must be the enterprise that has finished the place of origin registration, and the enterprise's English name should be consistent with that in the registration and filing at the Inspection and Quarantine Bureau. This item should not fill the name of middlemen like Hongkong, Taiwan and so on.

7.2.5.2 Goods consigned to

Type the consignee's name, address and country.

For example:

JENSON & JESSON, LANGE MUHREN 9, F-2000, HAMBURG, GERMANY

Note:

This item is generally to fill the name of the final consignee in the preference-giving country (the notify party of the B/L or the specially declared consignee stipulated in the L/C). This item cannot include Hong Kong, Taiwan and other middlemen. Under certain circumstances, this item can be filled with "TO ORDER" or "TO WHOM IT MAY CONCERN".

7.2.5.3 Means of transport and route

For example: SHIPMENT FROM NINGBO TO HAMBURG BY SEA

Note:

The place of origin of the transport route shall be the last departure from the Chinese mainland. If there is transshipment, the transshipment port shall be added. For example: FROM NINGBO TO PIRAEUS, GREECE VIA HONG KONG BY SEA. Means of transport include marine transport, land transport, air transport, combined sea and air transport, etc.

7.2.5.4 For certifying authority use only

This box shall be left blank. It is reserved for use by the certifying authority. The certifying authority will fill out the following contents:

1) In the case of issuing a delayed certificate, the certifying authority type "ISSUED RETROSPECTIVELY";

2) In the case of issuing a "duplicate" certificate, the certifying authority will indicate the number and date of the original certificate and declare the original certificate invalid as follows: THIS CERTIFICATE IS IN REPLACEMENT OF CERTIFICATE OF ORIGIN NO... DATED... WHICH IS CANCELLED. And the word "DUPLICATE" shall be typed there.

3) If the products exported to Japan have used Japanese raw materials, the certifying authority will type "SEE THE ANNEX NO..."

4) If the products exported to EU member states, Norway and Switzerland have used raw materials from these above importing countries, the certifying authority will type "EC CUMULATION" "NORWAY CUMULATION" or "SWITZERLAND CUMULATION".

7.2.5.5 Item number

If the consignee and the transportation conditions are the same, and there are different kinds of export goods, these goods can be listed according to the type as follows: "1" "2" "3" ...

7.2.5.6 Marks and numbers of packages

For example: JENSON,
ORDER NO.325952065
L/C E766896505
C/N 1-270

In this part, complete graphic marks and package numbers should be filled in accordance with the actual shipping marks on the goods and the invoice. The content of shipping marks in the same line shall not be printed in different lines.

Note:

1) *No words such as "HONG KONG" "MACAO" "TAIWAN" "R.O.C" or others which indicate the place of origin other than China shall appear in the shipping marks.*

2) *This item should not be left blank. When the goods have no shipping marks, "N/M" should be filled in. If the shipping marks are too long, please fill in the blank in Box 7, 8, 9 and 10.*

3) *If the shipping marks are complex with pictures and words, this box can be filled in with words "SEE ATTACHMENT", and attach a sheet. The attached sheet shall be in triplicate, with the top printed with "ATTACHMENT TO THE CERTIFICATE OF ORIGIN FORM A NO..." Referring to the certificate of FORM A, the issuing place and date, and the place and date of declaration shall be printed on the two sides at the bottom of the attached page respectively. At the bottom right, the visa seal of the applicant shall be stamped and it shall be signed by the applicant. The attached pages should be the same size as the FORM A certificate. If the importing country is Russia, the full English name of the institution directly under the Inspection and Quarantine Bureau should be added on the left side of the bottom of the attached page. For example: "NINGBO ENTRY-EXIT INSPECTION AND QUARANTINE BUREAU OF THE PEOPLE'S REPUBLIC OF CHINA".*

4) *The contents and format in this box must be the same as those actually printed on the outer packing box of the goods.*

7.2.5.7 Number and kind of packages; Description of goods

For example: SIX HUNDRED (600) CTNS OF SHRIMPS

*** *** *** ***

Note:

Never forget to fill in the number and kind of packages, and put the Arabic number in brackets after the English number expression of the package quantity. The name of the commodity should be filled in in detail to accurately determine the H.S. item number of the commodity. If the name of the commodity is general or misspelled in the L/C, the detailed description or the correct name of the commodity must be indicated in brackets. After listing the items such as the commodity name and so on, the cut-off line should be added at the last line to prevent foreign businessmen from adding forged contents. A foreign L/C sometimes requires a contract or the L/C number, etc., which can be added below the cut-off line in this box and begin with "REMARKS:".

For example: FIVE HUNDRED (500) CTNS OF SHRIMPS

*** *** *** *** ***

REMARKS:

L/C: 2846905067640

7.2.5.8 Origin criterion

This item has the least words, but it is the core item for the verification of foreign customs. The foreign customs is strict with the goods containing imported components, so the applicant should check the certificate carefully to avoid being refused by the foreign customs.

The general points are listed as follows:

1) For products sufficiently obtained, enter the letter -P-;

2) For products containing imported ingredients but meeting the origin criteria, it shall be filled in as follows when exporting to the following countries:

a. Norway, Switzerland, EU member states, Japan and Turkey: enter the letter -W-, followed by the four-digit tariff code for export goods under Harmonized System of Commodity Names and Codes (e.g. -W- 96.18). However, the imported raw materials from the preference-giving countries can be regarded as domestic raw materials. Therefore, for products containing imported ingredients completely from preference-giving countries, enter the letter -P-.

b. Canada: If the imported components account for less than 40% of the factory price of the products, enter the letter -F-.

c. Russia, Belarus, Ukraine and Kazakhstan: The imported ingredients shall not exceed 50% of the FOB price of the products, enter the letter -Y-, followed by the percentage of the value of the imported materials and parts in the FOB price of the export products (e.g. -Y- 35%).

d. Australia and New Zealand: Domestic raw materials and labor services shall be no less than 50% of the cost of production, and this box shall be left blank.

7.2.5.9 Gross weight or other quantity

For example: 1200KGS

Note:

This box should be filled in with the normal unit of measurement of the goods such as "piece" "pair" "set" "dozen" and so on. Type the gross weight if measured by weight. With net weight only, fill in the net weight but mark it as N.W. (NET WEIGHT).

7.2.5.10 Number and date of invoices

For example: SDAKF 0522
MAY 22, 2006

Note:

The content of the invoice must be consistent with that of the official commercial invoice, and this box shall not be left blank. To avoid misunderstandings, months are usually represented by abbreviations such as JAN., FEB., MAR., etc. The year in the invoice date shall be filled in completely. For example, the year "2006" can't be typed as "06". If the invoice number is too long and needs to be typed in another line, the line folding character "-" should be used. The invoice date shall not be later than the date of B/L and the date of declaration.

7.2.5.11 Certification

This item is to fill in with the issuing place and date, which is usually consistent with the declaration address and the date of the exporter. The certifying authority authorizes the issuing officer to sign this item and affix the seal of the certifying authority. For example: NINGBO, CHINA MAY 24, 2006.

If the importing country is Russia, the full English name of the Inspection and Quarantine Bureau shall be added in this item. For example: NINGBO ENTRY-EXIT INSPECTION AND QUARANTINE BUREAU OF THE PEOPLE'S REPUBLIC OF CHINA.

Note:

Only the original certificate shall be stamped by the issuing authority.

7.2.5.12 Declaration by the exporter

The manufacturing country horizontal line should be typed with "CHINA". The importing country horizontal line must be correctly filled in with the importing country, and the importing country should be the preference-giving country, which is the same as that of the final consignee or the port of destination. For goods shipped to EU member states, if the importing country is not clear, the importing country can be filled in with "E.U.".

The applicant should sign in this box, affix the registered visa seal in both Chinese and English, and fill in the place and date of application. The seal should be clear.

Note:

The declaration date should not be filled in with the legal rest day, the date should not be earlier than the invoice date and generally not later than the date of the B/L. If it is later than the date of the B/L, this box shall be sealed with "ISSUED RETROACTIVELY". Avoid covering the name of the importing country, the name of the country of origin, the declaration address and date when stamping and signing the original and all copies of the certificate. The declaration date of the amended certificate is generally the same as the original certificate, while the declaration date of the re-issued certificate shall be the current date.

7.2.5.13 Other instructions

1) Enterprises applying for a GSP certificate of origin must register with the local Inspection and Quarantine Institution in advance.

2) All the contents of FORM A should be completed in English or French, except box 2 and box 6 whose filling has no restriction on language.

3) When applying for a FORM A certificate, the applicant shall submit the printed commercial invoice from Enterprise Side Software of Certificate of Origin E-visa System (with the official seal and the legal person seal), and one original and two copies of the FORM A certificate.

4) If the export commodities contain imported ingredients but conform to the origin criterion, for example, if they are produced in Ningbo, the cost list of commodities containing imported ingredients shall be provided. If these goods are produced outside Ningbo, the GSP off-site survey results should be submitted.

5) If the date of declaration is later than the date of shipment, a copy of the original B/L should be provided when applying for a delayed certificate.

6) If the original certificate is lost or damaged, the applicant may apply to the original certifying authority for re-issuance. The lost certificate shall be invalidated in *China Door Times,* and then a written instruction by the applicant and the losing party, and a copy of the original certificate should be provided for the examination and approval of the Inspection and Quarantine Institution to re-issue a certificate.

7) If the raw materials imported from Japan are processed and then exported to Japan, the CERTIFICATE OF MATERIALS IMPORTED FROM JAPAN in triplicate and the invoice of raw materials imported from Japan shall be presented.

8) If the raw materials imported from EU, Norway and Switzerland are processed and exported to the above-mentioned countries, the invoice of the imported raw materials or Mobile Certificate Europe No.1 shall be submitted.

7.2.6 Clauses on a GSP Certificate of Origin in the L/C

There are some examples of clauses on a GSP certificate of origin in the L/C:

1. 46A: DOCUMENTS REQUIRED+CERTIFICATE OF ORIGIN GSP FORM A ISSUED BY THE OFFICIAL COMPETENT AUTHORITY. IF IT IS ISSUED ON A DATE AFTER THE B/L DATE, THE COLUMN NR.4 MUST STATE “ISSUED RETROSPECTIVELY”.

2. 1 ORIGINAL AND 1 COPY OF GSP CERTIFICATE OF ORIGIN FORM A ISSUED BY A GOVERNMENTAL AUTHORITY INDICATING ITS REFERENCE NUMBER. IF GSP C/O FORM A ISSUE DATE (BOX 11) IS LATER THAN B/L ON-BOARD DATE, IT MUST BEAR THE MENTION QUOTE ISSUED RETROSPECTIVELY UNQUOTE IN BOX 4.

3. ORIGINAL CERTIFICATE OF ORIGIN GSP FORM A ISSUED BY TRADE AUTHORITIES OF COUNTRY AND SHOWING FRANCE AS FINAL DESTINATION.

7.2.7 Samples of application forms for a GSP certificate of origin form A and a GSP certificate of origin form A

Sample 1

Application Form for a GSP Certificate of Origin Form A

普惠制产地证明书申请书

申请单位(盖章): 证书号: G015059/11/00121

组织机构代码: 132227717

申请人郑重声明: 注册号: 015059

本人被正式授权代表本出口单位办理和签署本申请书。

本申请书及普惠制产地证格式 A 所列内容正确无误，如发现弄虚作假，冒充格式 A 所列货物，擅改证书，自愿接受签证机关的处罚及负法律责任，现将有关情况申报如下:

生产单位	上海雷威进出口贸易有限公司	生产单位联系人电话	39587066
商品名称(中英文)	PRESSURE GAUGE(压力表) SPARE PARTS(压力表零件)	H.S. 税目号(以六位数码计)	902620 902690
商品 FOB 总值(以美元计)	12,193.76	发票号	QW20110404B

续表

最终销售国	加拿大	证书种类画“√”			加急证书	普通证书√	
货物拟出运日期		2011-12-22					
贸易方式和企业性质（请在适用处画“√”）							
正常贸易	来进料加工	补偿贸易	中外合资	中外合作	外商独资	零售	展卖
C√	L	B	H	Z	D	Y	M
包装数量或毛重或其他数量		3468PCS/218.00KGS					

原产地标准：

本项商品系在中国生产，完全符合该给惠国给惠方案规定，其原产地情况符合以下第 1 条：

(1)“P”（完全国产，未使用任何进口原材料）；

(2)“W”其 H.S 税目号为____________（含进口成分）；

(3)“F”（对加拿大出口产品，其进口成分不超过产品出厂价值的 40%）。

本批产品系：1. 直接运输从____上海____到____加拿大____；

2. 转口运输从____________中转国（地区）____________到____________。

申请人说明

领证人（签名）

电话：39587066

日期：2011 年 12 月 19 日

现提交中国出口货物商业发票副本一份，普惠制产地证明书格式 A(FORM A) 一正二副，以及其他附件　　份，请予审核签证。

注：凡含进口成分的商品，必须按要求提交《含进口成分受惠商品成分明细单》。

检验检疫局联系记录

上海出入境检验检疫局制

Sample 2

A GSP Certificate of Origin

ORIGINAL

1. Goods consigned from (Exporter's full name and address, country)
SHANGHAI YONGSHENG IMP &EXP. CO.
21 WEST ZHONGSHAN ROAD SHANGHAI, CHINA

2. Goods consigned to (Consignee's full name, address, country)
MAND ARS IMPORTS CO. LTD.
38 QUEEN'S WAY, 2008 UK

Reference No.

GENERALIZED SYSTEM OF PREFERENCES
CERTIFICATE OFORIGIN
(Combined declaration and certificate)
FORM A
Issued in THE PEOPLE'S REPUBLIC OF CHINA
(Country)
See Notes overleaf

3. Means of transport and route (as far as known)
FROM SHANGHAI TO LONDON BY SEA

4. For certifying authority use only

5. Item number	6. Marks and numbers of packages	7. Number and kind of packages; Description of goods	8. Origin criterion(see Notes overleaf)	9. Gross weight or other quantity	10. Number and date of invoice
1	MANDARS TXT200710 LONDON C/NO.:1-1000	LADIES DENIM SKIRT SAY TOTAL ONE THOUSAND (1000) CARTONS ONLY ************************	P	G.W. 140KGS	TX370 MAY 02, 2007

11. Certification
It is hereby certified that the declaration by the exporter is correct.

SHANGHAI MAY 22,07 萨姆森

Place and date, signature and stamp of the certifying authority

12. Declaration by the exporter
The undersigned hereby declares that the above details and statements are correct, that all the Goods were produced in

(The exporting country)
and that they comply with the origin requirements specified for those goods in the generalized system of preferences for goods exported to
(The importing country)
UK
SHANGHAI MAY 10, 2007 方达
Place and date, signature and stamp of the authorized signatory

7.3 Exercises

1. Fill in the Certificate of Origin according to the given particulars.

COMMERCIAL INVOICE

Consignee:
ABC TRADING CORP.,
123 BEACH STREET
SYDNEY, AUSTRALIA

INVOICE NO. YSM2019B
INVOICE DATE: NOV. 20, 2019
L/C NO. : KDTT875490
L/C DATE: SEP.20, 2019
S/C NO. : GD-75TX4607

Exporter:
SAMSON IMPORT & EXPORT CORPORTATION
156 JINJI ROAD, QINGDAO, CHINA

Transport details:
FROM QINGDAO TO SYDNEY, AUSTRALIA
BY VESSEL SAILING DATE: NOV. 25, 2019

Terms of Payment:
BY L/C

MARKS AND NUMBERS	DESCRIP. OF GOODS	QUANTYTY	UNIT PRICE	AMOUNT
ABC TRADING CORP.,	H.S.NO.: 6509.06			
86KCS06008	PLASTIC TOYS	20,000PCS	USD1.2/PC	USD24,000.00
NO.1-600				
MADE IN CHINA				

FOB QINGDAO USD24,000.00
TOTAL QUANTITY: 20,000 PCS PACKING: 600 CATRONS
TOTAL: US DOLLARS TWENTY FOUR THOUSAND ONLY.
SAMSON IMPORT & EXPORT CORPORTATION

<table>
<tr><td>1. Exporter</td><td rowspan="2">Certificate No.
CERTIFICATE OF ORIGIN
OF
THE PEOPLE'S REPUBLIC OF CHINA</td></tr>
<tr><td>2. Consignee</td></tr>
<tr><td>3. Means of transport and route</td><td rowspan="2">5. For the certifying authority use only</td></tr>
<tr><td>4. Country/Region of destination</td></tr>
</table>

Continued

6. Marks and numbers	7. Number and kind of packages; Description of goods	8. H.S code	9. Quantity	10. Number and date of invoices

11. Declaration by the exporter The undersigned hereby declares that the above details and statements are correct; that all the goods were produced in china and that they comply with the rules of origin of the People's Republic of China. .... Place and date, signature and stamp of the certifying authority	12. Certification It is hereby certified that the declaration by the exporter is correct. .... Place and date, signature and stamp of the authorized signatory

2. Fill in the GSP Certificate of Origin according to the given particulars.

COMMERCIAL INVOICE

Consignee:
MAND ARS IMPORTS CO. LTD
258 QUEENSWAY
NEWYORK, AMERICA

INVOICE NO. GD068
INVOICE DATE: FEB. 20, 2019
L/C NO.: 36036414256685
S/C NO.: D/267/95

Exporter:
SHANGHAI HUIYUAN IMP. & EXP. CO.
42 ZHONGSHAN ROAD
SHANGHAI, CHINA

Transport details:
FROM SHANGHAI TO NEWYORK
W/T HONG KONG BY VESSEL

Terms of payment:
BY L/C

MARKS AND NUMBERS	DESCRIP. OF GOODS	QUANTYTY	UNIT PRICE	AMOUNT
MAND ARS	H.S.CODE.: 5303.6900			
NEW YORK	COTTON PRINTED VELVET TOWELS			

15,000PCS USD2.5/PC USD37,500.00

CIF NEWYORK USD37,500.00

TOTAL QUANTITY: 15,000PCS PACKING: 150CATRONS

TOTAL: US DOLLARS THIRTY-SEVEN THOUSAND AND FIVE HUNDRED ONLY.

SHANGHAI HUIYUAN IMP. & EXP. CO.

<table>
<tr><td colspan="3">1. Goods consigned from (Exporter's full name and address, country)</td><td colspan="3" rowspan="2">Reference No.
GENERALIZED SYSTEM OF PREFERENCES
CERTIFICATE OF ORIGIN
(Combined declaration and certificate)
FORM A
Issued in THE PEOPLE'S REPUBLIC OF CHINA
(Country)
See Notes overleaf</td></tr>
<tr><td colspan="3">2. Goods consigned to (Consignee's full name, address, country)</td></tr>
<tr><td colspan="3">3. Means of transport and route (as for as know)</td><td colspan="3">4. For the certifying authority use only</td></tr>
<tr><td>5. Item number</td><td>6. Marks and numbers of packages</td><td>7. Number and kind of packages; Description of goods</td><td>8. Origin criterion(see Notes overleaf)</td><td>9. Gross weight or other quantity</td><td>10. Number and date of invoice</td></tr>
<tr><td></td><td></td><td></td><td></td><td></td><td></td></tr>
<tr><td colspan="3">11. Certification
It is hereby certified that the declaration by the exporter is correct.

Place and date, signature and stamp of the certifying authority</td><td colspan="3">12. Declaration by the exporter
The undersigned hereby declares that the above details and statements are correct, that all the goods were produced in
____
(the exporting country)
and that they comply with the origin requirements specified for those goods in the Generalized System of Preferences for goods exported to
(the importing country)

Place and date, signature and stamp of the authorized signatory</td></tr>
</table>

Chapter 8

Customs Clearance for Export

Customs is a government agency responsible for regulating shipments entering a country or a region. All shipments being sent to and from a country or a region should not be removed out of the customs' control without the written permission of the customs authorities, that is to say, customs must be cleared first.

Since regulations differ from country to country, traders must be fully aware of licensing, special provisions and restricted and prohibited goods in the country to which the goods are shipped.

8.1 Stages of customs clearance

There are four stages in customs clearance, i.e., declaration, inspection, tax payment (taxes, VAT, duties) and release.

8.1.1 Declaration

Before permission is given to remove the goods out of the customs' control, the owner or agent is required to submit a Bill of Entry, Customs Declaration, or Inward Permit, as may be prescribed by law, in the prescribed form to enable the customs authorities to examine, inspect and appraise the goods.

Filling in the customs declaration on the basis of the submitted data about the product, its volume and other details and submitting the customs declaration in an electronic or paper form starts the procedures of customs clearance.

Either by themselves or with the help of forwarders, the exporters have the goods available in compliance with the contract and book the shipping space. With all the relevant documents, the shippers fill in the forms in the customs authorities to declare the goods.

Attention should be paid to the documents and the time limit for declaration. Documents usually include the bill of lading, the invoice, the contract, and other documents required by customs authorities. The time limit for export is 24 hours before loading the goods while the time limit for import is calculated from the moment of the goods' arrival.

Clearance for those goods not to be levied or inspected by customs should be completed within one day from the declaration accepted.

8.1.2 Inspection

To ensure that the goods are in strict compliance with the particulars in the submitted declaration such as the goods' nature, value, quantity and specifications, the description of goods, the name of the ship, the port of shipment, the place of origin, etc., the customs authorities will check and inspect the goods imported or exported at docks, airports, stations, post offices, or customs. It is one way to carry out relevant foreign trade policies and supervise international trade.

Other inspection details as time, place, consignees and their agents, packing messages, the name of the goods, etc., will also be stated in the inspection.

The examination may be physical-visual inspection, counting, weighing, measuring, chemical test, etc.—or documentary, that is, calling for relevant documents such as the invoice, the banker's note, the policy of insurance for verifying the value, the quantity or the description of goods.

Within one day, the inspection notice will be issued upon the declaration application, and inspection will be completed within one day calculated from the moment the inspection facilities are available. Customs clearance will be completed within four hours from the moment the inspection is done.

8.1.3 Customs payments

According to the Customs Law, international shipments are often liable to import duties and taxes based on the import and export tariff set by governments. The import duty is what a country customs will charge traders when packages pass through the country's customs. Usually, it's the buyer's responsibility to clear customs and pay the relevant customs duties according to the country's tariff policy.

Tariffs are compulsory, at fixed rates, and non-refundable, including import duties, export duties, transit duties, import surtaxes, anti-dumping taxes, anti-subsidy duties, retaliatory duties, and emergency duties.

8.1.4 Release

After declaration and inspection, goods shall be released within two hours after the duties are paid. The customs will stamp to release the goods. Then the goods shall be at the disposal of the traders.

8.2 The documents required by customs clearance

It is vital to get the required documents in advance to avoid any hold-up at the border since the customs authorities will classify and process the shipment against the documents provided.

8.2.1 Documentation prepared by the exporters

8.2.1.1 Sales contract or sales confirmation

It is the foundation of any transactions between importers and exporters, which is countersigned.

All the items in the contract or confirmation must be clearly and precisely stated: Messrs, Contract No., Date of Conclusion, Product No., Production Description, Quantity, Unit, Unit Price, Amount, Total, Say Total, Payment, Packing, Port of Shipment, Port of Destination, Shipment, Shipping Mark, Quality, Insurance, Documents, Arbitration, Manager Signature of both the buyer and the seller.

8.2.1.2 Commercial invoice

It is a detailed description of the goods under transaction. It is named in different ways due to different purposes such as commercial invoice, shipping invoice, trade invoice, invoice, detailed invoice, certified invoice, manufacture's invoice, receipt invoice, sample invoice, and consignment invoice.

All the items of an invoice must be clearly and precisely stated: Drawee, Invoice No., Issuing Date, Transport Details, S/C No., L/C No., Term of Payment, Marks and Numbers, Description of Goods, Quantity, Unit Price, Amount, Total, SAY TOTAL, Special Terms, etc.

8.2.1.3 Packing list

It is the supplementary to the invoice, also called packing specification or detailed packing list.

All the items in the packing list must be clearly and precisely stated: Issuer, Drawee, Packing List No., Invoice No., Date, Marks and Numbers, Number and Kind of Packages, Description of Goods, G.W, N.W, Measures, Total, and SAY TOTAL.

8.2.1.4 Instruction for cargo by sea/sea

8.2.1.5 Inspection application form for export

8.2.1.6 Certificate of Origin

It refers to the following items: Certificate No., Exporter, Consignee, Means of Transport and Route, Country/Region of Destination, For Certifying Authority Use Only, Marks and Numbers, Number and Kind of Packages, Description of Goods, H. S. Code, Quantity, Number and Date of Invoice, Declaration by the Exporter, and Certification.

8.2.1.7 Generalized System of Preferences Certificate of Origin “Form A”

It refers to the following items: Goods consigned from..., Goods Consigned to..., Means of Transport and Route, For Official Use, Item Number, Marks and Numbers of Packages, Number and Kind of Packages, Description of Goods, Origin Criterion, Gross Weight or Other Quantity, Number and Date of invoice, Certification, Exporter, and Declaration by the Exporter.

8.2.1.8 Application form for inspection

8.2.1.9 Application for cargo transportation insurance

8.2.1.10 Customs declaration form for export

8.2.1.11 Collection order

8.2.1.12 Application for negotiation of draft under letter of credit

8.2.1.13 Bill of exchange

It’s also called Exchange Draft, including Draft No., Dated, Exchange for, At Sight..., Pay to the Order of, the Sum of, L/C No., Issuing Date, Issued by, To (drawee), and Authorized Signature.

8.2.1.14 Application for funds transfers (domestic)

8.2.2 Documentation issued by the parties concerned

(1) Notification of documentary credit

(2) Notification of amendment

(3) Dock's Receipt

(4) Delivery notice

(5) Certificate of inspection

(6) Cargo transportation insurance policy

(7) Airway bill/ ocean bill / railway bill of lading

(8) International freight forwarding special invoice

(9) Special invoice of VAT

…

8.3 Customs declaration form

8.3.1 What is customs declaration form

The import and export declaration is a legal instrument declaring goods' status, which is made by General Administration of Customs to regulate the uniform format and the filling standard, filled in by the consignor or the consignee or his agent. It is an important document by which the customs supervise import and export goods in accordance with the law, collect tariffs and other fees, compile customs statistics and deal with other customs brokerage.

An exporter has to apply to the customs for declaration of the commodity before the shipment. The customs officer will sign on the customs declaration form and release the goods if the goods are up to requirement.

The customs declaration form is in different colors, for example, the white one is made out for general trade and the pink one is used for processing trade. The contents of these documents are similar. We take the specification of an export customs declaration form for general trade as an example to show the method of filling in the document.

8.3.2 The main contents of the customs declaration form

(1) No. of Pre-record

(2) No. of Customs

(3) Port of Export

(4) Record number for checking

(5) Date of Export

(6) Date of Application

(7) Executive company

(8) Mode of Transportation

(9) Name of Transportation Tool

(10) Delivery Numbers

(11) Entrusting Company

(12) Mode of Trade

(13) Kind of tax

(14) Payment style

(15) License No.

(16) Name of Destination Country (Region)

(17) Designated Destination Port

(18) Original Place of Delivered Goods

(19) Number of Approved Documents

(20) Trade terms

(21) Freight

(22) Insurance Premium

(23) Additional Expenses

(24) Contract No.

(25) Number of packages

(26) Type of package

(27) Gross Weight

(28) Net Weight

(29) Container No.

(30) Attached Documents

(31) Manufacturer

(32) Marks, Numbers and Remarks

(33) Item No. and Number of Commodity

(34) Quantity and Unit

(35) Final Destination Country (Region)

(36) Unit Price

(37) Tax Paid or Not

(38) Applying Company (Seal)

8.3.3 Filling in the customs declaration form

(1) No. of Pre-record

It is given by the Customs.

(2) No. of customs

It is given by the dustoms.

(3) Port of export

It refers to the name of the Customs of exit.

(4) Record number for checking

It refers to the number given by the Customs to the corporation.

(5) Date of export

It refers to the date of completing exit formalities for the means of transport carrying the goods declared.

(6) Date of application

It is the date when the exporter applies to the Customs.

(7) Executive company

It refers to the name of the Chinese enterprise who signs or executes the contract with its registered code of 10 figures in the Customs.

(8) Mode of transportation

It is the mode of transportation, one declaration form for one means.

(9) Name of transportation tool

It is the name of conveyance (the name of the vessel or the number of the truck or the train), one declaration form for one name.

(10) Delivery numbers

It is the number of B/L, a copy of customs declaration can carry one piece of B/L's number only.

(11) Entrusting company

It refers to the manufacturer or entrusting party.

(12) Mode of trade

It should be filled in according to the situation and TRADE by Customs, one declaration form for one trade form.

(13) Kind of tax

It should be filled in according to relevant customs laws. When the corporation is wholly foreign-owned, a joint venture or a cooperative, the ways of levying the duty are different.

(14) Payment style

It refers to the actual ways of payment, such as the L/C, collection, remittance, etc.

(15) License No.

It refers to the number of Export License, one declaration form for one license.

(16) Name of destination country(region)

It refers to the final destination of the country (region) .

(17) Designated destination port

It is the final port of destination or the name of the city.

(18) Original place of delivered goods

It is the works that produce the goods for export.

(19) Number of approved documents

It refers to the number for the collection verification and writing-off of export proceeds in foreign exchange.

(20) Trade terms

It refers to as per FOB, CFR and CIF.

(21) Different kinds of charges should be filled in accordingly, including the freight, the premium or other charges.

(22) Freight

It refers to the transportation fee paid to the carrier and the currency name should be indicated.

Note:

Freight indication: "1" indicates freight rate; "2" indicates unit price of freight; and "3" indicates the total price of freight.

(23) Insurance premium

It refers to the insurance money under the terms of CIF or CIP and the currency name should be indicated.

(24) Additional expenses

It refers to the other charges except the freight and the premium and it should be in the name of RMB.

(25) Contract No.

It is the S/C number.

(26) Number of packages

It refers to the total number of packages, and it should be made out according to the B/L. Kinds of package refer to carton, bale, drum, etc.

(27) Type of package

It refers to carton, bale, drum, case, etc.

(28) Gross weight

It refers to the gross and net weight of the goods.

(29) Net weight

It refers to the total weight without packing and its unit is KG.

(30) Container No.

It is the container number.

(31) Attached documents

They refer to the names and copies of the relevant documents accompanied with customs declaration. Exporters can check the kind of accompanying documents (A or B) in the Customs licensed.

(32) Manufacturer

It refers to the final enterprise to make the export commodity. Unless it's known, just fill in the export name.

(33) Marks and remarks

They refer to the marks of the goods.

(34) Item No. and number of commodity

Two lines should be in cluded, the first line is the number of goods in the customs declaration form, and the second line is the registered number for goods in processing trade. It should be made out according to Commodity Classification for China Customs Statistics.

(35) Quantity and unit

They refer to the name of goods. When the goods and specification are more than one item, they should be filled in one by one. Therefore, a copy of declaration form can carry five kinds of name of goods only. When the unit of quantity is different from Commodity Classification for China Customs Statics or has a second unit, it should be also calculated into the stipulated unit in the Commodity Classification for China Customs Statistics. If the equipment is exported in partial shipment, "Partial shipment" should be indicated.

(36) Final destination country(region)

(37) Unit price

It refers to the unit price, the total amount and trade terms of the contracted goods. Currency should be indicated, e.g., USD 600.00/PC FOB London.

(38) Tax paid or not

It should be made out by a customs officer.

(39) Applying company(Seal)

It includes the name of the company, the name of the declarer and details of the contract, with the stamp of the company. Sometimes the seal is used.

8.3.4 Sample of a Customs Declaration Form

中华人民共和国海关出口货物报关单

222920190004208158

预录入编号：EDI198000076583335　　海关编号：222920190004208158 （航交办）　　页码/页数：1/2

境内发货人 (91510182MA6DHN3R5X) 四川寇客智能装备有限公司	出境关别 (2225) 外港海关		出口日期		申报日期 2019-11-08		备案号
境外收货人 NO DUC THANH HYDRAULIC PIPE COMPANY LIMITED	运输方式 (2) 水路运输		运输工具名称及航次号 CHUN JIN/1945S		提运单号 JJCSHIPK961475		
生产销售单位 (91510182MA6DHN3R5X) 四川寇客智能装备有限公司	监管方式 (0110) 一般贸易		征免性质 (101) 一般征税		许可证号		
合同协议号 09DT-2019	贸易国（地区） (VNM) 越南		运抵国（地区） (VNM) 越南		指运港 (VNM009) 海防（越南）		离境口岸 (310701) 外高桥
包装种类 (99) 其他包装	件数 34	毛重（千克） 26000	净重（千克） 25658	成交方式(2) C&F	运费 USD/500/3	保费 //	杂费 //
随附单证及编号							
标记唛码及备注 备注：集装箱标箱数及号码:TWCU4044544							

项号	商品编号	商品名称及规格型号	数量及单位	单价/总价/币制	原产国（地区）	最终目的国（地区）	境内货源地	征免
1	8412909090	活塞杆 0|1|用于液压油缸|无品牌|20	199.41千克 199.41千克	1.17 233.31 美元	中国 (CHN)	越南 (VNM)	(32199)东台	照章征税 (1)
2	8412909090	活塞杆 0|1|用于液压油缸|无品牌|25	749.65千克 749.65千克	1.04 779.64 美元	中国 (CHN)	越南 (VNM)	(32199)东台	照章征税 (1)
3	8412909090	活塞杆 0|1|用于液压油缸|无品牌|30等	5893.57千克 5893.57千克	0.99 5834.63 美元	中国 (CHN)	越南 (VNM)	(32199)东台	照章征税 (1)
4	8412909090	活塞杆 0|1|用于液压油缸|无品牌|180等	1809.73千克 1809.73千克	1.23 2225.97 美元	中国 (CHN)	越南 (VNM)	(32199)东台	照章征税 (1)
5	8412909090	活塞杆 0|1|用于液压油缸|无品牌|30	680.24千克 680.24千克	1.13 768.67 美元	中国 (CHN)	越南 (VNM)	(32199)东台	照章征税 (1)
6	8412909090	活塞杆 0|1|用于液压油缸|无品牌|80等	10753.04千克 10753.04千克	1.07 11505.75 美元	中国 (CHN)	越南 (VNM)	(32199)东台	照章征税 (1)

特殊关系确认：否　　价格影响确认：否　　支付特许权使用费确认：否　　自报自缴：否

报关人员　报关人员证号 22120542　电话	兹声明对以上内容承担如实申报、依法纳税之法律责任	海关批注及签章
申报单位 (913101097702360958H) 上海世洲国际货运代理有限公司	申报单位（签章）	

8.4 Exercises

Please fill in the customs declaration form according to the given materials.

Sales Contract

THE SELLER:

SHANGHAI IMPORT AND EXPORT TRADE CORPORATION

THE BUYER: TKAMLA CORPORATION　　S/C NO.: HX050224

DATE: JAN.1, 2005

DEAR SIRS,

WE HEREBY CONFIRM HAVING SOLD TO YOU THE FOLLOWING GOODS ON TERMS AND CONDITIONS AS SPECIFIED BELOW:

MARKS AND NO.	DESCRIPTION OF GOODS	QUANTITY	U/P	AMOUNT
	COTTON BLANKET		CIF OSAKA	
	ART NO. H10	500PCS	USD 5.50	USD 2,750.00
TKAMLA	ART NO. H11	500PCS	USD 4.50	USD 2,250.00
OSAKA	ART NO. H12	500PCS	USD 4.80	USD 2,400.00
C/NO.1-250	ART NO. H13	500PCS	USD 5.20	USD 2,600.00
	ART NO. HH22	500PCS	USD 5.00	USD 2,500.00
	250CTNS	2,500PCS		

LOADING PORT: SHANGHAI

PORT OF DESTINATION: OSAKA, JAPAN

PARTIAL SHIPMENT: PROHIBITED

TRANSSHIPMENT: PROHIBITED

PAYMENT: L/C AT SIGHT

INSURANCE: FOR 110 PCT OF THE INVOICE VALUE COVERING ALL RISKS AND WAR RISK

TIME OF SHIPMENT: LATEST DATE OF SHIPMENT MAR.16, 2005

THE BUYER: THE SELLER:

TKAMLA CORPORATION SHANGHAI IMPORT & EXPORT CORPORATION

LETTER OF DOCUMENTARY CREDIT

SEQUENCE OF TOTAL: 1/1

FORM OF DOC. CREDIT: IRRE.

DOC. CREDIT NO.: 23416523

DATE OF ISSUE: 050112

DATE AND PLACE OF EXPIRY: DATE 050317 PLACE IN THE COUNTRY OF BENEFICIARY

APPLICANT: TKAMLA CORPORATION RD 23 KAWARAMACH OSAKA, JAPAN

OPENING BANK: FUJI BANK LTD 1013, SAKULA OTOLIKINGZA MACHI TOKYO, JAPAN

BENEFICIARY: SHANGHAI TOOL IMPORT AND EXPORT CO., LTD 31, GANXIANG ROAD SHANGHAI, CHINA

AMOUNT: CURRENCY USD AMOUNT 12,500.00

AVAILABLE WITH/BY: ANY BANK IN CHINA BY NEGOTIATION

DRAFTS AT… : DRAFTS AT SIGHT FOR FULL INVOICE COST

DRAWEE: FUJI BANK LTD

PARTIAL SHIPMENT: PROHIBITED

TRANSSHIPMENT: PROHIBITED

LOADING ON BOARD: SHANGHAI CHINA

PORT OF DESTINATION: OSAKA JAPAN

LATEST DATE OF SHIPMENT: 050316

DESCRIPTION OF GOODS: COTTON BLANKET

ART NO. H10 500PCS USD 5.50/PC

ART NO. H11 500PCS USD 4.50/PC

ART NO. H12 500PCS USD 4.80/PC

ART NO. H13 500PCS USD 5.20/PC

ART NO. HH22 500PCS USD 5.00/PC

DOCUMENTS REQUIRED:

+ SIGNED COMMERCIAL INVOICE IN TRIPLICATE.

+ PACKING LIST IN TRIPLICATE.

+ CERTIFICATE OF ORIGIN GSP CHINA FORM A, ISSUED BY THE CHAMBER OF COMMERCE OR OTHER AUTHORITY DULY ENTITLED FOR THIS PURPOSE.

+ 2/3 SET OF CLEAN ON BOARD OCEAN BILLS OF LADING, MADE OUT TO ORDER OF SHIPPER AND BLANK ENDORSED AND MARKED “FREIGHT PREPAID” AND NOTIFY APPLICANT.

+ FULL SET OF NEGOTIABLE INSURANCE POLICY OR CERTIFICATE BLANK ENDORSED FOR 110 PCT OF INVOICE VALUE COVERING ALL RISKS AND WAR RISK.

+ CHARGES: ALL BANKING CHARGES OUTSIDE JAPAN ARE FOR ACCOUNT OF BENEFICIARY.

+ PERIOD FOR PRESENTATION: DOCUMENTS MUST BE PRESENTED WITHIN 15 DAYS AFTER THE DATE OF SHIPMENT BUT WITHIN THE VALIDITY OF THE CREDIT.

SUPPLEMENTARY MATERIALS

INVOICE NO.: XH05671

INVOICE DATE: FEB. 01, 2005

PACKING: G.W.: 20.5KGS/CTN; N.W.: 20KGS/CTN; MEAS: 0.2 CBM/CTN

PACKED IN 250 CARTONS OF 10 PCS EACH

PACKED IN TWO 20’ CONTAINER(CONTAINER NO.: TEXU2263000; TEXU2263001)

H.S. CODE: 5802.3090
VESSEL: NANGXING V.086
B/L NO.: COSCO0511861
B/L DATE: FEB. 26, 2005
POLICY NO.: SH09223
REFERENCE NO.: 20050819
FREIGHT FEE: USD 1000
注册号：7895478966
证书号：580511478
报检单编号：896541231
报检单位登记号：1254789479
生产单位注册号：12453Q
投保单编号：TB0562311
人民币账号：RMB061222
外币编号：WB68432114
海关编号：789866423
境内货源地：上海
生产厂家：上海毛巾厂
上海进出口贸易公司海关注册号：0387124666

中华人民共和国海关出口货物报关单

预录入编号：　　　　海关编号：　　　　页码／页数：

境内发货人	出境关别		出口日期		申报日期	备案号	
境外收货人	运输方式		运输工具名称及航次号		提运单号		
生产销售单位	监管方式		征免性质		许可证号		
合同协议号	贸易国（地区）		运抵国（地区）		指运港	离境口岸	
包装种类	件数	毛重(千克)	净重(千克)	成交方式	运费	保费	杂费
随附单证及编号 随附单证 1：				随附单证 2：			

续表

<table>
<tr><td colspan="9">标记唛码及备注

</td></tr>
<tr><td>项号</td><td>商品编号</td><td>商品名称及规格型号</td><td>数量及单位</td><td>单价 / 总价 / 币制</td><td>原产国（地区）</td><td>最终目的国（地区）</td><td>境内货源地</td><td>征免</td></tr>
<tr><td colspan="9">1</td></tr>
<tr><td colspan="9">2</td></tr>
<tr><td colspan="9">3</td></tr>
<tr><td colspan="9">4</td></tr>
<tr><td colspan="9">5</td></tr>
<tr><td colspan="9">6</td></tr>
<tr><td colspan="9">7</td></tr>
<tr><td colspan="9">特殊关系确认：　　价格影响确认：　　支付特许权使用费确认：　　自报自缴：</td></tr>
<tr><td colspan="7">报关人员　报关人员证号　电话　兹申明以上内容承担如实申报、依法纳税之法律责任

申报单位　　申报单位（签章）</td><td colspan="2">海关批注及签章</td></tr>
</table>

Chapter 9

Transport Documents

Transport documents lie at the heart of international trade transactions. These documents are issued by the shipping line, the airline, the international trucking company, the railroad, the freight-forwarder or the logistics company.

To the shipping company and the freight forwarder, transport documents provide an accounting record of the transaction, instructions on where and how to ship the goods and a statement giving instructions for handling the shipment.

There are various transport documents used in international shipment, such as the bill of lading, the packing list, the shipping instructions, the forwarder's instructions, the dock receipt, the mate's receipt and the captain's (or master's) protest. Among all the documents issued, the bill of lading (B/L) is the most important one.

9.1 Bill of lading

This is one of the three crucial documents in international trade, which is issued by a carrier that lists goods being shipped and specifies the terms of their transport to ensure that exporters receive payment and importers receive the merchandise. The other two documents are a policy of insurance and a commercial invoice.

9.1.1 Definition

A bill of lading (sometimes abbreviated as B/L or BOL) is a document issued by the carrier or its agent to a shipper, signed by the captain, the agent, or the owner of a vessel, furnishing written evidence regarding receipt of the goods (cargo), the conditions on which transportation is made (the contract of carriage), and the engagement to deliver goods at the prescribed port of destination to the lawful holder of the bill of lading.

A bill of lading is, therefore, both a receipt for merchandise and a contract to deliver it as freight. There are a number of different types of bill of lading and a number of regulations that relate to them as a group of transport documents. Since this is a negotiable instrument, the bill of lading may be endorsed and transferred to a third party while the goods are in transit.

A bill of lading must be transferable, and serves three main functions:

1. It is a conclusive cargo receipt, i.e., an acknowledgement that the goods have been loaded;

The principal use of the bill of lading is as a receipt issued by the carrier once the goods have been loaded onto the ship. This receipt can be used as proof of shipment for customs and insurance purposes, and also as commercial evidence of completing a contractual obligation, especially under such terms as CFR and FOB under INCOTERMS.

2. It contains or evidences the terms of the contract of carriage;

The bill of lading from carrier to shipper can be used as an evidence of the contract of carriage by the fact that the carrier has received the goods and upon the receipt the carrier would deliver the goods. In this case, the bill of lading would be used as a contract of carriage.

Many people think that

1) a B/L is a contract between the seller and the buyer.

2) a B/L is a contract of carriage between the carrier and the shipper.

Both notions are wrong in that

The contract between a buyer and a seller was already established when the buyer placed the order with the seller and they both discussed and agreed (verbally or in writing) the what, where, when, how and how much of the transaction in detail;

The contract between the shipper and the carrier was already established when the shipper or his agent made a booking with the carrier (the shipping line) to carry the cargo from port A to port B;

The B/L is the EVIDENCE of the contract of carriage entered into between the "Carrier" and the "Shipper or Cargo Owner" in order to carry out the transportation of the cargo as per the sales contract between the buyer and the seller.

3. It serves as a title to the goods.

When the bill of lading is used as a document of title, it is particularly related to the case of buyer. When the buyer is entitled to receive goods from the carrier, the bill of lading in this case performs as a document of title to the goods. There are two types of bill of lading that can perform as document of title. They are straight bill of lading and order bill of lading. The straight bill of lading is a bill of lading issued to a named consignee that is not negotiable. In this case, the bill of lading should be directed only to one specific consignee indicated on the bill of lading. An order bill of lading is the opposite from a straight bill of lading and there is no specific or named consignee. Therefore, an order bill of lading can be negotiated to a third party.

Note:

"STC": If the cargo cannot be effectively examined, such as goods in a sealed container, the carrier will issue a bill of lading describing the goods as "container (identified by number) ***said***

***to contain**" the contracted cargo. If the cargo within the container do not comply with the description, the consignee will take action against the seller, and the carrier will not be involved.*

9.1.2 Types of bill of lading

Bills of lading may take various forms, such as on-board and received-for-shipment, etc.

9.1.2.1 Shipped (On-board) B/L and received-for-shipment B/L

The shipped B/L is issued by the shipping company after the goods are actually shipped on board the designated vessel. Since the shipped bill of lading provides better guarantee for the consignee to receive the cargo at the destination, the importer will normally require the exporter to produce the shipped B/L and most bill of lading forms are preprinted as "Shipped Bill".

The received-for-shipment B/L arises where the word "shipped" does not appear on the bill of lading. It merely confirms that the goods have been handed over to, and are in the custody of the shipowner. The buyer under a CIF contract will not accept such a B/L because, in the absence of the date of shipment, he is in no position to anticipate the arrival of the consignment.

9.1.2.2 Clean B/L and unclean B/L

A clean bill of lading is the one that states that the goods have been "shipped in an apparent good order and condition". It is issued when the goods do not show any defects on their exteriors at the time of loading at the port of shipment. This type is favored by the buyer and the banks for financial settlement purposes.

If defects are found on the exteriors of the goods, or the shipping company does not agree to any of the statements in the B/L, the bill will be marked as "unclean" "foul" or "... packages in a damaged condition". An unclean B/L is usually unacceptable to the buyer and banks.

9.1.2.3 Straight, blank and order B/L

The straight bill of lading has a designated consignee. Under this bill, only the named consignee at the destination is entitled to take delivery of the cargo. As it is not transferable, it is not commonly used in international trade and normally applies to high-value shipment or goods for special purposes.

The blank B/L also called open B/L or bearer B/L, means that there is no definite consignee of the goods. There usually appear in the box of consignee words like "To bearer". Anyone who holds the bill is entitled to the goods the bill represents. No endorsement is needed for the transfer of the blank bill. Due to the exceedingly high risk involved, this bill is rarely used.

The order B/L is widely used in international trade. It means that the goods are consigned or destined to the order of a named person. In the box of consignee, "To order" "To order of the shipper" or "To order of the consignee" is marked. It can be transferred only after an endorsement is made. If the B/L is made out "To order of the shipper", the shipper will endorse the bill. If it is made out "To order of the consignee", the consignee will endorse the bill to transfer it. A blank endorsement is usually required for a "To order" bill.

9.1.2.4 Direct, transshipment, through bill of lading

A direct bill of lading is used when the goods are picked up by vessel and the same message will be delivered to its final destination.

A transshipment B/L means that the goods need to be transshipped at an intermediate port as there is no direct service between the shipment port and the destination port.

It is sometimes necessary to employ two or more carriers to get the goods to their final destination. In this case, usually the first carrier will sign and issue a through bill of lading. The on-carriage may be either by a second vessel or by a different form of transport.

9.1.2.5 Liner B/L, container B/L and combined transport B/L

The liner bill of lading is issued by a liner company for shipment on the scheduled port through scheduled routes.

The container B/L is becoming more common in use with the development of containerization. It covers the goods from port to port or from an inland point of departure to an inland point of destination.

The combined transport B/L is issued by a combined transport operator that covers the multi-modal transport on a door-to-door basis in one contract of carriage. It is ideal for container movements. It differs from a "through B/L" in that combined transport is operated by only one carrier.

9.1.2.6 Long form B/L and short form B/L

The long form B/L is more detailed with shipping contract clauses printed on the back of the page.

The short form B/L, as the name implies, is an abbreviated type of document, smaller and not containing the long list of detailed clauses that generally appear on bills of lading. In certain circumstances it may not, therefore, be considered a suitable form of evidence of contract or affreightment.

9.1.2.7 On Deck B/L, stale B/L, ante-dated B/L and advanced B/L

An on deck B/L is issued when the cargo is loaded on the ship's deck. It applies to goods like livestock, plants, dangerous cargo, or awkwardly-shaped goods that cannot fit into the ship's holds. In this case, the goods are exposed to greater risks and therefore usually specific insurance must be taken out against additional risks.

It is important that the bill of lading is available at the port of destination before the goods arrive or, failing this, at the same time. Bills presented to the consignee or the buyer or his bank after the goods are due at the port of destination are described as "Stale Bs/L". As a cargo cannot be collected by the buyer without the Bill of Lading, the late arrival of this all-important document may have undesirable consequences such as a warehouse rent, and therefore should be avoided. Sometimes especially in the case of short sea voyages, it is necessary to add a clause of "Stale B/L is acceptable".

Ante-dated B/L means when the actual shipment date is later than that stipulated in the L/C, the carrier sometimes, at the shipper's request, issues a B/L with a date of signature that suits the requirement so as to avoid non-acceptance by the bank. Due to the risk of the goods being rejected by the buyer arising from the issuance of such a bill, it is advisable to avoid this mal-practice even when it seems necessary in certain circumstances.

An advanced B/L is issued when the expiry date of the L/C is due but the exporter hasn't yet got the goods ready for shipment. The purpose of issuing such a bill is to negotiate payment with the bank in time within the validity of the L/C. It is also regarded as unlawful and risky and should be avoided.

Still there are some other types of B/L such as Groupage B/L, which covers a number of consignments from different shippers, and House B/L issued by a freight forwarder to each individual shipper, and so on. The house B/L is issued by the freight forwarder before he gets one groupage B/L from the shipowner.

All the above mentioned bills of lading are not independent of each other. Several types may be combined into one like "Clean on board, to order, blank endorsed B/L". A received-for-shipment B/L may also be a straight and clean B/L. Bills of lading are made out in sets, consisting of a number of originals (usually three) and a number of copies, marked with "original" and "copy" respectively. Only the originals signed by the carrier enable the consignee to take delivery of the goods. The copies are just for reference.

9.1.3 The main contents and notes of a B/L (on the face)

(1) shipper or consignor

(2) Consignee

(3) B/L No.

(4) Notify Party/Addressed to

(5) Vessel and Voyage No.

(6) Port of Loading

(7) Port of Discharge

(8) Mark and No.s

(9) No. of Packages and Kind

(10) Description of Goods

(11) Gross Weight & Measurement

(12) Total Number of Packages in Words

(13) Freight and Charges

(14) No. of Original B(s)/L

9.1.4 The Main Clauses of a B/L (across the face)

1) DEFINITION Wherever the term "Shipper" occurs hereinafter, it shall be deemed to include also Receiver, Consignee, Holder of this Bill of Lading and Owner of the goods.

2) JURISDICTION All disputes arising under and in connection with this Bill of Lading shall be determined by the court in the People's Republic of China.

3) DEMISE CLAUSE If the ship is not owned by or chartered by demise to the corporation by whom this Bill of Lading is issued (as may be the case notwithstanding anything that appears to the contrary), this Bill of Lading shall take effect only as a contract with the Owner or the demise charterer as the case may be as principal made through the agency of the said corporation who acts as agent only and shall be under no personal liability whatsoever in respect thereof.

4) HAGUE RULES This Bill of Lading shall have effect in respect of Carrier's liabilities, responsibilities, rights and immunities subject to the Hague Rules contained in the International Convention for the Unification of Certain Rules Relating to Bills of Lading 1924.

5) PACKING AND MARKS The Shipper shall have the goods properly packed accurately and clearly marked before shipment. The port of destination of the goods should be marked in letters of 5 cm high, in such a way as will remain legible until their delivery.

6) OPTIONAL STOWAGE (1) The goods may be stowed by the Carrier in containers or similar articles of transport used to consolidate goods; (2) Goods stowed in containers other than flats, pallets, trailers, transportable tanks or similar articles of transport whether by the Carrier or the Shipper, may be carried on or under deck without notice to the Shipper. Such goods whether carried on or under deck shall participate in general average.

7) DECK CARGO, PLANTS AND LIVE ANIMALS Cargo on deck, plants and live animals are received, handled, carried, kept and discharged at Shipper's or Receiver's risk and the Carrier shall not be liable for loss thereof or damage thereto.

8) FREIGHT (1) Freight and charges shall be deemed /earned on receipt of the goods by the Carrier and shall be paid by the Shipper and non-returnable and non-deductible in any event. Freight payable at destination together with other charges is due on arrival of the goods at

the place of destination and shall be paid before delivery of the goods. (2) For the purpose of verifying the freight basis, the Carrier reserves the right to have the goods and the contents of containers, trailers or similar articles of transport inspected in order to ascertain the weight, the measurement, the value or the nature of the goods. In case the particulars of the goods furnished by the Shipper are incorrect, the Shipper shall be liable and bound to pay to the Carrier a sum either five times the difference between the correct freight and the freight charged or to double the correct less the freight charged, whichever sum is the smaller, as liquidated damages to the Carrier.

9) LIEN The Carrier shall have a lien on the goods and any documents relating thereto for all sums payable to the Carrier under this Bill of Lading and for general average contributions to whomsoever due and for the cost of recovering the same, and for that purpose shall have the right to sell the goods by a public auction or a private treaty without notice to the Shipper. If on sale of the goods, the proceeds fail to cover the amount due and the cost incurred, the Carrier shall be entitled to recover the deficit from the Shipper.

10) TIME BAR, NOTICE OF LOSS In any event the Carrier shall be discharged from all liabilities under this Bill of Lading unless suit is brought within one year after the delivery of the goods or the date when the goods should have been delivered. Unless a notice of loss of or damage to the goods and the general nature of it be given in writing to the Carrier at the place of delivery before or at the time of the removal of the goods into the custody of the person entitled to delivery thereof under this Bill of Lading, or, if the loss or damage such removal shall be prima facie evidence of the delivery by the Carrier of the goods as described in this Bill of Lading. In the case of any actual or apprehended loss or damage the Carrier and the Shipper shall give all reasonable facilities to each other for inspecting and tallying the goods.

11) THE AMOUNT OF COMPENSATION (1) When the Carrier is liable for compensation in respect of loss of or damage to the goods, such compensation shall be calculated by reference to the invoice value of the goods plus the freight and the insurance premium paid. (2) Notwithstanding clause 4 of this Bill of Lading the limitation of liability under the Hague Rules shall be deemed to be RMB ￥700 per package or unit. (3) Higher compensation may be claimed only when, with the consent of the Carrier, the value for the goods declared by the Shipper which exceeds the limits laid down in this clause has been stated in this Bill of Lading and extra freight has been paid as required. In that case the amount of the declared value shall be substituted for that limit. Any partial loss or damage shall be adjusted pro rata on the basis of such declared value.

12) LOADING, DISCHARGING AND DELIVERY The goods shall be supplied and taken delivery of by the owner of the goods as fast as the ship can take and discharge them, without interruption, by day and night. Sundays and holidays included, notwithstanding any custom of the port to the contrary and the owner of the goods shall be liable for all losses or damages incurred

in default thereof. Discharge may commence without previous notice. If the goods are not taken delivery of by the the Receiver in due time from alongside the vessel, or if the Receiver refuses to take delivery of the goods, or in case there are unclaimed goods, the Carrier shall be at liberty to land such goods on shore or any other proper places at the sole risk and expense of the Shipper or the Receiver, and the Carrier's responsibility of delivery of goods shall be deemed to have been fulfilled. If the goods are unclaimed during a reasonable time, or wherever the goods will become deteriorated, decayed or worthless, the Carrier may, at his discretion and subject to his lien and without any responsibility attached to him, sell, abandon or otherwise dispose of such goods solely at the risk and expense of the Shipper.

13) LIGHTERAGE Any lighterage in or off ports of loading or ports of discharge shall be for the account of the Shipper or the Receiver.

14) FORWARDING, SUBSTITUTE OF VESSEL, THROUGH CARGO AND TRANSHIPMENT If necessary, the Carrier may carry the goods to their port of destination by other persons or by rail or other means of transport proceeding either directly or indirectly to such port, and to carry the goods or part of them beyond their port of destination, and to transship and forward them at the Carrier's expense but at the Shipper's or the Receiver's risk. The responsibility of the Carrier shall be limited to the part of the transport performed by him on the vessel under his management.

15) DANGEROUS GOODS, CONTRABAND

①The Shipper undertakes not to tender for transportation any goods which are of a dangerous, inflammable, radio-active, and/or any harmful nature without previously giving written notice of their nature to the Carrier and marking the goods and the container or other covering on the outside as required by any laws or regulations which may be applicable during the carriage. ②Whenever the goods are discovered to have been shipped without complying with the subclause ①above or the goods are found to be contraband or prohibited by any laws or regulations of the port of loading, discharge or call or any place or waters during the carriage, the Carrier shall be entitled to have such goods rendered innocuous, thrown overboard or discharged or otherwise disposed of at the Carrier's discretion without compensation and the Shipper shall be liable for and indemnify the Carrier against any kind of loss, damage or liability including loss of freight, and any expenses directly or indirectly arising out of or resulting from such shipment. ③If any goods shipped complying with the subclause ①above become a danger to the ship or cargo, they may in like manner be rendered innocuous, thrown overboard or discharged or otherwise disposed of at the Carrier's discretion without compensation except to the general average, of any.

16) REFRIGERATED CARGO

①The Shipper undertakes not to tender for transportation any goods which require refrigeration without previously giving written notice of their nature and the particular temperature range to be maintained. If the above requirements are not complied with, the Carrier shall not be liable for any loss of or damage to the goods howsoever arising. ②Before loading goods in any insulated space, the Carrier shall, in addition to the Class Certificate, obtain the certificate of the Classification Society's Surveyor or other competent persons, stating that such insulated space surveyor or other competent persons are fit and safe for the carriage and preservation of refrigerated goods. The aforesaid certificate shall be conclusive evidence against the Shipper, the Receiver and/or any Holder of the Bill of Lading. ③Receivers have to take delivery of refrigerated goods as soon as the ship is ready to deliver, otherwise the Carrier shall land the goods at the wharf at the Receiver's or the Shipper's risk and expense.

17) TIMBER Any statement in this Bill of Lading to the effect that timber has been shipped "in an apparent good order and condition" does not involve any admission by the Carrier as to the absence of stains, shakes, splits, holes or broken pieces, for which the Carrier accepts no responsibility.

18) BULK CARGO As the Carrier has no reasonable means of checking the weight of bulk cargo, any reference to such weight in this Bill of Lading shall be deemed to be for reference only, but shall constitute in no way evidence against the Carrier.

19) COTTON The description of the apparent condition of cotton or cotton products does not relate to the insufficiency of or torn condition of the covering, nor to any damage resulting therefrom, and the Carrier shall not be responsible for damage of such nature.

20) OPTIONAL CHARGE The port of discharge for optional cargo must be declared to the vessel's agents at the first of the optional ports not later than 48 hours before the vessel's arrival there. In the absence of such declaration the Carrier may elect to discharge at the contract of carriage, which shall then be considered as having been fulfilled. Any option must be for the total quantity of goods under this Bill of Lading.

21) GOODS TO MORE THAN ONE CONSIGNEE Where bulk goods or goods without marks or goods with the same marks are shipped to more than one consignee, the Consignees or Owners of the goods shall jointly and severally bear any expense or loss in dividing the goods or parcels into pro rata quantities and any deficiency shall fall upon them in such proportion as the Carriers, his servants or agents shall decide.

22) HEAVY LIFTS AND OVER LENGTH CARGO Any one piece or package of cargo which exceeds 2,000 kilos or 9 meters must be declared by the Shipper in writing before receipt by the carrier and/or stated clearly and durably on the outside of the piece or package in letters and figures not less than 2 inches high by the Shipper. In case of the Shipper's failure in his obligations aforesaid, the Shipper shall be liable for loss of or damage to any property or for personal injury arising as a result of the Shipper's said failure and shall indemnify the Carrier against any kind of loss or liability suffered or incurred by the Carrier as a result of such failure.

23) SHIPPER-PACKED CONTAINERS, ETC. ①If a container has not been filled, packed or stowed by the Carrier, the Carrier shall not be liable for any loss of or damage to its contents and the Shipper shall cover any loss or expense incurred by the Carrier, of such loss, damage or expense caused by negligent filling, packing or stowing of the container; or the contents being unsuitable for carriage in container; or the unsuitability or a defective condition of the container unless the container has been supplied by the Carrier and the unsuitability or the defective condition would not have been apparent upon reasonable inspection at or prior to the time when the container was filled, packed or stowed. ②The provisions of the sub-clause ①above also apply with respect to trailers, transportable tanks, flats and pallets which have not been filled, packed or stowed by the Carrier.

24) WAR, QUARANTINE, ICE, STRIKES, CONGESTION, ETC. Should it appear that war, blockade, pirate, epidemics, quarantine, ice, strikes, congestion and other causes beyond the Carrier's control would prevent the vessel from safely reaching the port of destination and discharging the goods thereat, the Carrier is entitled to discharge the goods at the port and the contract of carriage shall be deemed to have been fulfilled. Any extra expenses incurred under the aforesaid circumstances shall be borne by the Shipper or the Receiver.

25) GENERAL AVERAGE General average shall be adjusted at any port of place at the carrier's option.

26) BOTH TO BLAME COLLISION If the carrying ship comes into collision with another ship as a result of the negligence of the other ship and any act, neglect or default in the navigation or the management of the carrying ship, the Shipper undertakes to pay the Carrier, or, where the Carrier is not the Owner and in possession of the carrying ship, to pay to the Carrier as trustee for the Owner and/or the demise charterer of the carrying ship, a sum sufficient to indemnify the Carrier and/or the Owner and/or the demise charterer of the carrying ship against all losses or liability to the other or non-carrying ship or the Owner insofar as such loss or liability represents loss of or damage to his goods or any claim whatsoever of the Shipper, paid or payable by the other or non-carrying ship or the Owner to the Shipper and set-off, recouped or recovered by the other or non-carrying ship or the Owner as part of their claim against the carrying ship or the Owner or the demise charterer or the Carrier. The foregoing provisions shall also apply where the Owners, operations, or those in charge of any ship or ships or objects, other than, or in addition to, the colliding ships or objects, are at fault in respect to a collision, contact, stranding or other accident.

9.1.5 Relative descriptions of a bill of lading in the letter of credit or contract

1) FULL SET (3/3) OF CLEAN ON BOARD OCEAN BILL OF LADING MADE OUT TO APPLICANT AND BLANK ENDORSED MARKED FREIGHT TO COLLECT AND NOTIFY

THE ABOVE MENTIONED APPLICANT.

2) FULL SET, SHIPPED ON BOARD, OCEAN (PORT TO PORT) BILL OF LADING IN 3/3 ORIGINALS AND 3N/N COPIES ISSUED TO THE ORDER OF TOKYO COMMERCIAL BANK MARKED FREIGHT COLLECT AND MENTIONING FULL NAME AND ADDRESS OF THE APPLICANT AS NOTIFY PARTY.

3) FULL SET OF CLEAN ON BOARD OCEAN BILLS OF LADING, MADE OUT TO ORDER, BLANK ENDORSED, MARKED FREIGHT COLLECT NOTIFY THE APPLICANT.

9.1.6 Details in filling in a bill of loading

9.1.6.1 Name of shipper or consignor

It is usually the beneficiary under L/C or the seller/exporter under the collection. If a credit calls for a third party as a shipper, it must be completed as stipulated in the credit (e.g. the exporter's agent).

9.1.6.2 Name of consignee

There are three alternatives (demonstrative order, restrictive order and bearer order), so it can be made out to different orders:

If the demonstrative order is stipulated in the L/C as follows:

1) "Full set of B/L made out to order or to order of shipper"

2) "Full set of B/L made out to order of issuing bank"

3) "Full set of B/L made out to order of importer"

You should make out respectively:

1) "To order or to order of shipper"

"To order" indicates that the ownership of goods belongs to the exporter/shipper. So in effect, it is the same as "to order of shipper". When a bill of lading is made out this way, the exporter must make a blank endorsement to the bank. Once the goods arrive at the destination, they will be released to the holder of the original B/L.

Under collection, a bill of lading is often made out "to order" or "to order of shipper" in order to indicate the ownership of the goods retained to the exporter.

2) "To order of issuing bank"

Under a letter of credit, a B/L may be made "to order of issuing bank" in order to show the ownership of the issuing bank to the applicant before presentation to the carrier for the delivery of goods.

3) "To order of importer/consignee"

When a B/L is made out this way, no endorsement of the importer is required when he takes delivery of the goods. As banks cannot have the ownership of the goods, banks will be reluctant to accept the kind of B/L under the L/C.

If a restrictive order is made,

When a B/L is made out to a named consignee, it is a restrictive order and the named consignee is the importer. In this case, the importer can obtain the goods by presenting the original B/L upon his identification is proved. Under a restrictive order B/L, the exporter is at the risk of non-payment once the goods are delivered.

If a bearer order is made,

A bearer order B/L is made out to "to bearer". It can be transferred by delivery without endorsement and it is difficult to be replaced once lost. It is seldom used in practice.

When a B/L issued in Original(s) and consigned "TO ORDER" or "TO ORDER OF SHIPPER" or "TO ORDER OF XYZ BANK", it is termed as "Negotiable B/L or Order Bill".

9.1.6.3 B/L No.

The bill of lading number is created by the shipper to identify a unique shipment. The bill of lading number shall not be identical to the carrier pro number, the order number or the date.

9.1.6.4 Notify party/Addressed to

It is usually the consignee's agent with full name and the address as stipulated in the credit. According to the L/C, when a B/L is made out to order without the importer shown as the consignee, information of the importer or his agent should be shown in the notify party.

If not stipulated in a credit, this item can be left blank in order to keep documents and the credit identical, and the copy rendered to the shipping company must bear the applicant's complete name, address, telephone number, etc.

9.1.6.5 Ocean vessel and voyage No.

If transshipment is allowed, the second ship's name is filled in here; if transshipment is not allowed, the first ship's name.

9.1.6.6 Port of loading

The port is called the port of receipt, the port of loading or the port of shipment: the name of the port where the goods are loaded on board. Fill in the name of port, e.g. "Tianjin, China" "Qingdao, China", and it can not be written as "Chinese Port" on the CIF or CFR basis.

9.1.6.7 Port of discharge

And the other port is referred to as the port of destination, the port of discharge or the port of delivery. It refers to the name of the port where the goods are unloaded from the vessel. If the shipment arrives at the destination directly, fill in the port of destination; if transshipment is allowed, fill in the port that the cargo is unloaded after the first voyage.

9.1.6.8 Place of delivery

It should be in conformity with the stipulations of the L/C. If there is no L/C, it should be in conformity with the requirement of the contract and the invoice.

9.1.6.9 Marks and No.

According to the requirements of the L/C, if there is no marks, fill in N/M. It should be identical to the invoice and other documents.

9.1.6.10 Number and kind of container or packages

It is the same as the packing list. This shows how many boxes/cartons/cases into which goods are packed, e.g. 1,000CASES. If there is no package, fill in "in bulk" only.

9.1.6.11 Description of goods

As stipulated in the credit or according to the contract, the commodity name can be in general terms. A general or brief description of the goods will do. If the transaction is under a L/C, the credit number, the name of the issuing bank and the credit issuing date should be indicated here.

9.1.6.12 Gross weight & measurement

Fill in the gross weight in kilogram as calculating weight unit. If there is no package or in bulk, you can write "Gross for Net". Fill in the cargo's volume and three digits after a decimal point are needed.

9.1.6.13 Total number of packages in words

Fill in the total number of the containers and packages in capital letters. For example, SAY THREE HUNDRED AND TWENTY CARTONS ONLY.

9.1.6.14 Freight charges

Freight charges, usually, can be made as prepaid or collected , that is, if the term is CIF or CFR, fill in "Freight Prepaid"; if the trade term is FOB or FAS, fill in "Freight Collect" "Freight to Collect" "Freight to be Collected" or "Freight Payable at destination". When the voyage is chartered, write "AS ARRANGED" and if the exporter has known the rate or the carrier is reluctant to show this in the B/L, then write "Freight paid as arranged" "Freight as arranged" or

"Freight payable as per arrangement".

9.1.6.15 No. of original(s)

Two or three original bills of lading issued by the Carrier are needed, and are indicated in capital letters. This indicates how many original bills of lading will make a full set. In practice, a full set may contain two, three or four originals. An original B/L is one which is signed by the ship's master, or by an agent of the shipping company.

Notes:

Be the sole original bill of lading or, if issued in more than one original, be the full set as indicated on the bill of lading. (UCP 600 IV)

9.1.6.16 Place and date of Issue

The place of issue should be the loading place and the date of issue is the date of shipment, which is the date when the shipping company receives the goods for shipment and /or when the goods are loaded on board the ship, not later than the latest date stipulated in the credit or contract.

If the transaction is under a L/C, the B/L date should be made consistent with the stipulation of the credit and is usually be made between the invoice date and the latest date of shipment.

9.1.6.17 Signed for the carrier

The signature may be handwriting, seal, stamp, symbol or in any other mechanical or electronic way if not violating the law of the issuing country.

For a B/L to be original, it should be signed on behalf of the shipping company. Shipping companies often issue unsigned copies of a B/L for record purpose. These unsigned copies are not title documents and cannot be taken as an original B/L, such as "COSCO As Carrier or The Carrier" "ABC SHIPPING CO. As Agent for the Carrier COSCO", or "COSCO As Master or The Master".

9.1.7 Samples of bills of lading

Sample 1

Shipper

EAST ASIA (SHANGHAI) TRADING CO., LTD

NO.886 CAOYING RD, QINGPU DISCRACT, SHANGHAI, CHINA

B/L No.

ALSHA09100098

AMERASIA LOGISTICS (CHINA) LTD.

BILL OF LADING

Consignee TO THE ORDER OF THE CITY BANK LIMITED, DHAKA CHAMBER BRANCH	RECEIVED in an apparent good order and condition except as otherwise noted the total number of containers of packages or units enumerated below for transportation from the place of receipt to the place of delivery subject to the terms hereof, one of the original Bills of Lading must be surrendered duly endorsed in exchange for the Goods or delivery order on presentation of this document (duly endorsed) to the Carrier by or on behalf of the holder the rights and liabilities arising in accordance with the terms hereof shall (without prejudice to any rule of common law or statute rendering them binding on the Merchant) become binding in all respects between the Carrier and the holder as though the contract evidenced hereby had been made between them. IN WITNESS whereof the number of original Bills of Lading stated below has been singed, one of which being accomplished the other(s) to be void.
Notify Party PB TRADING LLC 29, BBC AVENUE DHAKA-1000, BANGLADESH AND THE CITY BANK LIMITED DHAKA CHAMBER BRANCH 65-66 MOTIJHEEL C/A, DHAKA-1000 BANGLADESH	
Pre-carriage by / Place of Receipt	
Ocean Vessel Voy No.: STADT ROSTOCK V.W004 / Port of Loading: SHANGHAI, CHINA	SEE TERMS ON REVERS
Port of Discharge: CHITTAGONG, BANGLADESH / Port of Delivery: CHITTAGONG, BANGLADESH	Final Destination (for the Merchant's reference only)

Marks and Numbers	No. of Pkgs. Or Units	Description of Packages and Goods	Gross Weight	Measurement
PB TRADING LLC	230CTNS	GYM EQUIPMENT CREDIT NO.074809010253 DATED AUGUST 12, 2009 ISSUED BY THE CITY BANK LIMITED DHAKA CHAMBER BRANCH, DHAKA, BANGLADESH IMPORTER'S NAME: PB TRADING LLC NAME, COMPLETE ADDRESS, PHONE NUMBER AND FAX NUMBER OF DELIVERY AGENT IN BANGLADESH: AMERASIA LOGISTICS (BANGLADESH) LTD. 89, CDB AVENUE DHAKA-1000, BANGLADESH PHONE NUMBER: 88-02-4012431 FAX NUMBER: 88-02-4012568	14,271.00 KGS FREIGHT	61.504CBM PREPAID
			ORIG	INAL
OOLU8187404/OOLA	SP9965/40'HC/230	CTNS/14271.00KGS/61.504CBM CY TO CY 1X40'HC SHIPPER'S LOAD, COUNT AND SEAL		

Continued

TOTAL NUMBER OF PACKAGES OR UNITS(IN WORDS)	SAY TWO HUNDRED AND THIRTY CTNS ONLY			
Freight and Charges	Revenue Tons Delivery Agent:	Rate Per	Prepaid	Collect
Ex. Rate	Prepaid at	Payable at	Place and date of issue SHANGHAI 20-OCT-2009	
	Total prepaid local currency	No. of original B(s)/L THREE	For and on behalf of AMERASIA LOGISTICS (CHINA) LTD. By Amerasia AMERASIA LOGISTICS (CHINA) LTD. AS CARRIER	
on Board Date 20-OCT-2009 By Samson				

Sample 2

Shipper Insert Name, Address and Phone		B/L No. CNS010108895
ABC LEATHER GOODS CO., LTD. 123 HUANGHE ROAD, SHANGHAI CHINA		中远集装箱运输有限公司 COSCO CONTAINER LINES TLX: 33057 COSCO CN FAX: +86(021)6545 8984 **ORIGINAL**
Consignee Insert Name, Address and Phone		
XYZ TRADING COMPANY 456 SPAGNOLI ROAD, NEW YORK 11747 USA		
Notify Party Insert Name, Address and Phone		
XYZ TRADING COMPANY 456 SPAGNOLI ROAD, NEW YORK 11747 USA		
Ocean Vessel Voy. No.	Port of Loading	
SUN V.126	SHANGHAI	Port-to-Port **BILL OF LADING** Shipped on board and condition except as other-…
Port of Discharge	Port of Destination	
LONG BEACH	NEW YORK	

Continued

Marks & No.s; Container/Seal No.	No. of Containers or Packages	Description of Goods	Gross Weight KGS	Measurement
XYZ 1234567 LONG BEACH NOS.1-500 YLMU259654/56789	5,000 PCS	LEATHER GOODS FREIGHT PREPAID	2,400KGS	20. 70 CBM
		Description of Contents for Shipper's Use Only (Not part of this B/L Contract)		
Total Number of containers and/or packages (in words) SAY FIVE THOUSAND PCS ONLY				

Ex. Rate:	Prepaid at	Payable at	Place and date of issue
		LONG BEACH	SHANGHAI MAY. 30, 2009
	Total Prepaid	No. of Original B(s)/L	Signed for the Carrier
		THREE (3)	COSCO CONTAINER LINES + + +
LADEN ON BOARD THE VESSEL DATE: MAY. 30, 2009 BY: COSCO CONTAINER LINES +++			

9.2 Shipment advice

The usual practice of international trade under FOB terms is for the seller to send a notice to the buyer before the agreed shipment date so that the buyer can arrange the relevant delivery vessel for delivering the consignment. The buyer, after receiving the relevant notice by the seller, should immediately notify the seller of the name of the vessel and the ETA (Estimated Time of Arrival). The seller should notify the buyer of the detailed information on shipment so that the buyer can make necessary arrangements for insurance and take delivery at the port of destination. Thus in the letter of credit, the required documents may include the beneficiary's certified copy of fax dispatched to the importer within several days after shipment advising the name of the vessel, the date, the quantity, the weight, the value of shipment, the L/C number and the contract number.

A piece of shipment advice usually contains the following points:

1) The date and the number of the bill of lading

2) The date and the number of the contract

3) The name of commodities and their quality and value

4) The name of the carrying vessel

5) The name of the shipping port/the loading port

6) The estimated time of departure

7) The estimated time of arrival

8) The name of the destination port

9) A list of the relevant shipping documents

Sample 1

SHIPPING NOTE

<table>
<tr><td rowspan="2" colspan="2">1. 出口商 Exporter
GUANGDONG IMPORT AND EXPORT CO. LTD
NO.4, NINGBO RD., GUANGZHOU, GUANGDONG PROVINCE</td><td colspan="2">4. 发票号 Invoice No.
MF88C573125</td></tr>
<tr><td>5. 合同号 Contract No.
JM349</td><td>6. 信用证号 L/C No.
R0319</td></tr>
<tr><td rowspan="2" colspan="2">2. 进口商 Importer
BIRMINGHAM IMPORT AND EXPORT TRADING COMPANY, 8TH FLOOR, EMPIRE BUILDING, BIRMINGHAM, UK</td><td colspan="2">7. 运输单证号 Transport document No.
B/L NO.: COSU52512</td></tr>
<tr><td colspan="2">8. 价值 Value
GBP 600,000.00</td></tr>
<tr><td colspan="2">3. 运输事项 Transport details
FROM GUANGZHOU,CHINA TO BIRMINGHAM, UK</td><td colspan="2">9. 装运口岸和日期 Port and date of shipment
GUANGZHOU, CHINA
DEC.25TH , 2019</td></tr>
<tr><td>10. 运输标志和集装箱号
Shipping marks; Container No.
BLOCK 2.0
S/C NO.: GIM-B02
BIRMINGHAM
C/NO: 1-2000
CONTAINER NO.:
COSU3298000
COSU3298001</td><td colspan="3">11. 包装类型及件数;商品名称或编码;商品描述
Number and kind of packages; Commodity No.; Commodity description
× × TREE BLOCK 2.0
250PCS/CTN
G.W.: 245.9 KGS
N.W.: 208.6KGS
MEAS: 0.2258CBM/CTN
PACKED IN 2,000CTNS</td></tr>
<tr><td colspan="2"></td><td colspan="2">12. 出口商签章
Exporter's stamp and signature
萨姆森</td></tr>
</table>

WE HOPE THE GOODS WILL REACH YOU AT THE DUE TIME AND WE LOOK FORWARD TO MORE OPPORTUNITIES OF SERVING YOU.

B. REGARDS,

GUANGDONG IMPORT AND EXPORT CO., LTD

Sample 2

NANJING TANG TEXTILE GARMENT CO., LTD.
HUARONG MANSION RM2901 NO.85 GUANJIAQIAO,
NANJING 210005, CHINA

SHIPPING ADVICE

TO: FASHION FORCE CO., LTD
P.O.BOX 8935 NEW TERMINAL, ALTA,
VISTA OTTAWA, CANADA

ISSUE DATE: MAR.21,2001
OUR REF. DATE: ____________

Dear Sir or Madam,

We are pleased to advise you that the following mentioned goods have been shipped out. Full details are shown as follows:

Invoice Number:	NT001FF004
Bill of Loading Number:	COS6314203208
Ocean Vessel:	HUA CHANG V.09981
Port of Loading:	SHANGHAI PORT
Date of Shipment:	MAR. 20, 2001
Port of Destination:	MONTREAL
Estimated Date of Arrival:	APR. 25, 2001
Containers/Seals Number:	MSKU2612114 / 1681316
Description of Goods:	SALES CONDITIONS: CIF MONTREAL/CANADA, S/C NO. F01LCB05127 LADIES COTTON BLAZER (100% COTTON, 40SX20/140X60) STYLE NO. PO NO. QTY/PCS USD/PC 46-301A 10337 2550 12.80
Shipping Marks:	FASHION FORCE F01LCB05127 CTN NO. MONTREAL

Quantity:	201 CARTONS
Gross Weight:	3,015.00KGS
Net Weight:	2,010.00KGS
Total Value:	USD32,640.00

Thank you for your patronage. We look forward to the pleasure of receiving your valuable repeat orders.

Sincerely yours,

NANJING TANG TEXTILE GARMENT CO., LTD.

9.3 Exercises

1. What is the definition of Bill of Lading?

2. What are the functions of a bill of lading?

3. Please modify the bill of lading according to the given materials.

...

❖ L/C No.: 894010151719

❖ PLACE AND DATE OF ISSUE: HONG KONG MAR 04, 2004

❖ APPLICANT: BERNARD & COMPANY LIMITED

UNIT 1001-3 10/F YUE XIU BLDG 160-174 LOCKHART ROAD WANCHAI HONG KONG

❖ BENEFICIARY: NANJING CANTI IMPORT AND EXPORT CORP. 120 MX STREET, NANJING, CHINA

❖ SHIPMENT: FROM SHANGHAI, CHINA TO SYDNEY, AUSTRALIA NOT LATER THAN APR. 04, 2004

❖ TRANSSHIPMENT: ALLOWED

❖ PARTIAL SHIPMENT: NOT ALLOWED

❖ INVOICE VALUE: USD37,200.00(SAY UNITED STATES DOLLARS THIRTY SEVEN THOUSAND AND TWO HUNDRED ONLY)

❖ DOCUMENTS REQUIRED:

— FULL SET OF CLEAN ON BOARD FREIGHT COLLECT OCEAN BILL OF LADING, MADE OUT TO ORDER OF SHIPPER AND BLANK ENDORSED, MARKED “NOTIFY ID COM CO., 79-81 WALES RD, NSW, AUSTRALIA” AND THE L/C NO.

— INVOICE IN TRIPLICATE

— PACKING LIST IN TRIPLICATE

❖ DESCRIPTION OF GOODS: LUGGAGE SET OF 8 PCS

❖ BENEFICIARY’S CERTIFIED COPY OF SHIPPING ADVICE TO THE APPLICANT

ADVISING MERCHANDISE, SHIPMENT DATE, GROSS INVOICE VALUE, NAME AND VOYAGE OF VESSEL, CARRIER'S NAME, PORT OF LOADING AND PORT OF DESTINATION IMMEDIATELY ON THE DATE OF SHIPMENT.

…

…

SUPPLEMENTARY MATERIALS:

❖ UNIT PRICE: USD 100.00/CTN FOB SYDNEY

❖ NAME OF VESSEL: MOONRIVER V.987

<table>
<tr><td colspan="4">SHIPPER:
NANJING CANTI IMPORT AND EXPORT LTD.
120 MX STREET, NANJING, CHINA</td><td colspan="2" rowspan="3">B/L NO.:

COSCO
OCEAN BILL OF LADING</td></tr>
<tr><td colspan="4">CONSIGNEE:
TO ORDER</td></tr>
<tr><td colspan="4">NOTIFY:
BERNARD & COMPANY LIMITED
UNIT 1001-3 10/F YUE XIU BLDG,160-174 LOCKHART ROAD
WANCHAI HONG KONG</td></tr>
<tr><td colspan="3">PRE-CARRIAGE BY</td><td>PORT OF LOADING
SHANGHAI, CHINA</td><td colspan="2">PORT OF RECEIPT
SHANGHAI, CHINA</td></tr>
<tr><td colspan="3">OCEAN VESSEL / VOYAGE NO.
BERLIN EXPRESS V.06W01</td><td>PORT OF DISCHARGE
SYDNEY, AUSTRIA</td><td colspan="2">PLACE OF DELIVERY
SYDNEY, AUSTRIA</td></tr>
<tr><td>MKS& NO.S
CONTAINER NO.
SEAL NO.</td><td>NO. AND KIND OF PKGS</td><td colspan="2">DESCRIPTION OF GOODS</td><td>GROSS WEIGHT</td><td>MEASURE-MENT</td></tr>
<tr><td>ID COM
PART OF 1 × 40'GP
MLCU4578618/C423776
FREIGHT PREPAID</td><td>372CNTS</td><td colspan="2">SAID TO CONTAIN:
LUGGAGE SET OF 5PCS</td><td>8,484.00KGS</td><td>47. 768CBM</td></tr>
<tr><td colspan="6">TOTAL NO. OF CONTAINERS
OR PACKAGES (IN WORDS): SAY THREE HUNDRED AND SEVENTY CARTONS ONLY</td></tr>
</table>

Continued

<table>
<tr><td rowspan="3">OVERSEA OFFICE OR DESTINATION PORT AGENT</td><td>NO. OF ORIGI-
NAL Bs/L
THREE (3)</td><td>FREIGHT PAYABLE AT
DESTINATION</td></tr>
<tr><td>ON BOARD DATE
2004-04-08</td><td>PLACE & DATE OF ISSUE
SHANGHAI, 04-04-08</td></tr>
<tr><td colspan="2">SIGNED BY:
AS AGENT FOR THE CARRIER</td></tr>
</table>

4. Please make out a piece of shipment advice according to EXERCISE 3.

Chapter 10

Negotiable Instruments

In international trade, payment can be made by negotiable instruments. A negotiable instrument is a specialized type of contract for the payment of money which is unconditional and capable of transfer by negotiation. The negotiable instruments as referred in this unit include the bill of exchange, the promissory note and check.

10.1 Bill of exchange

In documentary transactions, sellers make a written demand upon either a bank or the buyer to pay for the shipment of goods. This demand accompanies the documentation package the seller presents to the bank. Such a formal written demand for payment is called "Bill of Exchange" or "Draft", which is always used in the foreign trade.

A draft involves three parties: the drawer (usually the person who makes, signs and delivers it), the drawee (the person on whom the draft is drawn) and the payee (the person to whom the money is to be paid). Usually the drawer and the payee are the same person. The content of a draft must be in conformity with that of the relative contract.

A bill of exchange (draft) is usually drawn in two sets, which are dispatched separately so that if there is any delay in the receipt of the first copy of the bill, the second copy can be presented. Usually this takes the form of: "At... sight of the FIRST Bill of exchange (SECOND being unpaid)" and the drawee must be careful to accept only one copy of the bill.

10.1.1 What is a bill of exchange

A bill of exchange is an unconditional order in writing prepared by one party (the drawer) and addressed to another (the drawee) directing the drawee to pay a specified sum of money to order of a third person (the payee), or to the bearer, on demand or at a fixed and determinable future time.

In export transactions, drafts are generally drawn on either of two bases. The seller (the drawer) may initiate the draft as provided for in the contract of sales. In such cases the drawee is the purchaser or other person or agent mutually agreed upon. When this method of trade financing is used, it is known as collection draft financing, and final payment rests upon the ability to pay and the reliability of the drawee rather than the bank.

When a letter of credit financing is used, a draft may or may not be required. If required, the draft is drawn by the beneficiary under the terms of authorization in the letter of credit and in strict conformance with the conditions stated. Fundamentally, the letter of credit is formal authorization for the beneficiary/exporter to draw a draft or drafts, in the amounts specified, guaranteeing that they will be honored (paid) when presented for payment under the conditions specified. The draft must include the name of the issuing bank, with the credit number shown on its face.

The followings are the features of a bill of exchange:

1) A bill of exchange must be in writing and not oral.

2) It is an order to make payment.

3) The order to make payment is unconditional.

4) The maker of the bill of exchange must sign it.

5) The payment to be made must be certain.

6) The date on which payment is made must also be certain.

7) The bill of exchange must be payable to a certain person.

8) The amount mentioned in the bill of exchange is payable either on demand or on the expiry of a fixed period of time.

9) It must be stamped as per the requirement of law.

10.1.2 Parties to a bill of exchange

There are three parties to a bill of exchange: the drawer/creditor, the drawee/payer and the payee.

10.1.2.1 Drawer

The drawer is the one who issues the bill of exchange, through which he invites the drawee to pay the sum of money specified. The drawer is the first party of the draft. In certain transaction, the drawer is normally the supplier, the seller or the exporter. The payee is the person to whom the drawee has to pay on the due date. The payee can be the drawer himself or a third party to whom he might owe money.

10.1.2.2 Drawee

The drawee/payer is the one upon whom the draft is drawn. In other words, he is the person who has to pay the sum of money on the due date. And he must have a liability towards the drawer. It is quite usual that the drawee is the buyer or the importer in a transaction. If the drawee accepts the time bill of exchange by writing his name or the word "accepted" together with his name and the date on the bill, he now becomes the acceptor. By accepting the bill, the acceptor accepts the obligation to pay it when the bill matures.

10.1.2.3 Payee

The payee is the holder or the endorsee of a draft that is in possession of it or the bearer of it. The holder is normally the person who is legally entitled to the bill of exchange. The endorser is the person who endorses a bill of exchange. He writes such words as "Pay Bank of China" on the back of a bill of exchange and signs his name to transfer the bill. Usually, the seller is the first endorser.

The payee may change in the following situations:

1) In case the drawer has got the bill discounted, the person who has discounted the bill will become the payee.

2) In case the bill is endorsed in favour of a creditor of the drawer, the creditor will become the payee.

Normally, the drawer and the payee is the same person. Similarly, the drawee and the acceptor is the same person.

For example, Mamta sold goods worth USD 12,000.00 to Jyoti and drew a bill of exchange upon her for the same amount payable after three months. Here, Mamta is the drawer of the bill and Jyoti is the drawee. If the bill is retained by Mamta for three months and the amount of USD 12,000.00 is received by her on the due date, then Mamta will be the payee. If Mamta gives away this bill to her creditor Ruchi, then Ruchi will be the payee. If Mamta gets this bill discounted from the bank, then the bank will become the payee.

In the above-mentioned bill of exchange, Mamta is the drawer and Jyoti is the drawee. Since Jyoti has accepted the bill, she is the acceptor. Suppose the bill is accepted by Ashok, Ashok will become the acceptor.

10.1.2.4 Other parties

The acceptor is the party who signs on a time bill with his assent to the order given by the drawer.

The endorser is a payee or a holder who signs his name on the back of a bill for the purpose of negotiation.

The endorsee is the person to whom a bill of exchange is endorsed by the endorser. If the endorsee endorses the bill of exchange to another person, the endorsee will become a subsequent endorser.

A holder is a party who is in possession of the instrument. A holder can be the payee/bearer or the endorsee.

A guarantor is another third party who guarantees the acceptance and the payment of a bill of exchange.

10.1.3 Classification of bills of exchange

On the basis of different criteria, bills of exchange may be classified into the sight or time bill, the documentary or non-documentary bill, commercial acceptance or the banker's bill, etc.

1) According to the tender, the bill of exchange can be divided into the sight bill (demand bill) and the time bill (usance bill).

A sight bill of exchange is a draft that is payable when presented. A sight bill of exchange is used in the case where the exporter wants to sell goods to the importer for immediate payment.

A time or usance bill of exchange is a draft payable at a future fixed (specific) date or a determinable future date.

2) According to whether commercial documents are accompanied or not, we have the documentary bill and the non-documentary bill (clean bill).

A documentary bill of exchange is one that should be paid only when certain documents have been attached to and presented together with the bill of exchange. The accompanied documents are a commercial invoice, a bill of lading, an insurance policy and so on. A documentary bill of exchange is often used in international trade.

A clean bill of exchange is one that has no documents attached and is usually handed to a bank for collection in a foreign country. Such a draft may be drawn for many purposes, among which are the collection of an open account, the sale of stocks and bonds, the payment for services, and other transactions that arise in international trade but for which no shipping documents exist. Bank drafts are usually clean drafts.

3) According to different acceptors, the bill of exchange can be divided into the commercial acceptance bill and the banker's acceptance bill.

A commercial acceptance bill of exchange is a commercial time draft that is accepted by commercial firms. Both the drawer and the acceptor are commercial firms, so a commercial acceptance bill of exchange bases on the commercial credit.

A banker's acceptance bill of exchange is a time draft drawn by a business firm that is accepted by the bank. A bank, once it has accepted a draft, can either hold the paper until maturity or sell it in the money market. The accepting bank assumes some risk, although in most cases the credit risk is minimal, as banks generally deal only with tolerated companies.

4) According to different drawers, the bill of exchange can be divided into the commercial bill and the banker's bill.

A commercial bill of exchange is drawn by a commercial firm on another commercial firm or bank. A commercial bill of exchange is often used in international trade.

A banker's bill of exchange is drawn by one bank on another bank. It is used in settling payment obligations between banks.

10.1.4 The essentials of a bill of exchange

A bill of exchange is an important security. Only bills of exchange that have the statutory formal requirements and specify the statutory items shall have legal effect. Relevant matters include:

10.1.4.1 Words expressing it to be a bill of exchange

The word "exchange" on a bill of exchange can make it differentiate from other instruments, such as promissory notes and checks. According to the *Negotiable Instruments 1881*, a bill of exchange must indicate the word of "exchange". For example: "Exchange for USD120, 000.00".

10.1.4.2 An unconditional order to pay

An "unconditional order" means the order which should be carried out without any conditions. The bill must be an order which requires the payment instruction to be expressed in an imperative sentence. For example, "Pay to A company or order the sum of USD ONE THOUSAND ONLY". Also, the instrument must be made unconditional at the time of drawing. For example, "Pay to ABC company or order the sum of FIVE HUNDRED POUNDS ONLY providing the goods supplied in compliance with contract..." is not valid.

10.1.4.3 A sum certain in money

The sum on a negotiable instrument shall be specified in both capitalized words and numerical figures, and the two must be exactly the same. Otherwise, the instrument shall be null and void *(Article 8, Law of the People's Republic of China on China's Negotiable Instruments).* For example, USD100.00, SAY U.S. DOLLARS ONE HUNDRED ONLY.

10.1.4.4 Name of the payer or the drawee

The bill of exchange in every country requires that the draft must contain the name of the company or the name of the drawee. The name and address of the drawee shall be clearly stated so that the holder may present for acceptance or payment. For the payment of L/C, it is usually the issuing bank.

10.1.4.5 Name of the payee or the drawer

A bill of exchange must specify who is entitled to the money which the drawer authorized to be paid.

Usually, there are three kinds of writings to fill up the payee/drawer.

1) Restrictive order

Make out "pay ××× company only". This kind of bill can not be negotiable.

2) Demonstrative order

Make out "pay ××× company's order" or "pay to the order of ××× company". This kind of bill is negotiable with endorsements.

3) Payable to bearer/holder

Make out "pay to bearer/holder". This type requires no endorsement for negotiation.

10.1.4.6 Date and place of issue

The issue date is important because the drafts presentation validity and the tenor lie on the issue date. The date of issue has the important function of making sure the period of the presentation, the maturity of the instrument and the effectiveness of the issue.

If the place of issue is not specified in a bill of exchange, the business premises or the domicile or habitual residence of the drawer is the place of issue.

10.1.4.7 Tender

A bill of exchange must be payable on demand or at a fixed or determinable future time.

For Sight Bill/Demand Bill, bills must be payable at sight/on demand/on presentation without acceptance. If no words clearly identify the payment deadline, it should be paid at sight.

For Time/Usance/Term Bill, bills must be payable at a determinable future time, and needs acceptance. It includes:

Bills payable at... days/... month(s) after sight:

At 60 days after sight pay to...

Bills payable at... days/... month(s) after the date:

At 60 days after the date/two months after the date herein...

Bills payable at... days/... month(s) after the stated date:

At 60 days after 1st May, 2005 pay to...

Bills payable on a fixed future date (without acceptance)

On 30th of Jane fixed Pay to A Company...

Notice:

Where such words as "pay in a period of uncertainty" or "pay when an incident happens" are marked, a bill of exchange should not be set up.

When issuing a bill of exchange, the drawer always issues it in duplicate in order to avoid loss.

In order not to have it paid twice, such sentence reading as "FIRST OF Exchange (Second of the same tenor and the date being unpaid)" on the first copy of draft is necessary, whereas on the second copy the sentence should be "SECOND of Exchange (First of the same tenor and the date being unpaid)". This means that once either of them takes effect, the other automatically becomes void.

10.1.4.8 Signature of the Drawer

The drawer's signature serves as a means of authenticating a bill of exchange, usually the exporter/beneficiary.

A bill of exchange is void if any of the above-mentioned particulars is not specified thereon.

10.1.5 Acts of a bill of exchange

The acts of a bill of exchange refer to the legal acts carried out to bear the obligations to a draft. The acts of a bill of exchange include drawing, presentation, acceptance, payment, endorsement, dishonor and recourse, among which to draw is the main act.

10.1.5.1 Draw

To draw is to write and sign a draft and to deliver it to the drawee (payer) for acceptance or payment, so drawing comprises two acts to be performed by the drawer. One is to draw and sign a draft; the other is to deliver it to the payee. Delivery means to pass the draft to the drawee personally or to send it by mail. It states that whatever acts such as issuing, endorsement or acceptance without delivering would be an invalid act.

After being drawn and delivered to the drawee, the draft becomes irrevocable and in the meantime the drawer engages to the payee and the related holder that the draft should be paid or accepted. If it is dishonored by the drawee, the holder has the right of recourse against the drawer who is primarily liable thereon.

10.1.5.2 Presentation

Presentation is to be made by the holder to the one designated as the drawee for payment if it is a sight bill and for acceptance and payment if it is a time bill. As a general rule, a bill of exchange must be duly presented for payment, and if it is not so presented, the drawer and endorsers are discharged. This is a vitally important rule.

There are two types of presentation: presentation for acceptance and presentation for payment. A time bill needs to be presented for acceptance while a sight bill or an accepted time bill needs to be presented for payment. A sight bill needs presentation once, but twice for a time bill, the first one is for acceptance and the second is for payment.

Presentation has to be done within the agreed period. Many cases show the holder of a bill has lost his rights completely as against the drawer or endorsers, merely because he fails to observe the very strict rules related to presentation for payment.

(1) Presentation for payment

A holder of a draft shall make presentation for payment according to the following time limits:

One month after the date of issue for a bill payable at sight to be presented to the drawee;

Ten days after the date of maturity for a bill payable at a fixed date, at a fixed period after the date of issue or at a fixed period after sight to be presented to the acceptor;

Where the holder fails to present the bill for payment within the prescribed period, the acceptor or the drawee shall remain liable for the payment of the bill after the holder explains the situation.

(2) Presentment for acceptance

The bearer or the holder presents the bill of exchange to the drawee and demands a promise of payment from the drawee.

The holder of a draft shall make presentation for acceptance according to the following time limits:

Where a bill of exchange is drawn payable at a fixed date or at a fixed period after the date of issue, the holder shall present the bill to the drawee for acceptance before the date of maturity.

Where a bill of exchange is drawn payable at a fixed period after sight, the holder thereof shall present the bill to the drawee for acceptance within one month after the date of issue.

Where a bill of exchange is not presented for acceptance within the prescribed period, the holder thereof shall lose the right of recourse against his prior parties.

Usually, we have three channels to make presentment:

—to do over the counter of the paying bank

—to exchange the bill through a clearing house

—to dispatch the bill to the paying bank for acceptance or payment

(3) Acceptance

Acceptance is an act by which the drawee promises to make payment at the bill maturity.

Acceptance includes two acts—writing and delivering.

This is accomplished in a regular manner by writing the word "Acceptance", with the date and signature of the drawee, across the face of the bill. When the bill is accepted by the drawee, he is then known as an acceptor.

The purposes of acceptance are showed as establishing the liability of the parties, presenting the bill for payment and if necessary, giving notice of dishonor.

Presentation for acceptance is legally necessary in three cases:

1) Where a bill is payable after sight, presentation for acceptance is necessary in order to fix the maturity of the instrument.

2) Where a bill expressly stipulates that it must be presented for acceptance.

3) Where a bill is drawn payable elsewhere than at the residence or place of business of the drawee.

Except in the three cases listed above, it is not obligatory to present a bill for acceptance. The holder may await the maturity of the bill and then present it for payment.

Acceptance can be divided into general acceptance and qualified acceptance. A general acceptance is an acceptance by which the acceptor assents without qualification to the order given by the drawer. This is the most usual acceptance. A qualified acceptance is an acceptance by which the acceptor varies in express words the specified terms on the bill.

General acceptance:

ACCEPTED Oct. 20, 2019 For A Company (signed)

Qualified acceptance:

ACCEPTED Oct. 20, 2019 Payable on delivery of all documents For A Company (signed)

(4) Payment

Payment refers to that the drawee makes payment according to the draft. Under a sight bill, the drawee is required to make the payment when the bill is presented to him while for a time bill, the drawee is required to accept the bill when the bill is presented to him and make the payment at the maturity of the bill. When paid, the bill is retained by the payer while the receipt is made and signed by the holder of the bill.

(5) Endorsement

An endorsement is a legal formality to transfer the draft. In specific, it refers to the signature of the endorser on the draft, who should be the payee or the subsequent holder. The signature indicates the holder's intention to transfer his or her rights in the bill of exchange. It must be made for the whole amount of the draft.

An endorsement must satisfy three prerequisites:

1) Should be normally effected on the back of a draft and signed by the endorser

An endorsement shall be signed and the date of the endorsement should also be specified by the endorser.

An endorsement without a specified date is deemed to be made prior to the date of maturity.

2) Must be made for the whole amount of the draft

An endorsement which separately transfers a part of the sum payable by the bill of exchange to two or more endorsees shall be void.

3) Should be in succession

In the course of negotiation of an instrument, the signature of negotiation of an instrument, the signature of each endorser negotiating the bill and that of the immediate prior endorsee acquiring the bill shall be the same person's.

There are three main endorsements, namely special endorsement, blank endorsement and restrictive endorsement.

1) A special endorsement is one that specifies an endorsee to whom or to whose order the draft is to be paid, in addition to the signature of an endorser. For example,

Pay to the order of B Co., Singapore (the endorsee) For A Co., Singapore (the endorser) Signature (of the endorser)

2) A blank endorsement, also called a general endorsement or an endorsement in blank, is where the transferor merely signs the bill on its back. The bill becomes payable to the bearer. For example,

For A Co., Singapore (the endorser) Signature (of the endorser)

3) An endorsement is restrictive when it prohibits further transfer of the draft, such as "Pay... only" or "Pay... non-transfer". Once the bill is restrictively endorsed, it can't be transferred anymore. For example,

Pay to ABC Bank only (the endorsee) For A Co., Singapore (the endorser) Signature (of the endorser)

Pay to ABC Bank not negotiable (the endorsee) For A Co., Singapore (the endorser) Signature (of the endorser)

Pay to ABC Bank not transferable (the endorsee) For A Co., Singapore (the endorser) Signature (of the endorser)

Pay to ABC Bank not to order (the endorsee) For A Co., Singapore (the endorser) Signature (of the endorser)

(6) Dishonor

An act of dishonor is a failure or refusal of acceptance or payment of a bill of exchange when presented. When a bill duly presented for acceptance is not accepted within a customary time, the presenting person must treat it as dishonored by non-acceptance; while presented for payment, the holder must treat it as dishonored by non-payment.

When a bill is dishonored by non-acceptance, and the immediate right or recourse against the drawee and the endorser accrues to the holder, and presentation for payment at maturity is not needed.

If the drawee assents conditionally to the payment, the holder can take it or consider it as non-acceptance.

A notice of dishonor on which default of acceptance or of payment by the drawee or the acceptor is advised, to be given by the holder of a draft to the drawer and all the endorsers whom he seeks to hold liable for payment. The purpose of giving such notice is to inform the drawer and prior endorsers the default of acceptance or payment so that they may get ready to honor the payment.

(7) Protest

A protest is a written statement under seal drawn up and signed by a Notary Public or other authorized person in the dishonor place for the purpose of giving evidence that a bill of exchange has been presented by him for acceptance or for payment but dishonored. The holder carries out his right of recourse by means of such a protest.

According to *British Bills of Exchange Act 1882*, if the payer dishonors a foreign bill, the holder has to make a protest within one working day. If the non-acceptance bill is not protested, no presentation for payment is needed and it is needless to protest non-payment.

(8) Recourse

The right of recourse means that the holder of bills of exchange has the right to claim compensation from the drawer and the endorsers in the event the bill has been dishonored. The compensation should include the amount payable on the bill with interest, the fees for giving the notice of dishonor and protest and other incurred expenses.

The holder may exercise his right of recourse only when he has completed the following procedures:

1) Present the bill to the drawee for acceptance or payment and it is dishonored by non-acceptance or non-payment.

2) Give notice of dishonor to his prior party in one business day following the day of dishonor.

3) Make a protest for non-acceptance or non-payment in one business day following the day of dishonor.

(9) Discount

Discount means a bank purchase a time draft that has been accepted at a discount. When discounting the draft, the bank calculates the net present value of the face value of the bill and then pays the net proceeds to the holder of the bill. The present value is less than the face value because the interest from the date when the bill is transferred to the maturity date of the bill is deducted from the face value of the bill.

e.g.: suppose an accepted bill for USD 50,000.00 falls due on June 30 and the exporter takes it to a discounting bank on April 6. If the discount rate is 10%, the discount interest is:

Face value of the bill × the discount rate × the discount days/360 = Discount interest

50,000 × 10% × 85/360 = USD 1, 180.00

The amount the exporter can get is:

50,000−1180 = USD 48, 820.00

10.1.6 Procedures of accommodating a bill of exchange

1) The trader draws a time bill on an accepting house payable to himself and presents the bill to the drawee for acceptance.

2) The accepting house accepts the bill and returns it to the payee.

3) Before maturity, the payee discounts (sells) the bill to the discount house.

4) The discount house discounts (buys) the bill and makes the payment to the payee at an amount less than the face value of the bill.

5) The trader provides funds to the accepting house just before maturity so that the drawee can honor the bill at maturity.

6) At maturity, the discount house, as the new holder of the bill, presents the bill to the accepting house for payment.

7) The drawee makes payment to the discount house at the face value.

10.1.7 The General terms of a bill of exchange used in the L/C

1) The draft is drawn on us at 30 days' sight for 100% of the invoice value.

2) The draft is drawn on our bank (paying bank) at sight.

3) All drafts must be marked "Drawn under the Royal Bank of Canada, Montreal L/C No. ××× dated ××× and Citi Bank Tokyo Credit No. ××× dated ×××".

4) The draft at 90 days' sight, we are authorized to pay the interest at the rate of 9% p.a. (per annum) for the full invoice value.

5) The draft is drawn under... including the interest of USD 500 at rate of 10% per annum from date hereof to the maturity date.

10.2 Making a bill of exchange

In international trade, a documentary draft is used mainly as a certificate of payment by the exporter. When making out a bill of exchange, pay attention to the following items.

10.2.1 A bill of exchange under the Letter of Credit

The bill of exchange (draft) is one of the most commonly used bills in international payment. The drafts can be used in two ways, namely remittance and reverse remittance. The remittance is that the funds flow in a favorable direction to the payment instructions transmitted therefrom. The reverse remittance is that the funds flow in a contrary direction to the payment instructions transmitted therefrom. Most drafts under the letter of credit and collection are by reverse remittance.

10.2.1.1 Particulars in making a draft under the Letter of Credit

(1) Drawn under

All drafts drawn under this credit must contain the clause "Drafts drawn under Bank of ××× (opening bank) Credit No. ××× (L/C No.) dated ××× (date of issue)" to indicate the relationship with ××× bank.

(2) Number of the bill

Usually the invoice number or "AS PER INVOICE".

(3) Place and date of issue

—The place of issue is usually the place of the exporter.

—The date of issue shall be no earlier than the date of shipping documents and not later than the date of presentation and validity of the L/C. The place and date are usually on the upper right corner of the draft.

—The date must be stated in English, not Arabic numerals. For example:

March 10, 2019

(4)Amount of money (in both figures and words)

The total value is put after "Exchange for" in figures with the same currency name as that in the invoice and keeps two digits. For example: USD1,603.50; EUR1,000.00; GBP230.90.

After "the sum of" there is the total value in both figures and words. The two should be in accordance with each other and the word "only" is placed after word expression.

e.g.: SAY U.S. DOLLARS SEVEN THOUSAND TWO HUNDRED AND TWENTY ONLY.

The ways of expressing digits in words:

e.g.: USD 0.75

CENTS SEVENTY FIVE ONLY

... AND 75% ONLY

... AND 75/100 ONLY

Notice:

—*If there is no special provision in the letter of credit, the amount should be consistent with the invoice amount.*

—*If the amount of the bill of exchange stipulated in the letters of credit is a few percents of the amount of the invoice, such as 97%, then the amount of the invoice should be 100%, the amount of the draft is 97% and the difference of 3%, generally for the commission payable.*

—*If the letter of credit stipulates that part of the amount is to be made by a letter of credit, the rest by collection, then the drawer should issue two sets of draft. One is under a letter of credit with the opening bank as the drawee; the other is under collection with the customer (the importer) as the drawee. The invoice amount is the sum of two sets of draft.*

—*The amount on the draft must be the same in words and in figures. The amount of the bill shall not be altered, and the correction seal shall not be affixed.*

In the international practice of the letter of credit, the method "subject to the amount in words" can not be adopted, and the amount in figures must be the same as it in words.

(5) Tenor

The date of payment is one of the most important elements on a bill of exchange. If the date of payment is not specified on a bill of exchange, the bill is payable at sight.

—**Payable at sight**: put "—" or "***" between AT and SIGHT

For example: PAYABLE AT—SIGHT; AT***SIGHT

—**Payable after sight/date**: put " ××× days after" between AT and SIGHT/DATE

For example: PAYABLE AT **30 DAYS AFTER** SIGHT TO… ; PAYABLE AT **45 DAYS AFTER** DATE OF THE DRAFT TO… ; PAYABLE **AT 90 DAYS AFTER** B/L DATE (in this case, the drawer should indicate the date of the bill of lading on the blank of a draft)

—**Payable at a fixed date:** fill in the accurate date in the right place

For example: **ON Dec. 31, 2019 FIXED** PAY TO … ;

(6) Payee

Usually, there are three choices of wording the payee.

If the drawer and the payee are the same person, and it cannot be transferred, while in international trade, the payee is usually the exporter himself or his selected bank, so the column of the payee will be worded "Pay to… Only" or "Pay to… Not Transferable". If the payee is the original payee in the bill, or is the party to whom the original payee has transferred the instrument, then the column of the payee will be worded "Pay… or order" or "Pay to the order of…". With this kind of bill, the exporter may be paid or anyone to whom the exporter transfers the bill will be paid. If the payee is the bearer of the bill, the column of the payee will be worded "Pay Bearer" or "Payable to Bearer". This kind of bill need not to be endorsement and will be transferred by the mere presentation. Therefore, it enjoys the most dynamic circulation but contains the least security.

In accordance with international practice, drafts drawn under the letter of credit are generally made out a demonstrative order as PAY TO THE ORDER OF ×××, which is widely used at present and this kind of bill is negotiable with an endorsement.

In China, the payee under the letter of credit is always the negotiating bank.

(7) Payer

Put after "To" at the left bottom. Usually the drawee is the opening bank or the importer.

(8) Signature of the drawer

Under the letter of credit, the beneficiary is the drawer which is put at the right bottom. Without the signature and stamp, the bill of exchange is invalid.

10.2.1.2 Samples of bill of exchange under the letter of credit

Sample 1

BILL OF EXCHANGE

Drawn under________ L/C No.___________ Dated___________

Payable with interest @________%________ No. ____________

Exchange for __________________________ Shanghai

At _______ sight of this SECOND of Exchange (First of Exchange being unpaid)

Pay to the order of ______________________________________

The sum of ______________________________

____

To ___________________

____

(Signature)

Sample 2

BILL OF EXCHANGE

No. ____________

Exchange for __________________________ Shanghai date _____

At _______ sight of this FIRST of Exchange (SECOND of Exchange being unpaid)

Pay to the order of ______________________________________

The sum of ______________________________

____

Drawn under______________ L/C No. _______ Dated __________

To ___________________

____

(Signature)

10.2.2 A bill of exchange under collection

The bill of exchange (draft) under collection is basically the same as the bill of exchange under the letter of credit.

10.2.2.1 Particulars in making a draft under collection

(1) Drawn under

"Contract No. × × × + For Collection" should be filled in the blank after "Drawn under". For example: Drawn under SamOlMarch19-3 +For Collection

(2) Tenor

Put the relevant information between AT and SIGHT.

For example:

AT **D/P AT SIGHT** SIGHT

AT **D/P 30 DAYS** SIGHT

AT **D/A 45 DAYS** SIGHT

(3) Payee

Fill in the name of the collecting bank.

(4) Payer

Fill in the name and address of the importer or the buyer according to the contract.

(5) Signature of the Drawer

The drawer is the principal on collection terms. It usually covers the name of the drawer and the signature of the person in charge.

10.2.2.2 Samples of bill of exchange under collection

Sample 1

BILL OF EXCHANGE

No. ______ Exchange for ________________________ Shanghai

At _______ sight of this FIRST of Exchange (Second of Exchange being unpaid)

Pay to the order of ____________________________________

The sum of ________________________

____

To __________________

____

(Signature)

Sample 2

BILL OF EXCHANGE

No. ______ Exchange for ________________________ Shanghai

At _______ sight of this SECOND of Exchange (FIRST of Exchange being unpaid)

Pay to the order of ____________________________________

The sum of ________________________

____

To ____________________

____

(Signature)

10.3 Promissory note and check

A promissory note is sometimes used in international business especially when the settlement is made by means of remittance. According to *Bills of Exchange Act* (1882—the United Kingdom), a promissory note is an unconditional promise in writing made by one person to another signed by the maker, engaging to pay on demand or at a fixed or determinable future time, a sum certain in money, or to the order of a specified person or to the bearer. A promissory note is a negotiable instrument signed and issued by the maker promising to pay unconditionally the payee or the bearer a sum certain in money at sight.

10.3.1 Promissory note

10.3.1.1 Essentials of a promissory note

1) The "promissory note" must be in writing.

The promissory note must be in writing. The object of this requirement is to exclude oral engagement to pay from the purview of the above-mentioned *Act*, because mere verbal engagement to pay is not enough. The term "writing" includes printing, typewriting, lithographing, etc. Writing may be on any materials—papers, account books, etc.

2) The promise to pay must be unconditional.

A promissory note must contain an unconditional promise to pay. The promise to pay must not depend on the happening of a contingency. If it is uncertain or conditional, the instrument is invalid. For example, "I promise to pay B Rs.1500 seven days after JD's marriage." This instrument is not a promissory note because the promise to pay is coupled with a condition. "I promise to pay B Rs.500 on demand" is a note with an unconditional promise.

3) The promise must be to pay a certain sum.

The amount promised to be paid by the promissory note must be certain and definite. If the amount to be paid is uncertain, the instrument will not operate as a promissory note. For example: "I promise to pay some money on the occasion of his marriage." The above instrument is not a promissory note because the sum of money to be paid is uncertain.

4) It must be signed by the maker.

The signature of the maker on the face of the note is the most essential feature. In the absence of the signature of the maker, an instrument cannot be called a promissory note even if it is written by the maker himself and his name appears in the body of the instrument. His signature must be there. This may be done even with a pencil. If the maker cannot write his name, he may sign by a thumb mark.

5) The payee must be certain.

It is essential to the validity of a promissory note that the person who is to receive the money should be capable of being ascertained from the instrument itself. Where a document does not specify the person to whom the money is to be paid, it is not a promissory note. The payee should be certain on the face of the instrument and at the time of execution. The payee must be ascertained by name or by designation.

6) Other formalities

Formalities like number, place, date, attestation, etc. are usually found in the promissory note, but they are not essential to the validity of a promissory note. A promissory note should contain the name of the place where it is made or payable.

10.3.1.2 Differences between a promissory note and a bill of exchange

A promissory note is a "promise" to pay, whereas a bill of exchange is an "order" to pay. A promissory note only involves two parties: the maker and the payee, while the bill of exchange involves three parties: the drawer, the drawee and the payee. A promissory note is never accepted because the maker of it is the payer of it, whereas a bill of exchange can be accepted. The maker is primarily liable for a promissory note, while the drawer is primarily liable for a bill of exchange only before it is accepted. After the bill of exchange is accepted, the acceptor becomes primarily liable for it. A promissory note can be issued in an original note only, while a bill of exchange can be issued in a set of two copies.

10.3.1.3 A sample of promissory note

Patiala
September, 2019

On demand, I promise to pay Ms. Julia or order GBP 2,000.00(GBP two thousand only) with interest at 9 % per annum for value received.

(Stamp)

(Signature)

10.3.2 Check

Check, with a long history of development, is often seen in the circle of people's life and business activities. The check or cheque, a negotiable instrument, is an unconditional order in writing addressed by the customer (the drawer) to a bank (the drawee) signed by that customer authorizing the bank to pay on demand a specified sum of money to the order of a named person or to a bearer (the payee). Both the drawer and the payee may be natural persons or legal entities. When drawing the check, the drawer must note that the amount of the check cannot exceed the deposits of his designated account in the bank. Otherwise, the check is called a bounced check or a rubber check, which is dishonored by the bank and definitely prohibited by law. Besides, the check can be roughly divided into a cash check and a transfer check.

10.3.2.1 Essentials of a check

1) The cheque is in writing.

Every cheque has to be in writing. An oral promise to pay does not become a cheque. No particular form is prescribed; a promise contained in a letter will suffice. Writing includes printing or typing.

2) Parties of a cheque.

Usually, a check mentions three parties. The drawer is the one who draws the bill. The drawee is the one on whom the bill is drawn and the payee is the one who is entitled to receive the payment.

3) An unconditional order to pay.

The payment should be unconditional. The word "unconditional" has already been explained in connection with a promissory note and the same considerations apply here.

4) A sum certain in money.

It is necessary that the sum of money promised to be payable in a check should be paid with certainty and definiteness.

5) The cheque is always payable on demand.

Like a bill of exchange, a cheque can also be payable on demand. When a cheque is payable on demand, the drawee has to pay the bill amount whenever the drawer demands the payment. The instruments payable on demand are meant for immediate payment; therefore, no question arises for their maturity.

10.3.2.2 Differences between a check and a bill of exchange

A bill of exchange may be drawn upon any person, whereas a check must be drawn upon a banker. A check need not be accepted for it is payable only on demand, while a time bill of exchange can be accepted. The drawer is totally liable for a check, while the drawer is primarily liable for a bill of exchange only before it is accepted. After the bill of exchange is accepted, the acceptor becomes primarily liable for it. A check can be issued in an original one only, while a bill of exchange can be issued in a set of two copies.

10.3.2.3 A sample of check

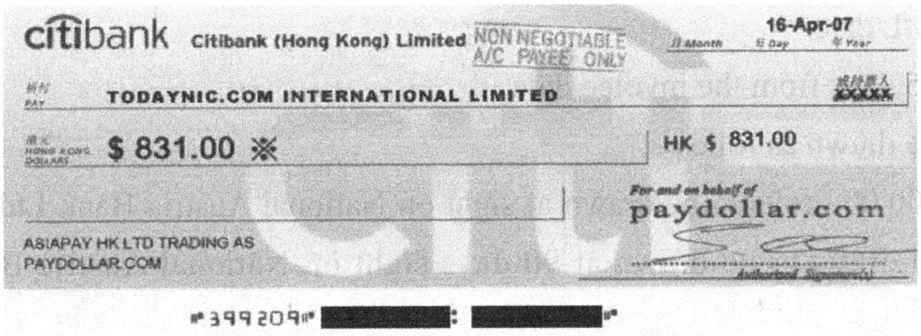

10.4 Exercises

1. Please draw a bill of exchange according to the following conditions:

Date: Feb. 24th, 2019

Amount: USD200, 300.00

Tendor: on demand

Drawer: General Motor Inc., New York

Drawee: The HSBC Bank Hong Kong

Payee: Sampson Incorporation's order

2. Please draw a bill of exchange according to the given materials.

OPENING BANK: FIRST CITY BANK, HONG KONG OEVO TOWER FLOOR 12 OWEF AVENUE, HONG KONG

ADVISING BANK: INDUSTRIAL AND COMMERCIAL BANK OF CHINA, DALIAN BRANCH

L/C No.: FCT1106

DATE OF ISSUE: NOV. 25TH, 2019

APPLICANT: HAPPY TRADE CO., HONG KONG

BENEFICIARY: KUAILE IMP.&EXP. CO.,LTD

DRAFT CLAUSE IN LETTER OF CREDIT: L/C AVAILABLE WITH ADVISING BANK NEGOTIATION BY YOUR DRAFTS AT SIGHT DRAWN ON OURSELVES FOR 100 PERCENT OF INVOICE VALUE TOGETHER WITH FOLLOWING DOCUMENTS...

INVOICE NO.: FPHK0648588

DATE OF INVOICE: DEC.14TH, 2019

3. Please translate the following sentences into Chinese.

1) We hereby issue our irrevocable documentary letter of credit No.09342 available by draft at 45 days after B/L date.

2) Draft at 35 days from the invoice date.

3) Draft to be drawn as follows:

"USD238,000.00-drafts to be drawn at sight on National Austria Bank Ltd. Vienna Branch. USD 122,000.00-drafts to be drawn at 90 days sight on National Austria Bank Ltd. Vienna Branch."

4) Usance drafts are to be negotiated at sight basis and presented to the drawee bank for a discount at the buyer's account.

5) 75% interest of 180 days should be paid by the applicant, the others paid by beneficiary.

6) Credit available with any bank in China, by negotiation, against presentation of beneficiary's drafts at sight, drawn on application in duplicate.

Chapter 11

Packing Documents and Beneficiary's Certificate

11.1 Packing documents

11.1.1 What are packing documents

Packing documents refer to the documents prepared by the shipper listing the kinds and quantities of commodities in a particular shipment. A copy of such packing documents is often attached to the shipment itself and another copy is sent directly to the consignee to check the shipment after arrival. The packing list is one of the main types of all packing documents.

11.1.2 Functions of packing documents

The packing documents play a vital role in transportation and customs clearance. The functions of them are shown as follows:

1) They're the supplement of a commercial invoice but without price information;

2) They're the foundation for the exporter to count the quantities of merchandise;

3) They're a reference document for customs clearance;

4) They can help the consignee to identify which contents may be found in which packages.

11.1.3 Main contents of packing documents

Generally, packing documents include the contract no., the invoice no., the date of issuance, the shipment mark, the name of commodity, the packing specification, the number of packing, the gross weight, and so on. All the information filled in the packing documents must be consistent with the bill of lading, the commercial invoice and the actual packing.

11.1.4 Types of packing documents

The importer requires different packing documents according to different kinds of merchandise, so the name and type of packing documents vary a lot in international trade.

The followings are usually used:

1) the packing list/ packing slip/ bill of parcels;

2) the packing specification;

3) the detailed packing list;

4) the packing summary;

5) the weight list/weight memo;

6) the weight certificate/certificate of weight;

7) the weight memo;

8) the measurement list;

9) the assortment list.

Cautions & notes:

1. *UCP 600 points out, "as long as the content of the packing documents conforms to the requirements of the letter of credit and can reflect the specified documents, the name of packing documents is not required to be identical with the letter of credit." But, when making the documents, the exporter should obey the requirements from the letter of credit strictly.*

2. *If the credit stipulates that inner packing must be fully stated in the documents, for example, the packing must be: Each piece in a poly bag, one dozen in a cardboard box and then 20 dozen in a carton.*

3. *Under the L/C, the bank doesn't check the details of each mathematical calculation in packing documents, but is only responsible for the total amount with the L/C and/or other documents.*

4. *If the name of packing documents required by the L/C is the certificate of weight, the sentence "We certify that the weights are true and correct" should be certified on the document.*

5. *Generally, packing documents should not show the unit price and the total amount of the goods, because the importer doesn't want to disclose the cost of the goods as long as the packing list and the goods are sold to a third party.*

6. *The description of goods may be consistent with the description of the goods in the L/C, or the general description of the goods may be used, but it shall not conflict with the description of the L/C.*

7. *Packing documents usually do not need to be signed. But when the packing document is marked "Certificate of...", it should be signed by the shipper.*

11.2 Making out a packing list

The packing list is a document issued by the exporter, indicating the details regarding the packing condition agreed by the importer and the exporter in the L/C or the contract. It is used by the Customs to apply certain types of duties, and is a required document for customs clearance. When clearing customs, specific duties require the packing list as they are applied on the physical nature of the goods, such as their pieces, weight or measure and this information comes from the packing list. Compound duties are applied as both Ad Valorem and specific tariffs together and thus both the commercial invoice and the packing list would be required for customs clearance. It is also used by shipping companies to identify the weight and dimensions of the product, and should be completed in a metric form. It does not usually require any value for the merchandise, but a very complete list of all the products, their packing (e.g. cartons, boxes, crates, barrels, bags), their gross and net weights, their cubic feet and cubic meters and any markings or handling issues.

11.2.1 Particulars in making out a packing list

There is no uniform format. Its main contents are as follows:

11.2.1.1 Exporter's name and address

The name and address of the exporter shall be consistent with the commercial invoice.

11.2.1.2 Name of document

The name of the document is usually in bold English. In practice, the packing list (note), packing specifications and specifications are used more. The name of packing documents should conform to the stipulation of the L/C, and if it is not stated in the L/C, the exporter can make his own option.

11.2.1.3 No. of packing list

Fill in the invoice number or the contract number.

11.2.1.4 Issuing date

The issuing date of the packing list is not earlier than the date of the invoice and is allowed to postpone 1 or 2 days after the invoice.

11.2.1.5 Shipping mark

The shipping mark shall be made in accordance with the stipulation of the L/C.

11.2.1.6 Name of commodity and specifications

The name of commodity and specifications shall be in accordance with the stipulation of the L/C including specifications of goods and specifications of packing. For example: Packed in polythene bags of 3 kg each, and then in inner boxes, 20 boxes to a carton.

11.2.1.7 Quantity

Fill in the actual pieces or cartons.

11.2.1.8 Unit

Fill in the numbers of outer packing, for example: carton, bag, drum…

11.2.1.9 Gross Weight

Fill in the weight of each outer packing.

11.2.1.10 Net Weight

Fill in the actual weight of each piece or carton.

11.2.1.11 Measurement

Fill in the total measurement of all goods (outer packages).

11.2.1.12 Signature

The issuer's signature shall correspond to the commercial invoice.

11.2.2 General clauses of a packing list used in the L/C

1) The signed packing list, original and nine copies.

2) The manually signed packing list in triplicate detailing the complete inner packing specifications and contents of each package.

3) The packing list in six fold.

4) The signed packing list in quadruplicate showing the gross weight, the net weight, the measurement, the color, the size and the quantity breakdown for each package, if applicable.

5) The detailed weight and measurement list showing in detail the colors, sizes and quantities in each carton and also NT. WT and G. WT.

11.3 Samples of packing list

Sample 1:

TIANJIN HONGHEGU CLOTHING MANUFACTURE CO., LTD
TAIHE DISTRICT, TIANJIN CHINA
TEL: 0086-022-63879833 FAX: 0086-022-63879822

PACKING LIST

INV. NO.:______
DATE: ________
L/C NO.: ______

TO:

SHIPPING MARK	DESCRIPTION OF GOODS	QTY (PCS)	CTNS	G. W. (KGS)	N. W. (KGS)	MEAS. (CBM)
TOTAL:						

SAY TOTAL ** ONLY.

TIANJIN HONGHEGU CLOTHING MANUFACTURE CO., LTD
Signature

Sample 2

SHENZHEN × × × CO., LIMITED

6TH FL, A1 BLDG, HUAFENGSHIJI SCIENCE PARK, TEL: 0086-755-23098768
HANGCHENG RD, XIXIANG FAX: 0086-755-23098767

PACKING LIST

MESSRS: REF INV. NO.: ________

DATE: ________

S/C NO.: ________

SHIP FROM: SHENZHEN TO: VENEZUELA

PACKING: BY STANDARD EXPORTING CARTON SHIPMENT: BY DHL

NO.	DESCRIPTION OF GOODS	Q'NTY	NW.	GW.
1-7	5inch high definition portable DVD player	70 CTNS	350KGS	420KGS
8-12	7inch high definition portable DVD player	50 CTNS	250KGS	300KGS
TOTAL:		**120CTNS**	**600KGS**	**720KGS**

SAY TOTAL: ALL OF THE GOODS ARE PACKED IN ONE HUNDRED AND TWENTY (120) CARTONS ONLY

WE HEREBY CERTIFY THAT ALL OF THE GOODS ARE PACKED IN THE STANDARD EXPORTING CARTONS.

SHENZHEN × × × CO., LIMITED

Signature

11.4 Beneficiary's Certificate

11.4.1 Basic introduction

11.4.1.1 What is beneficiary's certificate

The beneficiary's certificate is a document issued by the beneficiary in accordance with the requirements of the letter of credit certifying that the obligation has been fulfilled, such as the quality of goods, transportation, package, documents, etc.

11.4.1.2 Types of beneficiary's certificate

(1) Beneficiary's certificate for dispatch of documents

For example, CERTIFICATE FROM THE BENEFICIARY STATING THAT ONE COPY OF THE DOCUMENTS CALLED FOR UNDER THE L/C HAS BEEN DISPATCHED BY

COURIER SERVICE DIRECT TO THE APPLICANT WITHIN 3 DAYS AFTER SHIPMENT.

(2) Beneficiary's certificate for dispatch of shipment sample

For example, CERTIFICATE TO SHOW THAT THE REQUIRED SHIPMENT SAMPLES HAVE BEEN SENT BY FEDEX TO THE APPLICANT ON MARCH 15TH, 2019.

(3) Beneficiary's certificate for package and labeling

For example, A CERTIFICATE FROM THE BENEFICIARY TO THE EFFECT THAT ONE SET OF INVOICE AND PACKING LIST HAVE BEEN PLACED ON THE INNER SIDE OF THE DOOR OF EACH CONTAINER IN CASE OF FCL CARGO OR ATTACHED TO THE GOODS OR PACKAGES AT AN OBVIOUS PLACE IN CASE OF LCL CARGO.

(4) Others

For example, CERTIFICATE CONFIRMING THAT ALL GOODS ARE LABELLED IN ENGLISH.

BENEFICIARY'S CERTIFICATE CONFIRMING THEIR ACCEPTANCE OF THE AMENDMENT DATED 10/09/2005 MADE UNDER THIS CREDIT QUOTING THE RELEVANT AMENDMENT NUMBER.

11.4.2 Making out a beneficiary's certificate

11.4.2.1 Particulars in making out a beneficiary's certificate

(1) Issuer

It should be the beneficiary of the L/C.

(2) Name of certificate

It should be the same as that in the L/C. Usual names include "Beneficiary's Certificate" "Beneficiary's Statement" and "Beneficiary's Declaration".

(3) Date

It can be the same as that in the invoice. When the contents certified relate to the shipment or shipment advice, the issuing date shall be stipulated accordingly.

(4) L/C No., Invoice No., S/C No.

Unless otherwise stipulated, a beneficiary's certificate should have the number of credit and contract.

(5) Certification/ Statement

Such sentences should comply with the stipulation in the credit. If the L/C states "Beneficiary's Certificate certifying they have… ", in Beneficiary's Certificate "We hereby certify that we have…" should be used.

(6) Signature of issuer

It should be the company name of the exporter and the signature of the person in charge.

11.4.2.2 Some terms of a beneficiary's certificate used in the L/C

1) 1/3 ORIGINAL B/L AND ONE SET OF NON-NEGOTIABLE DOCUMENTS TO BE SENT TO APPLICANT WITHIN 3 DAYS AFTER SHIPMENT BY FEDEX (BENEFICIARY'S CERTIFICATE PLUS FEDEX RECEIPT ENCLOSED)

2) BENEFICIARY'S CERTIFICATE EVIDENCING THAT EACH PIECE/PACKING UNIT OF GOODS CARRIES THE NAME OF THE COUNTRY OF ORIGIN IN AN IRREMOVABLE AND INDELIBLE WAY.

3) BENEFICIARY'S CERTIFICATE STATING THAT 2/3 ORIGINAL B/L AND ONE SET OF NON-NEGOTIABLE DOCUMENTS HAVE BEEN AIRMAILED DIRECTLY TO XX CO. LTD.

4) BENEFICIARY'S CERTIFICATE CERTIFYING THAT ALL ITEMS MUST HAVE "MADE IN CHINA" LABEL.

11.4.3 A sample of beneficiary's certificate

GUANGDONG TEXTILES IMP. &EXP. NITWEARS COMPANY LTD

15/F., GUANGDONG TEXTILES MANSION 168 XIAOBEI RD. GUANGZHOU CHINA

BENEFICIARY'S CERTIFICATE

TO: JOHNSON'S S.A., NUBLE 1034 SANTIGO CHILE

DATE OF ISSUE: OCT. 5, 2006

NAME OF COMMODITY: GARMENTS (100% COTTON JERSEY BABY'S OVERALL)

L/C NO.: GDP976578

TOTAL GROSS WEIGHT: 1200KGS

TOTAL NET WEIGHT: 1000KGS

PACKING: 50PCS PER CARTON

WE HEREBY CONFIRM THAT FULL SET OF ORIGINAL INSURANCE POLICY HAS BEEN DISPATCHED TO JOHNSON'S S.A. BY FEDEX DIRECTLY.

GUANGDONG TEXTILES IMP. & EXP. NITWEARS COMPANY LTD

(signature)

11.5 Exercises

1. Please fill in the following packing list according to the given materials.

SELLER: SUZHOU IMPORT & EXPORT TRADE CORPORATION

321 FENGXIAN RD, SUZHOU, CHINA

BUYER: TANJIN-DAIEI CO., LTD. SHIBADAIMON

MF BLDG, 2-1-16, SHIBADAIMON MINATO-KU, OSAKA, JAPAN

NAME OF COMMODITY: BLACK TEA

UNIT PRICE AND QTY :	ART NO.555 USD 102.00/KG	100KGS
	ART NO.556 USD 100.00/KG	110KGS
	ART NO.557 USD 90.00/KG	90KGS

PACKING: ART NO.555 AND ART NO.556 ARE PACKED IN ONE CARTON OF 5 KGS EACH. ART NO.557 IS PACKED IN ONE CARTON OF 6KGS EACH

GROSS WEIGHT	NET WEIGHT	MEAS.
ART NO.555 USD 6KG/CTN	5KG/CTN	0.2CMB/CTN
ART NO.556 USD 6KG/CTN	5KG/CTN	0.2CMB/CTN
ART NO.557 USD 7KG/CTN	6KG/CTN	0.2CMB/CTN

SHIPPING MARK: BY SELLER'S OPTION

L/C NO.: XT124 DATE: MAY 12ND, 2019

INVOICE NO.: TX 093 DATE: JUNE 1ST, 2019

S/C NO.: TXT124

SHIPMENT: FROM SUZHOU PORT, CHINA TO OSAKA PORT, JAPAN NOT LATER THAN JUNE 20, 2019

SUZHOU IMPORT & EXPORT TRADE CORPORATION

321 FENGXIAN RD, SUZHOU, CHINA

TEL: 0086-512-68298589 FAX: 0086-512-68298590

PACKING LIST

INV. NO.:_______

TO: DATE: _________

L/C NO.: _______

From: To: By:

SHIPPING MARK	DESCRIPTION OF GOODS	QTY (PCS)	CTNS	G. W. (KGS)	N. W. (KGS)	MEAS. (CBM)
TOTAL:						

SAY TOTAL **ONLY.

____

____

2. Please fill in the following beneficiary's certificate according to the given conditions.

L/C clause: "Beneficiary's certificate certifying that non-negotiable shipping documents have been sent to applicant by DHL."

Additional materials:

BENEFICIARY: SHAMEI TEXTILES IMP. & EXP. CORPORATION, 48 DONGHUA RD, SHANGHAI, CHINA

L/C NO.: 07-J-38203   DATE: 07/09/10   INVOICE NO.: STC-23JULY

SHAMEI TEXTILES IMP. & EXP. CORPORATION 48 DONGHUA RD, SHANGHAI, CHINA ________________ L/C NO.__________ DATE:__________ INV. NO.__________ We hereby… ______________

Chapter 12

Export Verification System and Export Tax Refund

12.1 Export verification

Since 1st January, 1991, the State Foreign Exchange Administration of the People's Republic of China (State Administration of Foreign Exchange, SAFE) has implemented the export verification system with the approval of the State Council, which has lifted our management against export collection up to a new level. The export verification system can facilitate export collection and strengthen the management against it.

This system can control export collection directly by issuing the verification form, which has been one of the most essential certificates for following up and supervising export collection. Specifically, the State Administration of Foreign Exchange issues the verification form for shippers or their agents to fill in, which is needed in export declaration via the Customs, then the State Administration of Foreign Exchange can handle the case accordingly with the verification form checked and sealed by the Customs.

12.1.1 What is export verification

Export verification refers to the verification procedure that companies have gone through via local foreign exchange managerial institutions during a period after the cargo export, indicating that the export amount has been collected. Those entities include companies involving export business, import business and foreign-funded companies.

12.1.2 Procedures of export verification

1) The export unit obtains the import and export business right approved by the Ministry of Commerce or its authorized unit;

2) The export unit applies to the Customs for the "China E-port" access procedures, and

to the departments concerned for the "China E-port" corporate IC card and the "China E-port" business operator IC card through electronic authentication procedures;

3) The export unit of the material to the registered holders of the local foreign exchange bureau in writing off the registration and the foreign exchange bureau on preconditions for export units to register and establish export units in electronic field information;

4) The export unit applies for the written verification form of export proceeds online.

5) The export unit with the operator IC card, the verification card and the exporter contract (for the first time to provide) to the registration of the foreign exchange bureau to apply for the export verification form in paper.

6) The export enterprise applies to the customs offices for export verification forms the port for the record before the declaration by the "China E-port export exchange system";

7) The export unit makes a declaration.

8) The export unit may, after the customs declaration, pass the "China Electronic Port export collection system", which will be used for the verification of the export customs declaration and the one-way foreign exchange bureau.

9) After the export unit has handled the export proceeds in the bank, it shall go to the foreign exchange bureau for the formalities of verification and verification of the export proceeds.

12.1.3 Materials required for export verification

What materials should be provided when the export unit applies to the foreign exchange bureau for the verification of the export proceeds?

1) A letter of introduction and an application form.

2) The import and export enterprise qualification certificate of the People's Republic of China.

3) The business license (duplicate) of the enterprise's legal person or the business license (copy) and copies of the enterprise.

4) The original and photocopy of the organization code certificate of the People's Republic of China.

5) The original and photocopy of the customs registration certificate.

6) Other materials required by the foreign exchange bureau.

12.1.4 Sample of an export verification form

出口收汇核销单 存根 编号：194087153	出口收汇核销单 监制章 编号：194087153	出口收汇核销单 出口退税专用 编号：194087153

出口单位： 志麟实业有限公司
单位编码：20975364
出口币种总价： JPY70,000.00
收汇方式：L/C
约计收款日期： 2019.11.30
报关日期： 2019.12.15
备注：
此单报关有效期截止到 *************

出口单位： 志麟实业有限公司				
单位编码：20975364				
银行签注栏	类别	币种金额	日期	盖章
	***	***	***	***
海关签注栏：******				
外汇局签注栏： ** 年 ** 月 ** 日（盖章）				

出口单位： 志麟实业有限公司		
单位编码：20975364		
货物名称	数量	币种总价
半干李脯	2,400 CTNS	EUR 70,000
报关单编号：******		
外汇局签注栏： ** 年 ** 月 ** 日（盖章）		

12.2 Export tax rebate

As a financial incentive mechanism, the export tax rebate system has been widely applied and plays a positive role in many countries and regions of the world. In more than 100 WTO members, many countries and regions have actively used the export tax rebate policy as the international custom to promote the export of foreign trade products.

12.2.1 What is export tax rebate

The export tax rebate refers to the measure of the refunding to exporters some or all of the domestic tax which has been collected. The export tax rebate is an important part of the national revenue. Mainly through the tax refund to balance domestic taxes already paid, enterprises can reduce the cost of their products for access into the international market to compete with foreign products under the same conditions, thereby enhancing their competitiveness and increasing exports foreign exchange earnings.

12.2.2 Procedures of tax rebate (exemption)

1) Export enterprises should go through the procedure of export declaration.

2) Export enterprises should fill in the export commodities invoice issued by the State Tax Bureau.

3) Export enterprises should input relevant information via the tax rebate application system in computer for the administration of foreign exchange to verify export collection, and for the state tax bureau to examine correspondingly.

4) Once informed of successful handling on the tax rebate, the accountant of export enterprises should go through the procedure of tax rebate in the state tax bureau.

5) After the on-site tax rebate, export business shall receive the tax refund allocated from the relevant bank within 5 working days.

12.2.3 Required documents for some companies

1) For foreign trading companies, all the products purchased for export are taxed under the policy of refund after collection of the import value-added tax (VAT), and then enjoy tax refund after application to tax authorities. The specific tax refund amount can be counted by RMB price (the FOB price * the foreign exchange rate) multiplied by a tax refund rate.

2) For manufacturing companies, all the products produced for export are taxed under the policy of tax exemption, deduction and refund policy for the value-added tax (VAT).

When declaring tax exemption, deduction and rebate by productive enterprises, the following documents must be submitted:

1) Customs declaration forms (for export tax rebate use only)

2) The export commodities invoice (a commercial invoice not a proforma invoice)

3) The verification form of export collection (for export tax refund use only) and a medium & long term foreign exchange settlement statement

4) The export broker statement if any

5) The VAT special invoice

6) Other documents required by state tax authorities

12.3 Exercises

Please find out all the mistakes against the verification form of export collection (3) based on the letter of credit (1) and complementary information (2) listed below.

(1) Letter of Credit

Form of Doc. Credit	*40A: IRREVOCABLE
Doc. Credit Number	*20: LC-320-0254771
Date of Issue	*31C: 090922
Expiry	*31D: DATE 091222 PLACE CHINA
Applicant	*50: MARCONO CORPORATION RM1001, STAR BLDG. TOKYO, JAPAN
Beneficiary	*59: QINGDAO (SHANDONG) HUARUI CO. NO.35 WUYI ROAD QINGDAO, CHINA
Amount	*32: CURRENCY USD AMOUNT 70,000.00
Pos./Neg. Tol. (%) 39A:	5/5
Available with/by	*41D: ANY BANK BY NEGOTIATION
Draft at…	42C: DRAFTS AT SIGHT FOR FULL INVOICE VALUE
Drawee	42A: ROYAL BANK LTD, TOKYO
Partial Shipment	43P: ALLOWED
Transshipment	43T: NOT ALLOWED
Loading in Charge	44A: SHIPMENT FROM CHINESE MAIN PORT
For Transport to	44B: OSAKA, JAPAN
Latest Date of Ship	44C: 091210
Descript. of Goods	45A:

HALF DRIED PRUNE 2008 CROP

GRADE	SPECIFICATION	QTY (CASES)	UNIT PRICE (USD/CASE)
A L: 500CASE	M: 500CASE	1,000	22.00 CFR OSAKA
B L: 1,200CASE	M: 500CASE	2,400	20.00 CFR OSAKA

PACKING: IN WOODEN CASE, 12KGS PER CASE

TRADE TERMS: CFR OSAKA

Documents Required 46A:

FULL SET OF CLEAN ON BOARD OCEAN BILLS OF LADING MADE OUT TO ORDER OF SHIPPER AND BLANK ENDORSED AND MARKED “FREIGHT PREPAID” AND “NOTIFY MARCONO CORPORATION. RM1001, STAR BLDG. TOKYO, JAPAN”

+ MANUALLY SIGNED COMMERCIAL INVOICE IN TRIPLICATE (3) INDICATING APPLICANT’S REF. NO. SCLI-98-0474.

+ PACKING LIST IN TRIPLICATE (3).

Details of Charges	71B: ALL BANKING CHARGES OUTSIDE JAPAN ARE FOR ACCOUNT OF BENEFICIARY
Presentation Period	48: DOCUMENTS TO BE PRESENTED WITHIN 15 DAYS AFTER THE DATE OF SHIPMENT, BUT WITHIN THE VALIDITY OF THE CREDIT.

(2) Complementary information

发票号码：76IN-C001	发票日期：2011 年 9 月 8 日
提单号码：NSD220055	提单日期：2011 年 12 月 5 日
船名：FENGLEIV.66026H	装运港：青岛港
集装箱：2*20’ FCL CY/CY	出口口岸：青岛海关
TRIU 1764332 SEAL08003	合同号：HA1101
KHLU1766888 SEAL08004	SHIPPING MARKS:
出口商：青岛华瑞贸易公司	MQ
净重：12.00KGS/CASE	HA1101
毛重：14.00KGS/CASE	OSAKA
尺码：(20*10*10) CM/CASE	NOS1-3400

(3) Verification form of export collection

出口收汇核销单 存根 编号：964087153
出口单位： 青岛华瑞贸易公司
单位编码：15975364
出口币种总价： JPY70,000.00
收汇方式：T/T
约计收款日期： 2011.11.30
报关日期： 2011.12.15
备注：
此单报关有效期截止到 *************

出口收汇核销单 监制章 编号：964087153				
出口单位： 青岛华瑞贸易公司				
单位编码：15975364				
银行签注栏	类别	币种金额	日期	盖章
	***	***	***	***
海关签注栏：******				
外汇局签注栏： 青岛华瑞贸易公司 ** 年 ** 月 ** 日（盖章）				

出口收汇核销单 出口退税专用 编号：964087153		
出口单位： 青岛华瑞贸易公司		
单位编码：15975364		
货物名称	数量	币种总价
半干李脯	2,400 CASE	JPY 70,000
报关单编号：******		
外汇局签注栏： 青岛华瑞贸易公司 ** 年 ** 月 ** 日（盖章）		

Chapter 13

The Practice of Import Business

This chapter will introduce the procedures of import, because export and import are the two sides of a coin. When handling an import trade, some trade conditions and terms are just the opposite side of those we do in an export trade.

Under the FOB contract with terms of payment by a letter of credit, the general procedure of import business can be summarized as import controls, import contract, L/C issuance and amendment, shipment and insurance, document examination and payment, customs clearance, taking delivery and re-inspection, settlement of disputes.

13.1 Import control

The first step in an import transaction is to check whether the commodities you select fall in the restricted list because there must be prohibited items that can't be imported at all or there are import controls. The import license system is one of the forms that some countries use to control the imports. Sample of the import license is shown below:

中华人民共和国进口许可证

IMPORT LICENSE OF THE PEOPLE'S REPUBLIC OF CHINA

1. 进口商：编码 310123456 Importer 方正进出口贸易公司	3. 进口许可证号 Import Licence No. 07-JZ5661168
2. 收货人： Consignee 方正进出口贸易公司	4. 许可证有效期 Import Licence expiry date ______ 年 ____ 月 ____ 日
5. 贸易方式： Terms of trade 一般贸易	8. 出口国（地区） Country/Region of exportation 日本
6. 外汇来源 Terms of foreign exchange 银行购汇	9. 原产地国（地区） Country/Region of origin 日本
7. 报关口岸 Port of clearance 吴淞	10. 商品用途 Use of goods 自营内销

续表

11. 商品名称： Description of goods WRENCH　8,204.1100					
12. 规格、等级 Specification	13. 单位 Unit	14. 数量 Quantity	15. 单价 (USD) Unit price	16 总值 (USD) Amount	17. 总值折美元 Amount in USD
HEX DEYS WRENCH	套	1,000	10. 00	10,000.00	10,000.00
DOUBLE RING OFFSET WRENCH	套	1,500	10. 00	15,000.00	15,000.00
COMBINATION WRENCH	套	2,000	20. 00	40,000.00	40,000.00
ADJUSTABLE WRENCH	套	1,500	20. 00	30,000.00	30,000.00
18. 总计 Total	套	6,000		95,000.00	95,000.00
19. 备注 Supplementary details		20. 发证机关签章 Issuing authority's stamp & signature 中华人民共和国进口许可证 专用章 上海 21. 发证日期 Licence Date　2008 年 8 月 23 日			

中华人民共和国商务部监制 (2007)

13.2 Import contract

An import contract can only be worked out with good knowledge in a number of areas. Besides selecting the product to import, one should know the export regulations in the exporting countries and the capability and creditworthiness of the overseas supplier to fulfill the contract. Verification can be done by confidential reports about the supplier through embassies, banks, commercials and credit bureaus. The contents and formats are similar to the export contract mentioned above.

13.3 L/C issuance and amendment

Under the terms of payment with a letter of credit, the importer should apply for opening the L/C in time in favor of the exporter who would usually arrange production or shipment after receiving the formal letter of credit. The L/C should be made to fit the sales contract terms; otherwise, the exporter will ask the importer to amend the L/C, which will cause extra work and cost and may delay the shipment.

The exporter might request for L/C amendments after he has checked the L/C terms. If the request is made according to the contract terms, the importer should apply to the L/C opening bank for the exporter has agreed upon with the importer, and it is up to the importer to decide whether he accepts the request or not. If he wishes to entertain the request, he might want to ask the exporter to pay the amendment fee the L/C issuing bank will charge.

中国银行(加拿大)
BANK OF CHINA (CANADA)

To: Bank of China (Canada) Date:

Please establish by ☐ mail ☐ full telex / SWIFT an Irrevocable Documentary Credit as follows:

<table>
<tr><td>Documentary Credit No.</td><td>Expiry date and place:</td></tr>
<tr><td>Applicant</td><td>Beneficiary</td></tr>
<tr><td>Amount (in figures and words)</td><td>Advising Bank (if any)</td></tr>
<tr><td rowspan="4">Partial shipment ☐ allowed ☐ not allowed
Transshipment ☐ allowed ☐ not allowed

Place of Taking in Charge / of Receipt:
Port of Loading / Airport of Departure:
Port of Discharge / Airport of Destination:
Place of Final Destination / of Delivery:

Latest Date of Shipment:</td><td>Credit available with nominated bank:</td></tr>
<tr><td>☐ at sight ☐ by payment
☐ by negotiation</td></tr>
<tr><td>☐ at days ☐ after sight ☐ by negotiation
☐ after shipment date ☐ by deferred payment
☐ by acceptance</td></tr>
<tr><td>Against the documents detailed herein and
☐ beneficiary's draft(s) drawn on credit issuing bank</td></tr>
<tr><td colspan="2">GOODS:</td></tr>
<tr><td colspan="2">Documents required:
☐ Signed Commercial Invoice(s) in ________________ copies.
☐ Full set of clean "on board" Ocean Bills of Lading made out to Bank of China (Canada) / to order and endorsed in blank marked "Freight Prepaid" / "Freight to Collect" and notify applicant with full address.
☐ Clean Air Way bill marked "Freight Prepaid" / "Freight to Collect" consigned to Bank of China (Canada) / ________________ indicating the actual date of dispatch, flight no., airport of departure and airport of destination.
☐ Packing List in _______ copies.</td></tr>
</table>

Continued

☐ Insurance Policy(ies) or Certificate in ______ copies endorsed in blank for 110% invoice value showing claims payable at destination / ______ and covering All Risk and War Risk / Institute Air Cargo Clauses (A) and Institute War Clauses. ☐ Canada Customs Invoice(s) in ______ copies. ☐ Certificate of Origin / Certificate of Origin GSP Form A in ______ copies. ☐ Export License in ______ copies. ☐ Beneficiary's Certificate certifying that they have faxed and sent one set of non-negotiable shipping documents directly to the applicant by courier service immediately after shipment effected.
Applicant's initial:
OTHER TERMS AND CONDITIONS: ☐ All banking charges outside Canada including reimbursing charges are for account of beneficiary. ☐ All documents must be presented with ______ days after shipment date but within the validity of this credit. ☐ ______ % more or less in quantity and amount of the credit is acceptable.
"We acknowledge that this credit, if issued by you at our request, is subject to the terms and conditions of the Hypothecation of Term Deposit." / "General Trade Finance Agreement given by us in your favour, terms and conditions attached to this application form, and the Uniform Customs and Practice for Documentary Credits (2007) Revision, International Chamber of Commerce Publication No.600."

☐ Please debit our CAD / USD Account No. ______ ______ for your commission and charges. ☐ Please debit our CAD / USD Account No.______ ______ as 100% / ______ % margin deposit. ☐ For queries, please contact Mr. / Ms. ______ at Tel No. ______	______ **Applicant's Signature(s)**
FOR BANK USE ONLY	Signature(s) Verified by

13.4 Shipment and insurance

More coordination between the importer and the exporter will be needed under certain trade terms such as FOB. If the importer is responsible for shipment, he should arrange the transportation and keep the exporter informed of the progress in order to facilitate smooth delivery of the goods. The importer might also want to supervise the shipment at the loading port. If the insurance is to be arranged by the importer, the importer should ask the exporter to advise the shipment in time so that the goods can be covered by insurance without delay.

13.5 Document examination and payment

Document examination is a very important step and this should be done with great care. Either the L/C opening bank or the importer should scrutinize the documents to ensure that documents are delivered in accordance with L/C terms. Under the L/C arrangement, the exporter will make shipment and present the L/C with all the documents to a negotiating bank if it is available by negotiation. If the documents are in compliance with the terms of the L/C through carefully checking, the bank will negotiate the documents and send them to the issuing bank for reimbursement.

The opening bank must examine a presentation to determine, on the basis of the documents alone, whether or not the documents appear on their face to constitute a complying presentation. At the same time, the concerned bank shall have a maximum of five banking days following the day of presentation to determine if the presentation is complying. This period is not curtailed or otherwise affected by the occurrence on or after the date of presentation of any expiry date or the last day for presentation.

In practice, after examining all the documents presented carefully, the issuing bank may present those documents to the importer for verification within seven banking days. Once confirmed, the issuing bank will debit the importer's account when releasing the shipping documents to the importer. The whole transaction now comes to an end.

13.6 Customs clearance

All goods imported into a country have to pass through the procedure of customs clearance as they cross the border. The goods are examined, appraised, assessed, valued and then allowed to be taken out of charge of the customs for use by the importer. The entire process of customs clearance is complex and to carry out this procedure smoothly, the help of accredited customs clearing agents (also called Customs brokers) may be necessary, particularly for small companies that are not similar with the procedures or it is inefficient to keep their own personnel for customs clearance.

13.7 Taking delivery and re-inspection

The buyer or the consignee must take delivery of the goods when they have been delivered as contracted at the discharging port in the sea transportation. Consignees should settle all the charges and surrender the original bill of lading for switch of the local delivery order. Then, they could make necessary cargo clearance and take cargo delivery from the terminal.

A delivery order is issued by the carrier or his agent to enable the consignee or his forwarding agent to take delivery of the cargo (the import cargo) from the vessel. But specifically, the forwarding agent or the consignee should go through the customs clearance procedure (or formalities) by the delivery order and then apply for E/R (the equipment interchange receipt).

E/R is a document required when transferring a cargo container from one vessel to another, or to a shipping terminal. The receipt includes the container number, the vessel/voyage code, the stacking position and the stowage position.

The forwarding agent or the consignee can take delivery of designated containers and unload all the cargoes by E/R (out), then return all the empty containers as required. For detailed information, please see the following document attached: E/R (out)

PDA

大连港万通物流有限公司

DALIAN PORT WANTONG LOGISTICS CO.,LTD.

OUT出场

集装箱设备交接单

EQUIPMENT INTERCHANGE RECEIPT

No

用箱人/运箱人 (USER/HAULIER)	提箱地点 (PLACE OF DELIVERY)	发往地点 (DELIVERED TO)	返回/收箱地点 (PLACE OF RETURN)

船名/航次 (VESSEL/ VOYAGE NO.)	提单号 (B/L NO.)	目的港(DESTINATION)	中转港(T/S PORT)

集装箱号 (CONTAINER NO.)	铅封号 (SEAL NO.)	尺寸/类型 (SIZE / TYPE)	货名 (COMMODITY)	指定温度 (TEMP. SET POINT)

货重(NET)	总重(GROSS)	件数(QTY)	免费期限 (FREE TIME PERIOD)	入港日期 (DATE OF GATE IN)

出场目的/状态 (PPS OF GATE - OUT /STATUS)	进场目的/状态 (PPS OF GATE - IN/ STATUS)	运载工具牌号 (TRUCK,WAGON,BARGE NO.)

①码头·堆场

出场检查记录 (INSPECTION AT THE TIME OF OUTER CHANGE)

普通集装箱 (GP CONTAINER)	冷藏集装箱 (RF CONTAINER)	特种集装箱 (SPECIAL CONTAINER)	发电机 (GEN SET)
□ 正常 (SOUND) □ 异常 (DEFECTIVE)	□ 正常 (SOUND) □ 异常 (DEFECTIVE)	□ 正常 (SOUND) □ 异常 (DEFECTIVE)	□ 正常 (SOUND) □ 异常 (DEFECTIVE)

损坏记录及代号 (DAMAGE & CODE)

C	B	H	D	BR	M	DR	DL
割伤 (CUT)	擦伤 (BRUISE)	破洞 (HOLE)	凹损 (DENT)	破损 (BROKEN)	丢失 (MISSING)	污箱 (DIRTY)	危标 (DG LABEL)

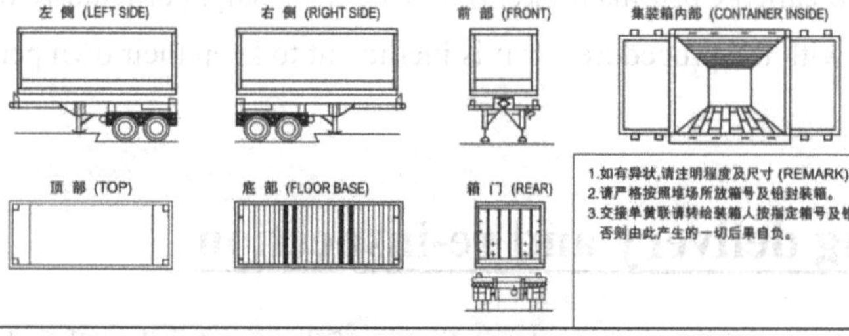

1.如有异状,请注明程度及尺寸 (REMARK)。
2.请严格按照堆场所放箱号及铅封装箱。
3.交接单黄联请转给装箱人按指定箱号及铅封装箱。否则由此产生的一切后果自负。

除列明者外，集装箱及集装箱设备交换时完好无损，铅封完整无误。

THE CONTAINER / ASSOCIATED EQUIPMENT INTERCHANGED IN SOUND CONDITION AND SEAL INTACT UNLESS OTHERWISE STATED

用箱人/运箱人/外理签署 (CONTAINER USER / HAULIER'S SIGNATURE/COSTACO)　　码头/堆场值班员签署 (TERMINAL/DEPOT CLERK'S SIGNATURE)

年　月　日　　年　月　日

After that, re-inspection should be carried out to confirm if the goods are up to the standard set in the sales contract, if problems such as weight shortage, inferior quality or damage are found and attributed to the exporter, if the loss or damage is due to the negligence of the carrier, the claim should be made against the carrier, if the loss or damage has been caused by the risks covered by insurance, the claim should be made against the underwriter.

13.8 Settlement of disputes

In case a claim can't be settled between the parties involved through negotiation, the dispute should be submitted to mediation or arbitration if that has been agreed upon. Otherwise, a lawsuit might be necessary to settle the dispute.

13.9 Exercises

1. Please review the import procedures in international trade.

2. Please fill in the import license according to the given materials.

预录入编号：EDI198000076583335 海关编号：222920190004208158 （航交办） 页码/页数：1/2

境内发货人 (91510182MA6DHN3R5X) 四川寇客智能装备有限公司	出境关别 (2225) 外港海关	出口日期	申报日期 2019-11-08	备案号
境外收货人 NO DUC THANH HYDRAULIC PIPE COMPANY LIMITED	运输方式 (2) 水路运输	运输工具名称及航次号 CHUN JIN/1945S	提运单号 JJCSHHPK961475	
生产销售单位 (91510182MA6DHN3R5X) 四川寇客智能装备有限公司	监管方式 (0110) 一般贸易	征免性质 (101) 一般征税	许可证号	
合同协议号 09DT-2019	贸易国（地区） (VNM) 越南	运抵国（地区） (VNM) 越南	指运港 (VNM009) 海防（越南）	离境口岸 (310701) 外高桥

包装种类 (99) 其他包装	件数 34	毛重（千克） 26000	净重（千克） 25658	成交方式(2) C&F	运费 USD/500/3	保费 //	杂费 //
随附单证及编号							
标记唛码及备注 备注：集装箱标箱数及号码:TWCU4044544							

项号	商品编号	商品名称及规格型号	数量及单位	单价/总价/币制	原产国（地区）	最终目的国（地区）	境内货源地	征免
1	8412909090	活塞杆 0|1|用于液压油缸|无品牌|20	199.41千克 199.41千克	1.17 233.31 美元	中国 (CHN)	越南 (VNM)	(32199)东台	照章征税 (1)
2	8412909090	活塞杆 0|1|用于液压油缸|无品牌|25	749.65千克 749.65千克	1.04 779.64 美元	中国 (CHN)	越南 (VNM)	(32199)东台	照章征税 (1)
3	8412909090	活塞杆 0|1|用于液压油缸|无品牌|30等	5893.57千克 5893.57千克	0.99 5834.63 美元	中国 (CHN)	越南 (VNM)	(32199)东台	照章征税 (1)
4	8412909090	活塞杆 0|1|用于液压油缸|无品牌|180等	1809.73千克 1809.73千克	1.23 2225.97 美元	中国 (CHN)	越南 (VNM)	(32199)东台	照章征税 (1)
5	8412909090	活塞杆 0|1|用于液压油缸|无品牌|30	680.24千克 680.24千克	1.13 768.67 美元	中国 (CHN)	越南 (VNM)	(32199)东台	照章征税 (1)
6	8412909090	活塞杆 0|1|用于液压油缸|无品牌|80等	10753.04千克 10753.04千克	1.07 11505.75 美元	中国 (CHN)	越南 (VN[illegible])	(32199)东台	照章征税 (1)

特殊关系确认：否 价格影响确认：否 支付特许权使用费确认：否 自报自缴：否

报关人员 报关人员证 电话 兹声明对以上内容承担如实申报、依法纳税之法律 海关批注及签章

中华人民共和国进口许可证

IMPORT LICENCE OF THE PEOPLE'S REPUBLIC OF CHINA

1. 进口商：编码 310123456 Importer	3. 进口许可证号 Import License No.
2. 收货人： Consignee	4. 许可证有效期 Import License expiry date ______ 年 ____ 月 ____ 日
5. 贸易方式： Terms of trade	8. 出口国（地区） Country/Region of exportation
6. 外汇来源 Terms of foreign exchange	9. 原产地国（地区） Country/Region of origin
7. 报关口岸 Port of clearance	10. 商品用途 Use of goods
11. 商品名称： Description of goods	

12. 规格、等级 Specification	13. 单位 Unit	14. 数量 Quantity	15. 单价 (USD) Unit price	16 总值 (USD) Amount	17. 总值折美元 Amount in USD
18. 总计 Total					
19. 备注 Supplementary details		20. 发证机关签章 Issuing authority's stamp & signature 中华人民共和国进口许可证 专用章 上 海 21. 发证日期 Licence Date 年 月 日			

中华人民共和国商务部监制 (2007)

References

Alan E. Branch，2008. Export Practice and Management[M]. 北京：清华大学出版社.
August, Ray，2006. International Business Law[M]. New York: Prentice Hall.
国际商会，2007. ICC 跟单信用证统一惯例（UCP600）[M]. 国际商会中国国家委员会，译. 北京：中国民主法制出版社.
黎孝先，王健，2011. 国际贸易实务：第五版 [M]. 北京：对外经济贸易大学出版社.
李月菊，2008. 进出口实务与操作（英文版）[M]. 北京：对外经济贸易大学出版社.
李月菊，2009. 国际贸易实务与操作（英文版）[M]. 上海：上海外语教育出版社.
屈韬，2010. 进出口贸易实务 [M]. 大连：东北财经大学出版社.
全国外经贸单证专业培训考试办公室，2016. 国际商务单证理论与实务 [M]. 北京：中国商务出版社.
盛美娟，梁志刚，2012. 国际贸易实务（英文版）[M]. 北京：中国人民大学出版社.
帅建林，2005. 国际贸易实务（英文版）[M]. 成都：西南财经大学出版社.
曾一志，周述谨，2017. 英汉国际贸易合同教程 [M]. 北京：外语教学与研究出版社.
赵立民，2006. 进出口业务操作（英文版）[M]. 北京：对外经济贸易大学出版社.
周瑞琪，王小鸥，徐月芳，2011. 国际贸易实务（英文版）[M]. 北京：对外经济贸易大学出版社.
邹勇，2006. 国际商贸英语实务 [M]. 成都：西南财经大学出版社.